THE SEASONS OF BUSINESS

The Marketer's Guide to Consumer Behavior

Judith Waldrop
with Marcia Mogelonsky

AMERICAN
DEMOGRAPHICSBOOKS.

To the women of American Demographics,
past and present

THE SEASONS OF BUSINESS
The Marketer's Guide to Consumer Behavior

INTRODUCTION
KEEPING UP WITH THE JONESES

The Joneses are your best customers. If you're a smart marketer, you already know them very well. You keep records on your own customers, and you keep up with the trends. You may have even been working with a consultant to do an in-depth study of the people who are most likely to purchase your goods and services.

Even though a detailed profile of your best customers can tell you a great deal, this type of analysis frequently tells you about only one point in time. Following your customers through an entire year in their lives would be extremely costly. But seasonal trends are important for developing marketing strategies—in business, timing is everything. To help you understand what seasonal factors may be shaping your customers' buying decisions, *The Seasons of Business* presents a month-by-month description of events, weather patterns, and health-care issues that influence consumer behavior.

The following is a monthly diary of a year in the life of a typical consumer, Mrs. Jones. She is a working wife and mother with two children, and she is the primary shopper for her family. At the beginning of the diary, her oldest child is about to have his eighth birthday. The baby is four. But other people outside the nuclear family also influence what Mrs. Jones does with her time and money. Her children's grandparents are still alive and active. Her husband has a teenaged son from a previous marriage who comes and stays with them for at least a few weeks every summer. Mrs. Jones is very close to her younger unmarried sister. Even close friends and co-workers influence Mrs. Jones's spending habits, and because Mrs. Jones cares about her community, she donates money, used clothing, and sometimes her time to causes she feels are worthy.

Mrs. Jones's diary begins in August because that is when she gets serious about spending for the school year. In July, having fun, rather than shopping, was the primary thing on her mind. Now she sees that if her growing kids are going to be ready for school, she has to get busy.

August

Mrs. Jones is frazzled. She would like to buy a new fall business outfit for herself, but she must take the kids school shopping instead. Her husband is out of town on business, and she regrets not going with him. His conference runs through Saturday

GOING WITH THE FLOW

Retailers must be prepared with the right products at the right time of the year. But the many seasons that ebb and flow during the year are important considerations for those who want to be sure that everything from their window dressing to their advertisements matches the mood of the consumer.

(peak seasons by month)

Peak seasons	Aug	Sep	Oct	Nov	Dec	Jan	Feb	Mar	Apr	May	Jun	Jul
School shopping	●	●										
Business travel	●	●	●	●								
Harvest			●	●	●							
Football season			●	●	●	●	●					
Peak fall colors		●	●									
Lent							●	●	●			
Flu season			●	●	●	●	●	●	●	●		
Winter sports		●	●	●	●	●	●	●	●			
Winter depression				●	●	●	●	●				
The holidays				●	●							
Diet season						●	●	●	●	●		
Tornado season									●	●	●	
Spring/summer sports	●	●	●						●	●	●	●
Pleasure travel	●								●	●	●	●
Prom season									●	●		
Wedding season	●								●	●	●	●
Violent crime	●	●							●	●	●	●
Hurricane season	●	●	●								●	●
Burglary/theft	●	●	●	●	●	●						●

afternoon—a measure the conference planners took to help attendees get better airfares—and she's never been to California. In the meantime, she's thinking it might be easier to go to the local shopping center than to battle the traffic on the way to the mall. A new children's clothing store just moved into the local center, and she hears they're having a great grand opening sale.

In August, a lot of people are torn between what they want to do for themselves and what they must do for others. August is a peak month for both business and pleasure travel. It is also a peak month for traffic and crime.

September

Now that school has started, Mrs. Jones is relieved. It was a bit of a hassle arranging day care for the four-year-old. But now all she has to do is pick up some colored

EATING HABITS

Mother's Day is the most popular holiday for all Americans to eat out. But each of us is more likely to eat out on our own birthday.

(*percent of adults who eat out at restaurants on selected occasions, 1988*)

occasion	share eating out
One's own birthday	47%
Mother's Day	39
Father's Day	24
Valentine's Day	22
Easter	16
New Year's Eve	13
St. Patrick's Day	10
Thanksgiving	10
Secretary's Day	8
Christmas Day	6
Grandparents' Day	5

Source: National Restaurant Association

pencils and supplies that Billy's third grade teacher requested. Billy's grandparents are sightseeing in Smoky Mountain National Park, but they sent him a check for his eighth birthday. Now he wants to go to the mall and spend it himself. Mrs. Jones said that would be O.K. as long as she could go along for the ride. She thinks it would be nice if Billy thanked his grandparents by sending them a Grandparents' Day card.

Labor Day marks the transition from summer fun to fall business-as-usual. While many people who are not tied to the school year enjoy taking advantage of fall travel opportunities, getting back to the fall and winter routine is critical for families with children. Retailers can look forward to continued strong sales in school-related products from books to shoes.

October

Mrs. Jones is feeling unusually domestic. Fresh apples at the farmers' market inspired her to bake. And because Mrs. Jones doesn't have the time to prepare fancy meals during the week, she loves to cook on weekends. Fixing some fresh-baked goods is the least she can do for her hard-working husband whose yearly task it is to take down the screens and put up the storm windows. He's a real sports fan, and she's sure there's something he'd like to be watching on television right now: baseball, football, basketball, or hockey.

The World Series and Halloween are important marketing events in October. The World Series captures the attention of nearly 50 million viewers. Each year, about one in three adults attends a Halloween party. But the season's first cold

HAPPY HOLIDAYS

Of course Christmas calls for lots of cards, but some less significant holidays like St. Patrick's Day and Grandparents' day inspire millions of Americans to purchase cards.

(number of Hallmark Cards purchased by type of holiday, 1991)

holiday	number sent (in millions)
Christmas	2,300
Valentine's Day	1,000
Easter	156
Mother's Day	150
Father's Day	101
Thanksgiving	40
Halloween	28
St. Patrick's Day	16
Rosh Hashana	12
Hanukkah	11
New Year's	10
Grandparent's Day	4
Sweetest Day	2
Passover	2
Secretary's Day	2
National Boss Day	1

Source: Hallmark Cards

breezes are a real incentive for making preparations for winter. In 1990, Americans spent almost $14 billion for winter outerwear.

November

When Mrs. Jones saw the first Christmas decorations go up, she was annoyed. But now she finds herself smiling when she hears Salvation Army bells or passes a particularly cheerful holiday display. She's especially happy that the mall is now offering a special Saturday children's activity program that entertains the kids while she shops. She knows she must begin shopping for holidays soon. Some presents will be shipped to people in other states, and one must be sent overseas. She also wants to buy a new centerpiece for her table, something that will go well with her grandmother's heirloom china. This year, her younger sister Emily will bring her new boyfriend for Thanksgiving dinner, and Mrs. Jones wants to make a good impression.

PHONE HOME

If you think these numbers are high, consider that a normal Sunday may send 60 million calls through the AT&T network. And some days can be worse. In 1991, an especially long July 4th weekend generated a backlog of telephone calls on Monday morning. The 156 million telephone calls that went through the AT&T network that day broke the previous record by 30 million calls.

(number of long distance calls in millions handled through
the AT&T network on major holidays in 1990)

holiday	calls
Christmas	85.5
Mother's Day	84.1
Father's Day	69.9
Easter	60.4
Thanksgiving	50.9

Source: AT&T

Almost 80 percent of Americans say their shopping patterns aren't influenced by holiday displays early in the season, according to Maritz Marketing Research of Fenton, Missouri. But marketers can't wait until the last minute to begin selling Christmas. And they'll find if they do it tastefully and make early shopping convenient for their customers, most will appreciate a little holiday cheer.

December

As far as Mrs. Jones is concerned, the holidays are the happiest time of the year. She has been busy making sure the holidays live up to her children's expectations by decorating the house, taking the kids to see Santa, and taking them to the latest Christmas movie special. But the season has also been filled with adult social events: dinner parties, office parties, and even charitable fund-raisers. One thing has made this holiday season especially joyful: sister Emily announced her engagement. The happy couple will be flying to Florida to introduce Emily to her future in-laws. The rest of the Joneses plan on spending a quiet New Year's Eve at home with just a few close friends.

In 1990, December retail sales totaled nearly $180 billion, compared with the monthly average of $151 billion. Sales for some retailers, like jewelry stores, can more than triple during this month. Even so, the holidays are more than just a time for people to buy presents for one another. Almost everyone entertains at home sometime during the holidays, and many people travel to visit friends and relatives at this time of year.

January

Mrs. Jones is feeling guilty. Over the holidays, she spent too much and ate too much. Now the bills are coming in, and she's seven pounds over her normal weight. She

PARTY ANIMALS

The last party (and first) of each year is the biggest party event of the entire year.

(percent adults who said they hosted or attended a party on selected occasions, 1989)

occasion	share hosting or attending a party
New Year's Eve	62%
The Super Bowl	37
Halloween	30
St. Patrick's Day	20
The World Series	17
Valentine's Day	14
The Kentucky Derby	7
Mardi Gras	4

Source: Research Alert's "Lifestyle Odyssey," data from the Crown Royal Report on American Entertaining.

feels she must lose these extra pounds, but she can't decide whether to join a formal program like Weight Watchers or just get a good book on dieting. Her husband could stand to lose a little weight, too, but she can't imagine dragging him away from the bowl games on television. There are such great bargains in the stores right now that Mrs. Jones thinks if she bought a new outfit, it might give her the incentive she needs to lose the weight.

Sales of self-help books and audio tapes and memberships in organizations that help people quit smoking or lose weight soar this month. And just because people are feeling a little guilty about overindulgence during the holidays doesn't mean retailers can't draw them out with a great sale. In the 1990s, America has become a nation of bargain hunters.

February

Mrs. Jones has cabin fever. Because the weather has been so bad, it seems like she's been stuck in the house all winter with nothing to do but watch television—not that the programming hasn't been great lately. But during the past three weeks, each member of the family has come down with the flu. She's tired of looking at her frumpy furniture. And she'd like to buy a home computer so she could catch up on her office work while she's home nursing the little one. If she knew her husband was making arrangements for a special Valentine's weekend at a nearby bed-and-breakfast inn, Mrs. Jones would probably feel better. But her most immediate concern is what to do for supper when she hasn't been to the grocery store in over a week. She thinks she'll just order a pizza.

February seems to be a low point for many Americans and many businesses. But

SUPERMARKET BLOSSOMS

Major holidays mean big sales at supermarket floral departments.

(average store sales for supermarket floral departments on major holidays, 1989)

occasion	average sales
Mother's Day	$8,120
Valentine's Day	6,200
Christmas	5,480
Easter Sunday	5,400
Thanksgiving	4,890
Secretary's Week	3,350
St. Patrick's Day	2,490
Secretary's Day	600

Note: Average weekly sales throughout the year are $1,920.
Source: The Survey of Supermarket Floral Retailing.

that doesn't mean the right incentive can't inspire consumers to get out and shop. Marketers can also reach consumers in their homes, through the media and with home delivery.

March

Mrs. Jones is eagerly anticipating spring. Despite cold weather, she bought a new spring outfit for Easter Sunday service, and she intends to wear it no matter what the forecast. She knows spring can't be too far away because her husband, the allergy sufferer, has already started sneezing. The topic of weather seems to dominate the news. One photo in the local newspaper shows college kids romping in the sun on Daytona Beach. On the same page is a photo of a residential neighborhood that was flattened by a tornado. Mrs. Jones was thinking about holding a garage sale to get rid of clothes the kids had grown out of and other things she didn't want. But now she thinks she ought to donate these things to the disaster victims.

Attendance at religious services swells nearly 60 percent during the Easter and Passover season. But March can be a confusing time for consumers. They want it to be spring, but the weather doesn't always cooperate.

April

Mrs. Jones is in the mood to clean. Everyone in the family has a job, even if it's just to "clean up your room." As usual, Mr. Jones is working outside, cleaning out the gutters, taking down the storm windows, and getting a spot in the yard ready for a garden. Billy is learning about the environment at school. Every day he comes home with a lesson for his parents about recycling or conserving energy or water.

MONTHLY SALES

December dominates the sales of many retail stores. But a smart marketer will find
(unadjusted monthly retail sales in millions of dollars by type of outlet)

KIND OF BUSINESS	January	February	March	April	May
Retail trade, total	$133,293	$128,033	$149,192	$145,803	$155,022
Total (excluding automotive group)	102,775	99,695	115,192	112,884	119,835
DURABLE GOODS, total	**$50,015**	**$47,400**	**$55,759**	**$54,665**	**$59,037**
Building materials, hardware, garden supply, and mobile home dealers	6,079	5,907	7,427	7,997	9,171
Building materials, supply stores, hardware	5,443	5,222	6,459	6,821	7,636
Building materials, supply stores	4,552	4,390	5,395	5,677	6,369
Hardware stores	891	832	1,064	1,144	1,267
Automotive dealers	30,518	28,338	34,000	32,919	35,187
Motor vehicle, miscellaneous automotive dealers	28,251	26,191	31,397	30,340	32,433
Motor vehicle dealers	27,218	25,078	29,798	28,414	30,566
Motor vehicle dealers (franch.)	25,047	22,988	27,344	26,175	28,188
Auto and home-supply stores	2,267	2,147	2,603	2,579	2,754
Furniture, home furnishings, and equipment stores	7,320	6,862	7,727	7,317	7,793
Furniture, home furnishings stores	4,136	3,860	4,401	4,190	4,422
Furniture stores	2,530	2,385	2,686	2,502	2,585
Floor-covering stores	941	892	1,023	1,006	1,066
Household appliance, radio and TV stores	2,547	2,369	2,652	2,495	2,762
Household appliance stores	756	695	800	792	895
Radio and TV stores	1,791	1,674	1,852	1,703	1,867
Sporting-goods stores and bicycle shops	949	998	1,177	1,122	1,233
Bookstores	681	474	480	475	515
Jewelry stores	808	979	937	956	1,201
NONDURABLE GOODS, total	**$83,278**	**$80,633**	**$93,433**	**$91,138**	**$95,985**
General merchandise group stores	12,192	12,809	16,350	16,114	17,153
Department stores (excluding leased departments)	9,736	10,144	13,299	13,046	13,700
Department stores (including leased departments)	10,063	10,523	13,740	13,475	14,102
Conventional department stores (including leased departments)	2,801	3,182	4,178	4,029	4,267

opportunities in every month.

June	July	August	September	October	November	December	TOTAL
$154,371	$149,719	$158,243	$146,335	$151,469	$156,086	$179,653	$1,807,219
119,440	116,151	123,811	115,330	119,866	127,133	153,146	1,425,258
$58,482	$56,090	$57,880	$52,561	$54,092	$52,271	$56,505	$654,757
9,052	8,558	8,543	7,707	8,082	7,443	6,558	92,524
7,620	7,397	7,428	6,736	7,049	6,522	5,733	80,066
6,351	6,212	6,315	5,640	5,905	5,410	4,549	66,765
1,269	1,185	1,113	1,096	1,144	1,112	1,184	13,301
34,931	33,568	34,432	31,005	31,603	28,953	26,507	381,961
32,103	30,842	31,625	28,439	28,882	26,388	24,064	350,955
30,327	29,164	30,108	27,149	27,698	25,286	23,212	334,018
28,027	27,142	27,928	25,017	25,681	23,343	21,501	308,381
2,828	2,726	2,807	2,566	2,721	2,565	2,443	31,006
7,731	7,494	7,750	7,377	7,710	8,118	9,784	92,983
4,348	4,183	4,380	4,131	4,366	4,528	4,620	51,565
2,534	2,358	2,511	2,390	2,438	2,517	2,562	29,998
1,061	1.058	1,061	1,015	1,134	1,069	964	12,290
2,765	2,710	2,689	2,580	2,668	2,859	3,919	33,015
920	924	869	800	868	914	1,093	10,326
1,845	1,786	1,820	1,780	1,800	1,945	2,826	22,689
1,255	1,151	1,275	1,122	1,065	1,138	1,773	14,258
515	517	708	738	588	601	1,000	7,292
1,076	1,020	1,072	943	1,025	1,323	3,062	14,402
$95,889	$93,629	$100,363	$93,774	$97,377	$103,815	$123,148	$1,152,462
16,913	15,466	17,702	15,970	17,027	21,783	32,454	211,933
13,650	12,475	14,356	12,898	13,778	17,533	26,130	170,745
14,048	12,852	14,802	13,302	14,199	18,034	26,871	176,011
4,075	3,666	4,464	4,073	4,305	5,672	8,853	53,565

MONTHLY SALES, *continued*

KIND OF BUSINESS	January	February	March	April	May
Discount department stores (*including leased departments*)	$4,984	$5,088	$6,543	$6,574	$6,880
National chain department stores (*including leased departments*)	2,278	2,253	3,019	2,872	2,955
Variety stores	452	476	559	602	585
Miscellaneous general merchandise stores	2,004	2,189	2,492	2,466	2,868
Food stores	28,045	26,903	30,499	29,064	30,950
Grocery stores	26,302	25,119	28,523	27,058	28,910
Meat, fish (seafood) markets	543	536	593	579	588
Retail bakeries	505	484	535	520	518
Gasoline service stations	9,660	9,003	10,014	10,046	10,683
Apparel and accessory stores	5,814	5,684	7,587	7,660	7,789
Men's and boys' clothing, furnishings	664	568	718	751	794
Women's clothing specialty stores, furriers	2,136	2,044	2,710	2,752	2,816
Women's ready-to-wear	1,826	1,807	2,456	2,497	2,563
Family clothing stores	1,491	1,575	2,112	2,052	2,173
Shoe stores	1,137	1,089	1,518	1,568	1,485
Eating and drinking places	13,476	13,252	15,221	15,034	15,736
Eating places	12,595	12,402	14,247	14,077	14,755
Restaurants, lunchrooms, cafeterias	6,870	6,756	7,662	7,661	7,948
Refreshment places	5,519	5,473	6,357	6,164	6,527
Drinking places (*alcoholic beverages*)	881	850	974	957	981
Drug and proprietary stores	5,405	5,043	5,429	5,489	5,653
Liquor stores	1,480	1,421	1,606	1,575	1,693
Nonstore retailers[1]	4,006	3,702	4,108	3,837	4,040
Mail-order houses (*department store merchandise*)	305	297	388	370	381
Other mail-order	2,364	2,007	2,271	2,077	2,139
Fuel and ice dealers	2,077	1,587	1,408	1,044	860
GAF, total[2]	29,940	29,933	36,540	35,765	37,966
Miscellaneous shopping goods stores	4,614	4,578	4,876	4,674	5,231

1. Includes establishments primarily selling merchandise through coin-operated vending machines, by house-to-house
2. GAF represents stores that specialize in department store type of merchandise.

June	July	August	September	October	November	December	TOTAL
6,945	6,342	7,096	6,387	6,846	8,628	12,309	84,622
3,028	2,844	3,242	2,842	3,048	3,734	5,709	37,824
557	544	613	530	593	684	1,081	7,276
2,706	2,447	2,733	2,542	2,656	3,566	5,243	33,912
31,211	30,855	31,622	30,010	29,970	30,472	32,809	362,410
29,214	28,825	29,557	28,124	28,055	28,526	30,448	338,661
585	597	597	541	544	578	732	7,013
512	512	530	510	528	557	618	6,329
10,896	10,988	12,112	11,781	12,562	12,271	11,709	131,725
7,675	7,150	8,542	7,599	7,728	8,807	12,696	94,731
805	660	705	718	779	882	1,490	9,534
2,710	2,550	2,782	2,625	2,716	3,042	4,239	33,122
2,488	2,333	2,536	2,411	2,451	2,740	3,780	29,888
2,254	2,128	2,661	2,204	2,284	2,829	4,242	28,005
1,463	1,355	1,773	1,500	1,405	1,546	2,051	17,890
16,156	16,253	16,654	15,176	15,289	14,722	15,075	182,044
15,140	15,287	15,685	14,203	14,269	13,680	14,000	170,340
8,095	8,231	8,510	7,787	7,830	7,460	7,554	92,364
6,760	6,855	6,974	6,202	6,222	6,039	6,213	75,305
1,016	966	969	973	1,020	1,042	1,075	11,704
5,549	5,481	5,770	5,454	5,841	5,943	7,500	68,557
1,778	1,794	1,820	1,666	1,694	1,785	2,501	20,813
3,809	3,835	4,000	3,922	4,684	5,224	5,096	50,263
385	339	399	368	422	538	547	4,739
2,049	2,059	2,160	2,166	2,671	3,168	3,104	28,235
741	729	1,000	1,032	1,295	1,529	1,830	15,132
37,456	35,023	39,381	35,986	37,614	44,880	66,621	467,105
5,137	4,913	5,387	5,040	5,149	6,172	11,687	67,458

canvass and from mail-order.

Note: U.S. and group totals include kinds of business not shown separately.
Source: U.S. Department of Commerce

A SPORTING CHANCE

With 66 million people over the age of 6 participating at least once each year, swimming is America's most popular sport. Exercise walking and cycling rank second and third.

(America's top ten sports activities by number of people aged 7 and older participating at least once a year, in millions, 1987)

sport	number participating
Swimming	66.1
Exercise walking	58.1
Bicycle riding	53.2
Fishing	45.8
Camping	44.2
Bowling	40.1
Exercising with equipment	34.8
Motor boating	30.9
Billiards/pool	29.3
Basketball	25.1

Source: National Sporting Goods Association.

It's got Billy's father thinking about how much lower his heating and cooling bills would be if he replaced those old windows. But then, there are so many things that Mr. Jones would like to do around the house. If he did them all, he would have to get a home-improvement loan.

In the 1990s, a majority of every age, education, and income group consider themselves environmentalists. But spring weather also inspires householders into action, cleaning and fixing up their homes. Sometimes these projects go beyond the simple repair and can lead to major expenses.

May

Mrs Jones is excited about buying a new bicycle for herself. The weather has been beautiful, and with the addition of her bicycle, the whole family will be able to go on outings together. She also thinks she needs a new bathing suit this year, but they're so expensive, and she never did lose the weight she picked up last winter. Maybe it's time to join a health club. Every year, her husband sends her flowers for Mother's Day, and the whole family goes out to eat at her favorite restaurant. Later that evening, Mr. and Mrs. Jones call their own mothers to wish them a happy Mother's Day and make sure that they received the flowers they sent. But Mrs. Jones also bought some special Mother's Day cards this year: one for her youngest child's day-care provider and another to her older son's after-school care provider.

As the weather warms up, getting in shape becomes a priority for many

SPORTING EVENTS

Among televised sports, football still commands the greatest number of hours, but other sports saw the greater gains during the 1980s.

(number of hours aired by sports category, 1976-1988)

Sport category	Hours aired, 1988	Percent change, 1976-1988
Football	423	28.2
Olympics	270	157.1
Basketball	263	71.9
Golf	218	101.9
Baseball	184	26.9
Anthologies	138	-7.4
Other	110	93.0
Tennis	90	-18.2
Bowling	36	16.1
Total	**1732**	**45.8**

Source: Nielsen Media Research

consumers. But retailers who depend on summer sales must be ready before the impulse to buy hits their customers. Studies show that once the weather turns, shoppers interested in sports equipment make a quick dash to the store and usually buy the brand they have in mind. Mother's Day is also big business, not only for gift shops, but also for restaurants, telephone companies, florists, and greeting-card companies.

June

Mrs. Jones is under a great deal of stress. Her sister is getting married at the end of this month, and Mrs. Jones has consented to be the matron of honor. Her sister is depending on her help with everything, from registering her china pattern to picking out the bridesmaids' dresses, flowers, and catering service. Even more stressful is the arrival of Sam, her husband's 16-year-old son from a previous marriage. Sam spends a few weeks every summer with the Joneses. But this year, Mrs. Jones is more worried than ever that she's not prepared to be the mother of a teenager. Sam has his driver's license, and he's looking for a summer job. Mrs. Jones wanted to do something for her tenth wedding anniversary, which is coming up this month, but it looks like their celebration will have to take a backseat to everybody else's needs.

The happy events that come in June—weddings, graduations, moves, and even vacations—can add up to a great deal of stress. Even though only a small share of the population marries or graduates each year, these events affect millions of Americans. About 38 percent of adults attends or participates in a wedding every year.

July

Mrs. Jones is enjoying herself. That new gas grill that she bought her husband for Father's Day is really paying off by keeping her out of the kitchen during these hot summer days. And she's finally going to get the vacation she feels she deserves. Billy will be at camp, and the grandparents have agreed to take care of the little one for a week. Sam will be staying with friends, and the dog and cat will be boarded at the local kennel. She really wanted to go to Europe this summer, but she feels the trip they're taking to the U.S. Virgin Islands will be cheaper and safer, with less hassle.

In the summer, Americans are committed to having a good time. But family obligations and financial considerations often shape their final vacation decision. Still, despite the economic woes of 1991, nearly two-thirds of Americans took a summer vacation trip of 100 miles of more.

Seasonal trends can be skewed by major events that don't take place every year. Unemployment goes down during the years in which a decennial census count is taken. Spending on advertising typically swells 1.5 percent in years in which the Olympic Games and Presidential elections take place, says Martin Flemming of the Cahners Publishing Company. But seasonal trends will always be with us. While some marketing strategies, like the introduction of year-round friendship cards, attempt to reduce seasonal fluctuations in an individual industry, other relatively new innovations, like Grandparents' Day, create new seasonal opportunities.

Most seasonal events are not wholly created by the Hallmark corporation. The weather, sporting events, the school year, fiscal calendars, and other events all work together to create seasonal atmospheres, from winter doldrums to spring fever, summer fun, and fall frenzy. The seasons influence not only what consumers buy, but how they feel and think during different times of the year.

Seasonal marketing means more than just picking out the right window dressing. It includes knowing when to offer special services—like home delivery when snow or illness keeps people inside—and understanding why a bride thinks her June wedding should get a retailer's complete attention. Taking seasonal factors into account will help you know your customers better and make it easier for you to keep up with the Joneses.

PART 1

THE MARKETING SEASON BEGINS

For marketers, August is a beginning. The summer season is ending and back-to-school shopping has just begun. Marketers who get established now will be prepared for a profitable holiday season to come.

AUGUST WEATHER
■ ■ ■ ■ ■ ■ ■ ■ ■ ■ ■

The combination of heat and rain makes people in Miami and Mobile miserable, but Californians wish they had a little more rain in August.

	TEMPERATURE		PRECIPITATION	
	low	*high*	*inches*	*days*
Albuquerque, NM	62.8°F	89.4°F	1.51	9
Atlanta, GA	68.7	87.6	3.41	9
Bismarck, ND	54.2	83.3	1.69	9
Boise, ID	56.7	87.3	0.40	3
Boston, MA	63.9	79.8	3.68	10
Buffalo, NY	59.6	78.2	4.16	11
Burlington, VT	56.6	77.6	3.87	12
Charlotte, NC	68.2	87.6	3.75	10
Chicago, IL	61.7	82.1	3.53	9
Cleveland, OH	60.5	80.3	3.38	10
Dallas, TX	73.7	97.3	1.76	5
Denver, CO	57.0	85.8	1.53	9
Detroit, MI	59.4	81.5	3.21	9
Great Falls, MT	53.0	82.0	1.31	8
Honolulu, HI	73.6	88.3	0.60	6
Houston, TX	72.1	93.1	3.66	9
Indianapolis, IN	62.7	83.7	3.46	9
Jacksonville, FL	71.8	90.2	7.15	14
Juneau, AK	46.6	62.6	5.02	18
Los Angeles, CA	64.0	76.5	0.10	0
Memphis, TN	70.8	90.3	3.74	8
Miami, FL	76.5	89.2	7.02	17
Milwaukee, WI	60.2	78.4	3.09	9
Minneapolis, MN	60.3	80.9	3.64	10
Mobile, AL	72.9	90.7	6.75	14
New Orleans, LA	73.1	90.2	6.02	13
New York, NY	67.1	83.7	4.03	10
Norfolk, VA	69.6	85.7	5.33	10
Oklahoma City, OK	69.4	92.8	2.40	6
Omaha, NE	64.2	86.2	4.10	9
Philadelphia, PA	66.0	84.6	4.10	9
Phoenix, AZ	77.5	102.3	1.02	5
Portland, OR	55.8	78.6	1.13	5
Salt Lake City, UT	59.7	90.0	0.92	6
San Francisco, CA	54.2	71.8	0.05	0
Sault Ste. Marie, MI	52.4	73.4	3.46	11
Seattle, WA	54.3	73.9	1.27	6
St. Louis, MO	66.6	87.4	2.55	8
Washington, DC	68.7	86.4	4.40	9
Wichita, KS	67.9	91.5	2.80	8

Source: U.S. Department of Commerce, Bureau of the Census, Statistical Abstract of the United States 1991. Average daily minimum and maximum temperatures and average monthly precipitation were measured over a standard 30-year period.

AUGUST
THE GRAND OPENING

At first glance, it seems like just a few more lazy weeks of summer, but there's an underlying sense of urgency. For school children, August is the last chance for summer fun—it is also time to get serious about getting back to school. Shoppers are torn between the summer close-out sales and the new fall fashions. Business people planning the winter season must get back on the road now. Pleasure travelers are also active in August. And the traffic is terrible. Long hot summers are noted as prime times for crime. Many consumers won't visit places they consider dangerous. People are having fun, but it is by no means the same kind of carefree, laid-back fun that characterized July.

BACK-TO-SCHOOL SHOPPING

Because August is an important transitional period from summer fun to autumn routine, businesses often schedule store openings, promotions, and sales for this time. Back-to-school sales segue naturally into the fall pre-holiday sales, the frenzy

AUGUST'S BEST BUYS
(items most likely to be on sale in August)

- Automobiles (new)
- Baby carriages
- Camping equipment
- China
- Coats
- Draperies & curtains
- Fans
- Garden supplies
- Infants' clothing
- Lamps
- School clothing
- Summer clothing
- Tires

Source: DOLLAR$ENSE Magazine, *1987*

of Christmas shopping, and finally the post-holiday sales. August can really kick off six months of healthy store revenues, says Francesca Turchiano, president of InFact, a consulting firm in New York City.

"August is still a relatively quiet month. It gives retailers a chance to refine their product mix, streamline their operating systems, and organize their point-of-sale strategies in time for the back-to-school sales," Turchiano points out.

Many regional economies have become very dependent on mall businesses. About 8 percent of the U.S. labor force worked in the nation's 30,600 shopping centers in 1987. They generated $586 billion in sales, or 13 percent of the country's gross national product, says Turchiano. Pension funds, insurance companies, and foreign investors have made major monetary commitments to the industry. Ten billion dollars of pension-fund money is allocated to real estate every year, and one-third of that investment is in shopping centers, according to *Institutional Investor*.

But shopping malls are headed for trouble. The share of adults who frequently shop at malls declined from 42 percent in 1987 to just 36 percent in 1991, while the share who never shop at malls increased from 12 percent to 18 percent. Long-term changes in lifestyle and shopping habits, as well as the 1991 recession, are the most likely reasons for malls' decline in popularity, according to a study by the Roper Organization of New York City.

Adults aged 18 to 30 are the most frequent mall patrons. About 16 percent of these young adults say they visit malls very often, and another 27 percent say they visit fairly often, says Roper. But attendance shrinks with age—among people aged 60 and older, only 9 percent visit very often, and just 18 percent visit fairly often.

More than 80 percent of mall shoppers say they go to the mall because it is an easy, comfortable way to visit more than one store. Many shoppers go because they are attracted to a particular store. About half go because they think it is a pleasant place to shop, and only one-third go for the selection of eateries in the mall. Entertainment serves as a magnet for one in four shoppers, and just one in five goes to the mall in hopes of running into friends and acquaintances. Fully half of women say they enjoy going to the mall, compared with just 35 percent of men.

Shop 'Til You Drop?

There are a number of reasons the shopping malls are becoming less popular. Turchiano says the main problems are "shopping fatigue," "marketing myopia," the decline of the department store, and the graying of America. The changing shopping preferences of working women, the high cost of adequate security, the rise of first-rate mail-order offerings, the growing acceptance of electronic retailing, and the shortage of entry-level workers in most regions of the country further drive this trend. The outlook is not good, says Turchiano.

"Shopping fatigue," a syndrome first identified by the *Wall Street Journal*, is an attitude affecting former shopping addicts who are tired of high prices, mediocre quality, and the lack of customer service. "'Shop 'Til You Drop' was the motto of many consumers during the 1980s. It may soon be replaced by a very different one: 'Fashion Free and Proud of It,'" says Turchiano.

The disgruntlement of shoppers has resulted because many malls suffer from nearsightedness in their marketing strategies, placing rates of return and profit margins above the needs of their customers. The results of this attitude are poor housekeeping, confusing signs, stores that appear either too upscale or too downscale, outdated mall directories, and too many redundant clothing stores.

"To compete and prosper in the retail environment of the 21st century, shopping center management groups must see each of their centers as a single superstore—an integrated entity that competes with all other channels of distribution," says Turchiano. "Each center needs to be designed, leased, and marketed in a way that its target audience will find compelling and its competitors will find hard to duplicate."

The department store, once the big drawing card for mall shoppers, is losing ground as its customer base dwindles. Department stores have de-emphasized customer service in the name of operating efficiency, and the results have been devastating. Busy customers who feel they are being neglected take their business elsewhere. Others who are displeased with their surroundings do not take the time to browse. As Turchiano points out, less browsing means less buying.

Department stores must meet the needs of their changing customer base. If they don't, the results can be disastrous. Sears made the mistake of focusing too strongly on the middle class—a shrinking segment of its business. Shoppers today are looking for either upscale specialty shops or bargain stores, and Sears could not fit the bill in either category.

Although Sears introduced "everyday low prices" in the late 1980s, "it is still not competitive in the mind of the consumer, and it doesn't have the prestige of upscale specialty shops," says Leonard Berry, director of the Center for Retailing Studies at Texas A&M University in College Station, Texas. But Sears is still hard at work trying to reshape its image in the 1990s. Today, it offers a "WearOut Warranty" on children's clothing, offering free replacements if the clothing is damaged before the child grows out of the size. The emphasis is on value, a word that means both high quality and low price to consumers.

The aging American population is another problem mall managers must deal with. Even though they spend only 24 percent of their retail dollars in their favorite department store, shoppers between the ages of 25 and 34 account for 27 percent of department store sales. On the other hand, people aged 65 and older spend 39 percent of their retail dollars in department stores, but they account for only 5 percent of all dollars spent by department store customers. Currently, the older population is smaller and less affluent than young adults. But as their numbers grow, their contribution to mall revenues will become increasingly important.

One way to get older people in malls is to provide them with an exercise program. Nearly 2,000 malls offer special walking programs, and as many as 3 million

Americans get their exercise by walking in malls. Walkers take advantage of malls' security and climate control before the malls open for business. But older Americans are not necessarily finding anything to keep them there once business hours begin.

Many older shoppers are happier sitting at home with their feet up, making their purchases from a stack of mail-order catalogs. Except for security, "the intangible qualities sought by older adults are not easily found in malls," says Francesca Turchiano. To attract older customers, accessible washrooms, enough comfortable seating, legible mall directories and informational signs, and personable salespeople are as important as the right stores.

Could malls go the way of platform shoes, love beads, and bell-bottoms? Not if shopping-center owners and managers make a commitment to understanding the people who live and work in each center's trading area, says Turchiano. In communities with many older people, malls should have large-type directories and a large assortment of spoil-the-grandchild items. Malls in ethnically diverse areas should have multilingual signs. Stores with products catering to Asians, Hispanics, or blacks should be encouraged to become tenants in malls that serve those groups.

The Small Mall

The neighborhood strip mall is making a comeback. In the 1960s, strip malls were designed to provide essential services—grocery stores, dry cleaners, pharmacies—in small, user-friendly but architecturally nondescript shopping areas—easy in, easy out.

But the image of the local strip mall is changing as retailers rethink their marketing strategies. Strip malls accounted for 87 percent of all shopping malls and 51 percent of total shopping center retail sales in 1990. And 85 percent of new shopping centers under construction that year were strip malls, according to the International Council of Shopping Centers (ICSC). With strip malls becoming so popular, the corner grocer, dry cleaner, and pharmacist have some new neighbors: home furnishing, electronics, toys, and even contemporary fashion stores.

These retail outlets choose strip malls as their new targets with good reason. Even though just 24 percent of adults shop exclusively at strip malls, 89 percent patronize them at least once during an average month, according to a 1990 survey by ICSC. But loyal strip-mall shoppers visit them more than seven times a month, while adults who shop at regional malls do so less than four times each month.

Strip malls appeal most to married women who are full-time homemakers with children. They find the convenience of local one-stop shopping appealing, according to the 1990 National Benchmarks Study by Stillerman Jones & Company in Indianapolis. As jaded consumers and busy adults find that shopping is no longer recreation but responsibility, the local shopping center will become more attractive.

The attraction will be spiritual, too. No longer will the strip mall be the slightly down-at-the-heels amalgam of variety stores clustered around an independent grocer. It will instead consist of small groups of niche-targeted specialty shops grouped together to provide fast and friendly service to a familiar regular clientele.

Shopper's Hell

When it comes to the question of who does the most shopping, women win hands down. Wives are primarily responsible for buying everything from groceries to clothing, furniture, and other durable goods for 92 percent of both dual-earner and single-earner couples with children.

Eleven million married shoppers with children don't like to shop, according to a study by Eugene H. Fram of the Rochester Institute of Technology, and Joel Axelrod, president of BRX/Global in Rochester, New York. Half of the primary shoppers in dual-earner families and 35 percent of those in single-earner families feel that shopping adds stress to their lives. Parents in two-earner families are more likely than others to feel that their time for shopping is slipping away.

But parents must face the challenge of back-to-school shopping. Many turn to tried-and-true timesaving devices to help get them by. About 70 percent of dual- and single-earner parents rely on catalogs at least for information about shopping, and about 50 percent make at least occasional purchases from catalogs, according to Fram and Axelrod. Some parents buy clothes that are big enough for kids to wear more than one season. Others use the express checkout lines, preferring to shop more frequently than to stay in the store a minute longer than they need to. But many shoppers feel too busy to think. Only 22 percent make shopping lists, and just 13 percent plan ahead.

Some customers don't have the time to buy, prepare, and eat the food they need to keep up their frenetic lifestyles. Fast-food restaurants, supermarket ready-to-eat food, and restaurant take-out menus are the order of the day for many families. As a result, supermarkets are stocking more microwavable and ready-to-eat foods. In order to get customers in and out as quickly as possible, they offer more checkout stations and express lines. They have relocated their deli and fresh-prepared departments closer to the front of the store. And they are providing in-store services like bank machines, post offices, fax stations, and video rentals near the take-out food section. "A store that wastes people's time will be committing competitive suicide," says Texas A&M's Leonard Berry.

FALL FASHIONS
■ ■ ■ ■ ■ ■ ■ ■ ■ ■

Long before the leaves begin to turn, fall colors appear in retail stores everywhere. Demographic trends indicate a strong market for women's clothing, but the market for women's apparel is as unpredictable as Indian summer. Between 1984 and 1985, the average household's annual expenditure for women's apparel rose from $440 to almost $500, according to the Bureau of Labor Statistics' Consumer Expenditure Survey. Spending slipped to $470 in 1986, rose to nearly $520 in 1987, and then dropped to $490 in 1988. But it rose to $564 in 1989 and $585 in 1990.

Fashion Statement

Middle-aged women are the most affluent, so they can afford to spend more on clothing. Sixty percent of women aged 35 to 54 have household incomes of $30,000 or more, according to a 1989 study by Simmons Market Research Bureau of New York City, compared with only 40 percent of younger women and 25 percent of older women. Almost 70 percent of middle-aged women are employed, compared with 65 percent of younger women and only 20 percent of older women.

Economic independence has made middle-aged women choosy about clothing. "When women first started working, they needed clothing to suit their new role," says Patty Cohen of DKNY, a fashion design house in New York City. In 1977, *The Woman's Dress for Success Book* advised working women to project the same image as businessmen. But "today's women are much more secure. They're not competing with men," says Cohen. A modern woman's day includes work, family, social, and recreational activities. "Clothes have to work morning to night," she explains. A working woman's wardrobe is therefore "not about size. It's about comfort and attitude."

Women aged 35 to 54 are 20 percent more likely than other women to buy a suit each year, and they are 40 percent more likely to buy a blazer, according to Simmons' 1989 survey. Sixty percent of middle-aged women buy four or more dresses a year, compared with 40 percent of younger women and fewer than 30 percent of older women. Women aged 35 to 54 also pay more for most of the items they buy. They are 30 percent more likely than other women to spend $100 or more on a single pair of shoes, for example. Younger women outspend the middle group on designer jeans, and older women are more likely to buy pantsuits. But women aged 35 to 54 dominate the market for most other kinds of apparel.

"The fashion industry has to change to fit working women," says Beate Ziegert, senior lecturer in the Department of Textiles and Apparel at Cornell University . "For baby boomers, quality is much more important than price." While boomers' entry into the labor force is an important factor changing the women's apparel market, Ziegert says that other trends are also critical. The aging population affects size and tastes, for example. But while the average American woman's dress size is getting larger, immigration is bringing in Hispanic and Asian customers who often wear smaller sizes. As a result, the fashion industry must offer a wider selection of sizes.

Not listening to the needs of women can be disastrous. Designers got a chilly reception when the 1987 fall fashions featured miniskirts. Already fed up with the rising costs of clothing and further perturbed by the fashion industry's lack of concern for their real clothing needs, women stopped buying—sending a shock wave through the retail clothing industry. Designers listened, and while their fashions still feature above-the-knee skirts, they are now keeping the professional and older woman in mind by offering a wider range of choices.

One-third of adult women are now aged 35 to 54. By 2000, this powerful segment will grow to 40 percent of the women's apparel market. To survive, designers must follow the needs of busy women, instead of expecting them to follow fashion.

The Executive Wardrobe

For many women, clothes are an expression of their personality on and off the job. Young single women feel that clothing and appearance are important ingredients in defining their identities, according to a 1991 nationwide mail survey conducted by *Mademoiselle* magazine. Of women between the ages of 18 and 24, 43 percent say their clothing and appearance help define who they are. Fully 57 percent of career-oriented women aged 18 to 24 feel this way.

Some busy women literally have no time to shop. For them, a personal shopper is a must. A personal shopper, most often another woman, is hired to select, coordinate, and accessorize a working woman's wardrobe. At Dayton Hudson stores alone, sales attributed to personal shoppers or wardrobe consultants rose from $3 million in 1985 to $15 million in 1988.

Deciding whether or not a personal shopper is in order is based on a number of factors, according to a 1990 study by Sandra Forsythe, Sara Butler, and Robert Schaeffer, published in the *Journal of Retailing*. Of the 373 employed midwestern women they surveyed in 1990, 6 percent had used a personal shopper and another 8 percent were considering using this type of service. Important criteria include the perception women have of themselves as career-oriented and the length of time they have held their current position.

How much money women set aside for their professional wardrobes is another key factor. The share desiring this shopping service rises as budgets increase, but peaks at 28 percent among women whose annual workclothes budgets ranged from $1,000 to $1,499. The percentage slips to 11 percent of those spending between $1,500 and $1,999 and to 13 percent of those spending $2,000 or more. Women with mid-range budgets can afford to buy the clothing, but they can't afford to make fashion mistakes, say Forsythe, Butler, and Schaeffer.

In general, women are spending less on their clothes, according to Walter K. Levy, a New York retail consultant. He points out that designer lines are being replaced by mid-priced clothes, making "high-priced designer clothes particularly vulnerable." With the proliferation of off-price stores, factory outlets, and markdown racks in department stores, women are discovering that they can still look professional without overspending.

CRIME AND TRAFFIC
■ ■ ■ ■ ■ ■ ■ ■ ■ ■ ■ ■ ■

Summer means different things to different people. Unfortunately, criminals see it as a good season to rip people off. Hot summers exacerbate not only property-related crimes like robberies, break-ins, and motor-vehicle thefts, but also murders, rapes, and other violent crimes. As crime becomes more common and more visible in our communities, people are beginning to limit their activities both at home and while they're away.

Mean Streets

Fearful of crime, one-third of Americans limit the places and times that they go shopping, according to a 1991 survey by Shulman Ronca Bucuvalas for the National Victim Center. Sixty percent of adults say that fear of crime keeps them from going some places by themselves. Fully 48 percent fear being attacked or robbed while traveling on vacation or for business.

More burglaries occurred in August than in any other month in 1990, according to the FBI's Uniform Crime Reports. August has been the leading month for burglaries for a number of years. Thefts—pickpocketing, shoplifting, purse-snatching, auto and bicycle thefts, and thefts from buildings and coin-operated machines—were also high in August.

Violent crimes—murder, rape, and aggravated assaults—are at their peak in July and August. Because women are especially vulnerable, they try to avoid poorly lit parking areas and alleyways between shops. Even though the longer days of summer provide more daylight hours for shopping, women are still wary of deserted streets or parking lots.

Crime is the number-one concern of Americans, according to a 1991 survey conducted by the Roper Organization of New York City. A person's concern about crime increases with age and income. While 35 percent of those between the ages of 18 and 29 are concerned about crime, 43 percent of people over the age of 60 are concerned. Forty-six percent of people whose household income is $50,000 or more consider crime a major concern, compared with 37 percent of adults whose annual household income is under $15,000.

Geographic locale also affects people's feelings about crime. About 38 percent of both Northeasterners and Westerners are concerned about crime. Concern is lowest in the Midwest (33 percent) and highest in the South (46 percent), according to Roper. Southerners' fears may be well founded. While New York, Chicago, and Los Angeles have the largest number of break-ins per year, Sunbelt cities rank far ahead when the number of break-ins are compared with the number of households, according to Mary Granfield of *Money* magazine.

In 1990, Atlanta and Fort Worth tied for first place, with 61 burglaries for every 1,000 households. Dallas, San Antonio, and Miami followed. Chicago, with just 29 break-ins for every 1,000 households, was 37th on the list. New York, with 25 break-ins per 1,000 households, and Los Angeles, with 24, were even further down on the list.

When Getting There Isn't Half the Fun

Traffic adds to shopping fatigue and discourages shoppers. In August, just when back-to-work and back-to-school shopping is at its height, traffic on both rural and urban roads is at its heaviest, according to 1990 figures from the Federal Highway Administration. Americans logged more than 2 trillion vehicle miles in 1988, compared with 1 trillion in 1970.

MURDERS AND MILES

In August, the combination of business and pleasure travel generates traffic. But summer crime reports may convince some shoppers to avoid certain areas.

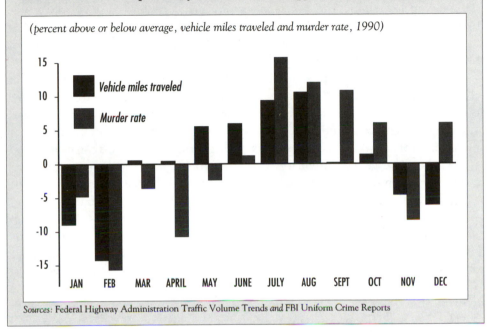

(*percent above or below average, vehicle miles traveled and murder rate, 1990*)

■ Vehicle miles traveled

■ Murder rate

Sources: Federal Highway Administration Traffic Volume Trends *and* FBI Uniform Crime Reports

Who is most likely to get caught in a traffic jam? Young adults (aged 18 to 29), people with annual household incomes of $50,000 or more, and working parents, according to a 1991 survey by the Roper Organization. People over the age of 60 are the least likely to be stuck in traffic—most retirees can wait until off-peak hours to use their cars and avoid much of the heavy traffic.

States with the fast-growing populations experienced the greatest gains in mileage. Between 1970 and 1988, Nevada had a 116 percent rise in population and a 160 percent gain in vehicle miles driven. In Arizona, the number of vehicle miles driven nearly tripled in 18 years. But large increases in traffic are not limited to rapidly growing states. North Dakota's population gain was only 8 percent, but the number of miles driven there increased by 102 percent between 1970 and 1988. New York lost population, but the number of miles driven grew more than 50 percent.

Commercial traffic is responsible for much of the gain. Between 1975 and 1985, the annual number of miles driven by trucks increased from 282 million to nearly 500 million, a 77 percent increase. The total number of vehicle miles driven increased just 33 percent over this time period. But even in 1985, commercial traffic accounted for just 28 percent of all vehicle miles driven. The proliferation of two-job, two-car families is also fueling the driving bonanza.

The Automobile Society

As traffic jams become a way of life, people adapt to the challenge of spending hours crawling along at a snail's pace. Nowhere is the art of living in traffic more highly developed than in the City of Los Angeles.

Los Angeles's traffic, the butt of jokes for years, is getting progressively worse. In 1989, it took about 30 minutes to drive 10 miles in the Los Angeles basin. That time could double by 2010, according to David Stein, a transportation planner for the Southern California Association of Governments.

Californians are using their creative talents to cope with the situation. Cellular telephones now include built-in answering machines and speakers for hands-free conversations. Some even have ports to allow the attachment of fax machines and photocopiers. Laptop computers, microwave ovens, coffee machines, and other appliances are being designed for use in cars. Electronic-map systems can be installed on dashboards—especially useful for discovering the way off crowded freeways. Top-of-the-line automobile sound systems, incorporating compact-disc players, tape decks, and multiple amplifiers and speakers, can cost more than $25,000.

Traffic-bound consumers are a captive audience, and Los Angeles is like heaven for radio and billboard advertisers. A new type of advertising, one in which the driver is an interactive participant, is also popular. Called Drive Buy Radio, the advertiser posts an FM radio frequency on a sign in its parking lot. When drivers turn to that frequency, they hear a taped message about whatever special deals the advertiser has that day.

The Campbell Soup Company predicts that by the year 2000, 25 percent of all cars will have microwave ovens. If traffic continues to build and the demand for more in-car conveniences increases, before too long the L.A. freeway system could resemble an RV park, with accessorized automobiles rather than trailers providing all the comforts of home.

THE BUSINESS TRAVELER
■■■■■■■■■■■■■■■■■■

August is a peak time for both business and travel. Summer vacationers are still trying to squeeze in some fun before Labor Day, and business people are gearing up for the upcoming busy holiday months. In 1990, the combination of business and leisure activity made August the busiest month for travel. Of the more than 70 million trips taken that month, one-third were for business purposes.

Travel, for Fun and Profit

Every year, more travelers are mixing business with pleasure. However, the image of the business traveler from out of town—party hounds drinking to excess and wearing lampshades—is changing. Today, when business mixes with pleasure, the whole family is likely to join in. Only 28 percent of all business travelers take another

SUMMER BREEZES

H URRICANE CELIA came ashore at the little island community of Port Aransas, Texas, in August 1970. The 200-mile-per-hour winds swept through Corpus Christi, a city of more than 200,000, and caused damage another 50 miles inland. The damage totaled more than $450 million, but few people were killed. Most of Port Aransas's 1,500 residents and their tourist guests evacuated early, fearing the rising waters would cut off their links to the mainland.

The returning residents were grateful that Celia had been relatively dry, unlike the more deadly Carla, which struck nine years earlier, killing 46 people. They were also grateful that their town had no major industrial development that could ignite fires, like the ones the islanders saw burning on the mainland each night for a week.

Among the first on the island after the storm were members of the National Guard, the American Red Cross, and other volunteer groups providing food, water, clothing, and medical services. The Department of Housing and Urban Development provided temporary housing. Soon, construction teams funded by Small Business Administration loans were rebuilding the little tourist and fishing village—only bigger and better.

The next year, a direct hit by hurricane Fern caused only minor damage. And although Port Aransas felt the winds from hurricane Allen, which hit Brownsville in 1980, the eye of a major storm has not passed over the town since 1971.

Although storms can occur at almost any time of the year, the official hurricane season runs from June 1 to October 31. August, September, and October are the peak months for hurricanes. Of the 144 hurricanes that formed in the North Atlantic Ocean, the Caribbean, or the Gulf of Mexico between 1900 and 1985, 24 percent developed in August and 41 percent in September. October had the next highest share, 15 percent, and 10 percent formed in July.

Areas in the Southeast, especially along the Gulf Coast, are most likely to be hit. But on August 19, 1991, Hurricane Bob roared up the eastern seaboard and landed at Newport, Rhode Island. With winds up to 125 miles per hour, the storm left 18 people dead and at least 700,000 homes and businesses without electricity. Flooding was a problem in low-lying areas from North Carolina to Maine, and the storm did $1.5 billion in damage. But storm watchers were grateful that the hurricane did not pack the power of Hugo, a storm that struck South Carolina in September 1989. That storm, classified as a Category 4, with winds between 131 and 155 miles per hour, killed 26 people and caused a record $7 billion in damage.

Over the past century, hurricanes have become less deadly and more costly. But the southern coastal areas of the United States that are most likely to be struck by hurricanes are also some of the fastest-growing areas in the country. That spells potential disaster, because many of the new residents in hurricane-prone areas have never experienced a direct hit by a major storm.

In 1988, more than 15 million people lived in areas with a high probability of receiving a direct hit from a hurricane every 20 years. This high-risk population is expected to grow more than 20 percent by the year 2000. Over half of these residents live in areas that can expect a hurricane every ten years. One of the greatest concerns of the National Weather Service is that coastal residents have come to believe that advanced technology will prevent major loss of life from future storms. Camille, in 1969, was the last storm classified as "catastrophic," the most severe type of hurricane, and the lack of a major hurricane experience among the new residents of rapidly growing coastal areas has resulted in general apathy.

On average, 10 major storms form each year during hurricane season, and 8 of them reach hurricane strength. The 10- to 13- year cycle of sunspots significantly influences storm patterns. More storms seem to occur when sunspots are at a minimum, but the storms seem to be more intense when sunspots are at a maximum. The last sunspot minimum was in 1986.

Monroe County, in the Florida Keys, tops the list of counties likely to experience a major storm. Looking at a century of data, Monroe County is hit on average once every five years. Its 1988 population, not including tourists, was 76,000, and the county is expected to grow more than 30 percent by the year 2000.

The most populated area in the danger zone is the rapidly growing Florida Gold Coast, including Dade, Broward, and Palm Beach counties. The combined population of these counties could top 5 million by the end of the 20th century. Although low-level storms have passed over southern Florida almost every year, no major hurricane has hit the Gold Coast or the Florida Keys since 1950. Since the probability is high that these counties will be struck every ten years, it appears they are living on borrowed time.

member of their household along. But half of business travelers who extend a trip for recreational purposes bring another household member, according to the U.S. Travel Data Center of Washington, D.C.

Between 1987 and 1989, the total number of business trips taken within the U.S. grew from fewer than 160 million to nearly 170 million, according to the U.S. Travel Data Center. During the same period, the share of business trips that were extended to include leisure activities increased at the rate of 1 percentage point a year. Nearly one in four business travelers includes some time for recreation. Half of these travelers arrange leisure activities that double the length of a stay. Business travelers are especially likely to extend their trips when meetings take place at resorts.

Low round-trip airfares often depend on a Saturday night stay, so employers frequently save money when employees stretch their business trips, says Bernice Rosmarin, an agent at VTS/Edison Travel in Edison, New Jersey. Sometimes the savings in airfare are enough to justify the expense of spending Saturday night in a hotel. Business-oriented hotels are more likely to be filled from Monday through Friday. To encourage business travelers to stay, they frequently offer special weekend rates.

People who combine business trips with pleasure are most likely to be younger (under the age of 35) or older (aged 45 or older) than other business travelers. Frequent business travelers are less likely than occasional travelers to extend any given trip for leisure pursuits. Twenty-four percent of all business trips include leisure activities, compared with 13 percent of trips taken by frequent business travelers. Still, business travelers in general average only 5 trips each year, while frequent business travelers average 19.

Business travelers who add leisure activities to a trip are less affluent than those who don't. Forty percent of pleasure-seeking business travelers have household incomes of less than $35,000, compared with 35 percent of all business travelers. More than one-third (37 percent) of the pleasure-seekers are self-employed, compared with 29 percent of all business travelers; 51 percent use their own cars, compared with 44 percent of all business travelers.

Between 1987 and 1989, the number of business trips taken by women increased from 47 million to 54 million. Today, they are one-third of all business travelers. Twenty-eight percent of women extend their business trips for recreational purposes, compared with 22 percent of men. Businesswomen are more likely than men to be visiting a place for the first time, so they may have a greater incentive to stay and explore. Fewer businesswomen earn top salaries, so they also may be more likely to take a vacation if some of the expenses are covered by the company.

The Executive Traveler

For many top executives, mixing business with pleasure is not always what they have in mind, especially when it means interrupting a vacation to keep up with business. Seventy percent of executives with household incomes above $125,000 say the office knows where they are at all times; 30 percent check in constantly, according to a 1991 survey of 500 executives by Hyatt Hotels and Resorts.

These top business people rarely think of their vacations as fun, Mark Yanofsky of Hyatt told *USA Today*. He explains that they are opportunities to "prevent burnout, increase productivity on the job, and improve personal relationships."

As the lines between business travel and vacation travel become more blurred, many people are beginning to feel the leisure-time/work-time crunch even more intensely. Forty-two percent of men and 39 percent of women say they work to make it possible to get the leisure time they want. Just 37 percent of men and 35 percent of women feel that work is more important to them than leisure, according to the Roper Organization.

Most Americans say that having free time is as important to them as making money, according to a 1991 survey conducted by the Hilton Corporation. With so many people treasuring their leisure time, it is no wonder that almost half of American workers say they would give up a day's pay to get an extra day off.

Businesses realize how much their employees value leisure time and have responded with some innovative new programs. A concept known as incentive travel, offering vacations as bonuses, is proving a popular alternative to the usual cash bonuses.

Spending on incentive travel in the U.S. topped $5 billion in 1989, an increase of 13 percent over 1988, according to the 1990 *Incentive Travel Fact Book*. Offering incentive travel boosts healthy competition among salespeople. At the same time, it offers them paid vacations with their families—a boon to those who feel that leisure time and quality family time are slipping away from them.

The secret behind the success of incentive travel may lie in the fact that, for successful men and women, the rewards of travel are like nothing else. "If they have been in the achiever end of the marketplace, they're probably earning a comfortable living. Cash is probably not the best incentive. What incentive travel offers is something that applies to a higher level of lifestyle satisfaction," says Jane E. Schuldt, a Minneapolis businesswoman who is president of the Society of Incentive Travel Executives, a trade organization based in New York City.

Business + Pleasure = Golf

The idea of mixing golf and business is as old a tradition in America as the sport itself. A century ago, a young Scot named Donald Ross made a prediction: "I knew the day would come when the American businessman would relax and want some game to play, and I knew that game would be golf." Ross spent his life designing 400 American golf courses. His most famous is in Pinehurst, North Carolina, a mecca for golfers and the location of the PGA's World Golf Hall of Fame.

More than 30 other golf courses are located in Pinehurst and prosperous Moore County, North Carolina. They provide a money-making proposition for the county's 60,000 permanent residents.

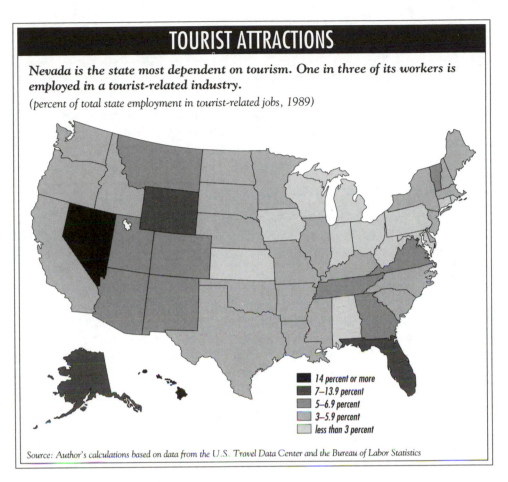

TOURIST ATTRACTIONS

Nevada is the state most dependent on tourism. One in three of its workers is employed in a tourist-related industry.

(percent of total state employment in tourist-related jobs, 1989)

- 14 percent or more
- 7–13.9 percent
- 5–6.9 percent
- 3–5.9 percent
- less than 3 percent

Source: Author's calculations based on data from the U.S. Travel Data Center and the Bureau of Labor Statistics

Pinehurst was conceived by aging New England businessman James W. Tufts in the 1890s as a resort area, complete with hotel, stores, cottages, tennis courts, and other amenities. It was designed to provide a place for New Englanders of modest means and advancing years to spend a winter vacation away from the bitter winter weather of Boston or Philadelphia.

The idea took root, and in 1990 there were close to 14,000 golf courses in the United States, or about one 18-hole golf course for every 23,000 people, according to the National Golf Foundation (NGF). The location of many courses makes it clear that they are meant primarily for the business traveler who wants to unwind with a few quick holes.

At the Washington Duke Inn and Golf Resort adjacent to Duke University in Durham, North Carolina, for example, "no one checks out early on weekends," says hotel manager Adriano Moscatelli. As the only hotel in the Research Triangle with both corporate meeting rooms and golf facilities, the Washington Duke is more than just a corporate pit stop. Businesspeople linked to the university are the hotel's primary market. "Contracts don't get signed on the greens, but there's plenty of time to talk in between shots," says John Rooney, professor of geography at Oklahoma State University. "And here you can get a good feel for the people you're playing with. How they manage themselves on the golf course says a lot about how they'll manage themselves in the office."

About 23 million adults play golf each year, according to Simmons Market Research Bureau of New York City. Golfers are 66 percent more likely than others to have household incomes of $50,000 or more. Many are professionals, managers, or administrators. One in five employees of the Fortune 500 companies is a golfer. Two million golfers play at least 60 days a year, according to Simmons. This number should increase as baby boomers age. More than one-third of all golfers are aged 45 or older, but almost two-thirds of frequent golfers are that old.

As the sport increases in popularity, there may come a day when the golf courses are too crowded to squeeze in another player. In 1988, 211 new golf courses opened around the country. In 1989, this figure was 290, and in 1990, 289 new golf courses opened. Prior to this boom, the average number of openings per year was 150, according to NGF figures. New openings were highest in Florida for the sixth year in a row, followed by South Carolina and California. All three states have warm weather and are retirement- and vacation-oriented.

And while old Mr. Ross and Mr. Tufts may have envisioned golf as the businessman's sport, that image is no longer totally accurate. Women are an increasingly large share of participants. While only 21 percent of new players in 1983 were women, women accounted for 41 percent of new players in 1987, according to NGF figures.

The sport has changed in many other ways, too—spawning a whole range of related industries from apparel and equipment retailers to real estate developments with a golf course as their centerpiece. Its importance as a spectator sport has also grown, and professional golfers compete for purses that exceed $25 million annually, according to Rooney and Robert L. Adams, professor of geography at the University of New Hampshire.

More 20th-century chief executives favor golf than any other hobby. George Bush's news-conferences-on-the-fairway may be the ultimate example of mixing business and pleasure. His presidential soul mates include Gerald Ford, John F. Kennedy, Dwight D. Eisenhower, Warren G. Harding, Woodrow Wilson, and William Howard Taft, according to a 1991 exhibition entitled "Hobbies" at the Gerald R. Ford Museum in Grand Rapids, Michigan.

THE SOUNDS OF SUMMER

Aside from the flurry of back-to-school shopping, packed highways, and busy travel schedules, the last month of summer can also provide a measure of culture in our harried lives. August is Artists' Appreciation Month. The month definitely holds memories for the half-million people who attended the Woodstock Music and Art fair in 1969, and it is still a great time to attend music festivals around the country. The Grand Teton Music Festival in Jackson Hole, Wyoming, promises superb scenery and concerts by first-rate musicians. At the Glimmerglass Opera in Cooperstown, New York, Beethoven co-exists with the Baseball Hall of Fame. Music festivals also flourish at Aspen, Colorado; Santa Fe, New Mexico; and Santa Cruz, California. Theater afficionados can enjoy the drama of the Oregon Shakespeare festival in Ashland or the Bumbershoot in Seattle, Washington. For dance lovers, there's Jacob's Pillow in Lee, Massachusetts.

Some states hold special celebrations in August. Oklahoma celebrates Victory Day, and Texas honors its favorite son, Lyndon Johnson. In Vermont, Bennington Battle Day even commemorates a Revolutionary War battle that "wasn't really fought in Vermont, but very close by," according to Tom White of the Vermont Department of Personnel.

SEPTEMBER WEATHER
■■■■■■■■■■■■■■■

In September, temperatures in the high 70s and 80s indicate that weather is still beautiful throughout the U.S.

	TEMPERATURE		PRECIPITATION	
	low	*high*	*inches*	*days*
Albuquerque, NM	54.9°F	83.0°F	0.85	6
Atlanta, GA	63.6	82.3	3.17	8
Bismarck, ND	43.2	71.4	1.38	7
Boise, ID	48.7	77.6	0.58	4
Boston, MA	56.9	72.3	3.41	9
Buffalo, NY	52.7	71.4	3.37	11
Burlington, VT	48.7	68.8	3.20	12
Charlotte, NC	62.3	81.7	3.59	7
Chicago, IL	53.9	75.5	3.35	10
Cleveland, OH	54.0	74.2	2.92	10
Dallas, TX	67.5	89.7	3.31	7
Denver, CO	47.7	77.5	1.23	6
Detroit, MI	52.2	74.4	2.25	10
Great Falls, MT	44.2	70.5	1.03	7
Honolulu, HI	72.9	88.2	0.62	7
Houston, TX	68.1	88.7	4.93	9
Indianapolis, IN	55.3	77.9	2.74	8
Jacksonville, FL	69.4	86.9	7.26	13
Juneau, AK	42.3	55.9	6.40	20
Los Angeles, CA	62.5	76.4	0.15	1
Memphis, TN	64.1	84.3	3.62	7
Miami, FL	75.7	87.8	8.07	17
Milwaukee, WI	52.5	71.2	2.88	9
Minneapolis, MN	50.2	71.0	2.50	10
Mobile, AL	69.3	87.0	6.56	10
New Orleans, LA	70.1	86.8	5.87	10
New York, NY	60.1	76.4	3.66	8
Norfolk, VA	64.2	80.2	4.35	8
Oklahoma City, OK	61.9	84.7	3.41	7
Omaha, NE	54.0	77.5	3.50	8
Philadelphia, PA	58.6	77.8	3.42	8
Phoenix, AZ	70.9	98.2	0.64	3
Portland, OR	51.1	74.2	1.61	8
Salt Lake City, UT	50.0	80.0	0.89	5
San Francisco, CA	54.3	73.4	0.19	1
Sault Ste. Marie, MI	45.3	64.2	3.90	13
Seattle, WA	51.2	68.7	2.02	9
St. Louis, MO	58.6	80.7	2.70	8
Washington, DC	62.0	80.1	3.22	8
Wichita, KS	59.2	82.0	3.45	8

Source: U.S. Department of Commerce, Bureau of the Census, Statistical Abstract of the United States 1991. Average daily minimum and maximum temperatures and average monthly precipitation were measured over a standard 30-year period.

SEPTEMBER

A LEARNING EXPERIENCE

For parents of school-aged children, September is time to reorganize. For children and young adults who attend school or college, it is the month of the "three r's"—rules, restrictions, and responsibilities. But for child-free couples and empty nesters, September is a wonderful month for travel and relaxation as the summer crowds desert the beaches and mountains. September is a great month for off-peak travel rates, and people who aren't tied to the school calendar can take advantage of these bargains.

But the need to establish routine is critical for families with children. For those who have children in preschool, grade school, high school, or even college, there is a certain challenge associated with September. Summer patterns can be hard to break, especially when the weather is still warm and the days are still long.

Even so, September is an exciting time for school children. Back-to-school shopping is still strong. September is one of the biggest months for bookstores, shoe stores, and general merchandise stores. As classes begin and students bring home lists of required readings, gym equipment, and art supplies, sales in these categories pick up.

SEPTEMBER'S BEST BUYS

(items most likely to be on sale in September)

- Automobiles (new)
- Bicycles
- Carpets and rugs
- China
- Fabrics and notions
- Furniture
- Glassware
- Hardware
- Lamps
- Paint

Source: DOLLAR$ENSE Magazine, 1987

PRESCHOOLERS
■■■■■■■■■■■

While most people have heard about the baby boom that started in 1946 and lasted until 1964, few realize there is an annual baby boom that starts in mid-summer and peaks in September. For example, figures from the National Center for Health Statistics (NCHS) reveal that 12,100 babies were born every day in September 1990, compared with a daily average of 11,400 for the entire year.

September's Children

Although hospitals have known about this cycle for years, the increase in births brought on by baby-boom women in their peak childbearing years is putting a strain on the system. Doctors are less likely to take vacations during peak months, and nurses may be shifted from other parts of the hospital to handle the increase. But how much a hospital is affected by the increase in births depends on its mix of patients and how many Cesarean sections it performs. In some community hospitals, where obstetrics account for 40 percent of the volume, seasonal variations may significantly increase revenues.

The September peak can be traced back more than 100 years, according to Joseph Lee Rogers, associate professor of psychology at the University of Oklahoma. But he adds that seasonal variations present a real paradox. "When you interview people, you find that they most want to have a baby in the spring—April. And they least want to have a baby in August or September. But the smallest number of babies are born in April, and the largest number in August and September," explains Rogers.

To understand these seasonal variations, Rogers and associate Richard Uldry developed the "misinformed reproducers hypothesis." "Couples who want to have a baby must decide when to stop using contraceptives. They figure they'll do this nine or ten months before they want the baby. But it takes them three or four months to conceive," says Rogers. Consequently, their babies are born exactly when they don't want them.

This explanation is just one of the many theories for the seasonal variations in fertility. There may also be biological reasons, like sperm count and ovulatory patterns. David A. Seiver of Miami University has documented a link between temperature and fertility rates. His research indicates that seasonal variations are less distinct in the cooler northern states than in the South, and that the proliferation of air conditioning is reducing seasonality.

Even though seasonal variations may be cooling down, differences by day of the week are intensifying. Each year, relatively fewer children are born on weekends and holidays and more are born Tuesdays through Fridays. Cesarean deliveries are a primary reason for increases in weekday births, according to NCHS. More than one-third of Cesareans are repeat procedures, and physicians are unlikely to schedule these deliveries during the weekend. Tuesday is the biggest day for births. On an average Tuesday in 1988, 11,700 children were born, 9 percent more than the daily average for the year. Tuesday's children are not only full of grace: they also account for a disproportionately high number of birthday sales—especially when they're born in September.

Bringing up baby is still fun, but it is a lot more costly than it used to be. In 1990, a baby cost almost $5,800 in its first year of life, about twice as much as it did 30 years earlier, after adjusting for inflation. Food and feeding equipment account for $855 the first year, while diapers add $570 to the bill. Furniture for the nursery averages $995, while bedding and bath supplies come to $223, and medicines (including vitamins and personal care products) amount to $396. Almost $200 goes to toys. Among the most expensive items is day care, which costs over $2,000 during baby's first year.

Mothers of Invention

Preschoolers are one of the fastest-growing American markets. In 1990, the number of births stood at 4.2 million—the second year in a row that the total topped 4 million. These are the highest numbers since 1961. If this boom continues, the number of preschool-aged children could reach 20.2 million in 1994—almost as many as the 20.3 million in the peak year of 1960.

But because over half of new mothers return to work before their child's first birthday, the question of what to do with the kids is critical. Finding child-care providers from outside the family is essential for many new mothers. In 1985, nearly 16 percent of working mothers left their preschool children with their fathers while they worked. Another 16 percent of mothers depended on their children's grandparents. About 22 percent placed their children in the home of a nonrelative. Only 6 percent had a nonrelative watch the children in their own home. The largest share of working mothers, 23 percent, used organized day care—nearly double the proportion that used this service in 1977.

Preschool can be very costly. At $109 weekly, Boston may be the most expensive city for day care, according to a 1990 survey conducted by Runzheimer International in Rochester, Wisconsin. Costs were based on a 3-year-old who spends 40 hours each week in a for-profit day-care center in a suburban community surrounding the central city. The next two most expensive cities are New York City, at $95, and Anchorage, Alaska, at $91. Ogden, Utah, at $38 weekly, was the least expensive, followed by Mobile, Alabama, at $42, and Jackson, Mississippi, at $44.

But for many parents, cost does not equal satisfaction. Only 8 percent of the parents of preschoolers believe the child-care system is working very well, according to a 1989 survey by Louis Harris and Associates. While 38 percent have little faith in the capabilities of the child-care system, 53 percent say it is working somewhat well. Parents are dissatisfied with the cost, availability, and quality of child care. And this dissatisfaction is almost universally felt by both rich and poor parents.

For some parents, the cost of child care is simply too much of a burden on the household finances. For that reason, a growing number of parents have split-shift jobs. To make sure one parent is always around for the child, one parent works days and the other works nights or evenings. As of 1985, more than one out of every six working mothers with children under age 14 worked evenings, nights, or on a rotating shift, according to University of Maryland demographer Harriet Presser. One in five fathers also worked this schedule.

Industry was slow to recognize its role in child care. Only 2 percent of nonagricultural businesses with ten or more employees offered day-care centers for their employees' children in 1987, according to the Bureau of Labor Statistics. Three percent helped pay for child-care expenses, and 5 percent offered information and referrals to child-care facilities in the area.

But more recent information indicates that companies will become increasingly involved in day care in the future. Twenty-nine percent of companies affiliated with the International Foundation of Employee Benefits Plans (IFEBP) offered child-care resources or referrals in 1990, but 74 percent plan to offer these services by the year 2000. While 12 percent currently subsidize child-care expenses, 52 percent say they will offer some assistance by 2000. The number of on- or near-site child-care facilities is also expected to rise, from 7 percent in 1990 to 35 percent in 2000.

The financial burden of day-care costs, after-school activities, sick days, and other unforeseen events adds to the stress of coordinating work lives and private lives. Recognizing that stress impairs productivity, more companies are planning sick-child facilities or home-based care alternatives. Although only 3 percent of member companies offered these services in 1990, this share should rise to 28 percent by 2000, according to IFEBP.

American businesses may lose as much as $3 billion each year because of absences related to sick children or disrupted child-care service. Child Care Inc., a nonprofit private resource-and-referral agency in Manhattan, has been helping companies cope with emergency child care since 1989. To take part in the service, companies must pay an annual membership fee. When a child is sick or the regular caregiver is suddenly unavailable, Child Care Inc. arranges for an emergency caregiver. Most companies pay for the full cost of the emergency caregiver for the first three days and then half of the fee for the next three days. Employees appreciate the service so much that abuse is rare.

Helping parents of young children manage their time is becoming an important business. Kinder-Care Learning Centers of Montgomery, Alabama, which has more than 1,260 centers across the country, has extended its services beyond day care. The company, which minds some 130,000 children, offers a broad range of services to parents, from evening child care to handing the family's dry cleaning.

Kinder-Care is also getting together with national merchandisers to offer additional services to busy parents. Instead of requiring parents to supply the diapers and baby food their children use while at the day-care center, for example, the company has arranged for Procter & Gamble to provide Pampers and Beech-Nut to supply Special Harvest baby foods. Parents are charged supermarket prices, but they save the trouble of having to go out and purchase the supplies themselves.

As the number of children in this age group increases, so will the amount of money parents spend on them. Retail sales of clothing, baby-care supplies, juvenile furniture and nursery accessories, toys, and baby feeding supplies reached nearly $19 billion in 1990, according to the New York-based Packaged Facts, Inc. The market will experience steady sales increases for the next several years, making average annual gains of about 7 percent. At this rate, sales are expected to exceed $26 billion by 1995.

In 1990, clothing for infants, toddlers, and preschoolers accounted for almost half of overall sales of infants, toddlers, and preschool products. And clothing sales are expected to grow to $12 billion by 1995. Many of the leading marketers—Oshkosh, Carter, Gerber, JC Penney, Stride Rite, and Sears—are extending their product lines and devoting more of their marketing energy to preschoolers.

Other areas of the industry are making impressive gains, and there is increased competition among marketers. Mennen has increased its investment in skin care and toiletries with new products like Baby Magic Lite baby oil and Baby Magic baby powder with oatmeal. Marketing across broad category lines has become common. Fisher-Price, a manufacturer of baby toys, now has a clothing line. And a new toiletries line launched by S.C. Johnson is also licensed under the Fisher-Price name.

The number of births, especially first births, has contributed greatly to the increased sales of these products. But the rising number of mothers in the work force, their increased affluence, and something called the "daddy syndrome" are also contributing to bigger sales, says David A. Weiss, president of Packaged Facts. "The daddy syndrome is where you work harder to make more money to give to your kids, because you can't be with them—because you're working harder to make more money," says Weiss. When both parents suffer from the syndrome, dual-earner parents have double the guilt and twice as much money to spend for relief.

GRADE SCHOOL KIDS
■ ■ ■ ■ ■ ■ ■ ■ ■ ■ ■ ■ ■ ■

The rush to get organized in time for the school bus—lunches packed, backpacks filled, kids dressed, breakfast eaten—is a well-established routine by the end of September. But in the early days of the month, it can be a harrowing prospect.

K Through 8
The number of elementary-school students will increase by 8 percent between 1990 and 2000, according to the Population Reference Bureau (PRB) of Washington, D.C. But growth is not guaranteed in every school district. Overall, school enrollment will fall by at least 5 percent in Iowa, Kentucky, Montana, North Dakota, and West Virginia. Smaller declines are projected for Arkansas, Idaho,

Indiana, Louisiana, Michigan, Nebraska, Ohio, Oklahoma, Pennsylvania, Tennessee, Wisconsin, and Wyoming. But school enrollments in Alaska, California, Florida, and New Hampshire will grow by at least 20 percent. Arizona and New Mexico can expect gains of more than 30 percent.

For businesses, the changing characteristics of the school-aged population will be even more important than its rate of growth. By the year 2000, one in every three schoolchildren will be from a minority group. Minorities are already a majority in half of the nation's 100 largest school districts, according to PRB. In Oakland, Washington, D.C., Atlanta, New Orleans, Detroit, Newark, and San Antonio, minorities account for more than 90 percent of students.

Increasing ethnic diversity means greater cultural and language differences. It also means that the spending power of the school-aged market may not increase as rapidly as its size, because black and Hispanic children are three times more likely than non-Hispanic white children to live in poverty.

If current trends persist, PRB predicts that 42 percent of white children and 86 percent of black children will spend at least some of their childhood in a single-parent home. And the majority of children growing up in the 1990s will never know anything but a working mother.

The Latchkey Kids

An increase in the number of working parents is paralleled by an increase in the number of school-aged children who must look after themselves after school and before their parents come home from work. In 1984, about 7 percent of children aged 5 to 13 were latchkey kids, according to the Census Bureau.

Over two-thirds of eighth-grade students care for themselves at least one hour weekly after school, says a study published in the September 1990 issue of *Pediatrics*. Twenty-four percent of the students reported having to care for themselves between one and four hours each week after school. About 16 percent took care of themselves for 5 to 10 hours, and almost 29 percent for 11 hours or longer.

Almost half of these latchkey kids began caring for themselves in elementary school. Although girls and boys looked after themselves about the same number of hours each week, boys were more likely than girls to have begun self-care in elementary school.

Almost 70 percent of the eighth-graders lived with both parents, while 21 percent lived only with their mother, and 9 percent lived with their father, grandparents, or foster parents. Children living with two parents were less likely to care for themselves more than 11 hours weekly than those living with just one parent.

Children who cared for themselves for 11 hours or more after school performed equally well in their studies as those with more supervision. But the risk of unexcused absences from school was significantly higher for the children who were left on their own longer, according to the findings of the *Pediatrics* study.

The latchkey kids were more likely than others to cite their friends as their major source of influence. They were more likely than children with more supervision to go to parties. And they were more likely than others to be risk takers. They also reported a higher incidence of stress, anger, and fear when left alone. Children who took care of themselves for 11 hours or more had a higher rate of substance use for cigarettes, alcohol, and marijuana. Those who initiated self-care during elementary school were at higher risk for heavy alcohol and marijuana use than their counterparts who began self-care in junior high.

The survey did not include children who attended private or remedial schools. But ethnic differences indicate that white children are more likely than minority children to be in self-care. Self-care is associated significantly with higher, rather than lower, socioeconomic status.

Quality Time

Even though more mothers split their time between home and the office, today's parents spend more time in activities with their children than those of the 1970s did. Parents of children aged 7 to 17 do many more things with their children than parents who answered the same question in the late 1970s, according to a 1991 Roper Organization survey. The activities they share include going out to eat together, watching television, enjoying recreational activities, and just sitting and talking.

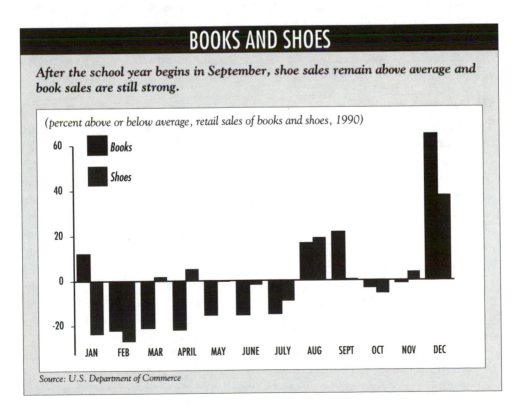

BOOKS AND SHOES

After the school year begins in September, shoe sales remain above average and book sales are still strong.

(*percent above or below average, retail sales of books and shoes, 1990*)

■ Books

■ Shoes

Source: U.S. Department of Commerce

Today's families do only one thing less frequently than parents did in the 1970s—eat meals together. Baby-boomer parents are strong believers in "quality time," but meal-time is sometimes sacrificed. With work, school, and after-school activities using up more late-afternoon and early-evening hours, arranging meal times that fit each household member's schedule is becoming increasingly difficult.

Businesses are working to help busy parents cope with shopping and services. Those that provide services to school-aged children, from orthodontia to music lessons, will profit by offering flexible schedules and help with transportation. And service businesses can no longer assume that all parents work from nine to five on weekdays, either. Just as the number of parents who must work split shifts is increasing, so too is the number of parents who work on weekends. One in four employed women and one in three employed men work on weekends, according to PRB.

Many retailers are making sure the shopping experience is positive for parents who must (or want to) shop with their children. Some do this by helping family members avoid conflicts, by providing "no candy" checkout lanes or diaper changing areas. Others strive to enhance the complete shopping experience. At the West Point market in Akron, Ohio, shopping carts are provided for "little shoppers only," turning a mundane grocery shopping trip into an adventure. The market provides other incentives for parents who bring kids shopping—they offer "cookie credits," a West Point currency that can be exchanged at the in-store bakery for fresh chocolate-chip cookies. It also provides a rainbow of balloons at the register where the store photographs the little shoppers manning their carts. "We call this strategy 'plussing the business.' It's a way of enhancing the shopping environment to a degree that sets your store apart from the competition," says West Point Market's Russell Vernon.

Kids' Spending Power

The buying power of 4-to-12-year-olds has been steadily rising. The average per capita income of this age group increased 46 percent from 1984 to 1989, according to a survey conducted by James McNeal, professor of marketing at Texas A&M University in College Station, Texas. In 1984, children aged 4 to 12 "earned" an average of $158 each year, primarily from gifts and allowances from parents and relatives. This figure reached $230 in 1989. While children still spend the majority of their income, they have become better savers over the years. In 1984, the average child managed to save only $16. But in 1989, the average child put away $70, an increase of 335 percent.

But even though children are saving more of their own money, they still spend at very high levels. American children spent just over $6 billion in 1989, 41 percent more than in 1984. While 4-year-olds spend just 83 cents weekly, 6-year-olds spend $2.59 a week, and 12-year-olds spend $6.90, according to McNeal.

Children spend most of their money on food and toys. In 1989, they spent about $2 billion on candy, soft drinks, frozen desserts, fruits, and other snacks such as potato chips, popcorn, and peanuts. They spent $1.9 billion on toys, games, and crafts—everything from toy cars and board games to bicycles, skateboards, and video game cartridges.

Clothing is another big spending area. Kids spent almost $700 million on clothes in 1989, usually brands that their parents consider too expensive. They also spend over $600 million on movies, spectator sports, and live entertainment. Video arcades and video games accounted for $486 million, and the remaining $264 million went for other expenditures, including televisions, portable stereos, telephones, cosmetics, compact discs, and video movie rentals.

Children enjoy shopping, and many visit stores on their own before they get into grade school. Half of 6-year-olds make a purchase themselves at least once a week. About three-quarters of 7-to-9-year-olds make independent trips to stores, visiting an average of two stores each week. By age 10, virtually all children buy things on their own at least twice a week, in at least two different stores.

Children are willing consumers, according to McNeal: "They know a lot about stores, and they remember small details. Retailers should take note that making their stores child-friendly now could yield an important source of customers in the future."

The Tweens

Children aged 8 to 13 feel very strongly that school and family are the most important elements of their day-to-day lives, says Irma Zandl, president of Xtreme, Inc. in New York City. These tweens have a need to fit in, according to her interviews with young people. The majority of tween-aged children do not want to stand out from the crowd; they prefer instead to follow the mainstream.

Team sports, especially contact sports, are important to boys in their tween years, and this trend continues in their teenage period. Soccer is very popular with the 8-to-13 set, but it declines in popularity as the children get older. Other contact sports, however, remain popular.

Like women of all ages, tween girls love to dance. They list it not only as their favorite activity but also as their favorite hobby. Zandl predicts that this love of dancing will lead to a revival of the 1970s disco-dancing craze during the next five years. Unfortunately, boys do not feel the same way about dancing and see social events where dancing takes place in a totally different way than girls do. They see parties as a way of making social contact with their peers. The concept of "partying" is strictly male. While girls dance, boys interact on a more verbal level. Girls may fantasize about dancing with "Mr. Right," but boys think about sex, according to Zandl.

Both boys and girls like humorous commercials, but the sexes react differently to different subject matter, Zandl explains. Tween-aged boys favor commercials that advertise food, entertainment, and athletic wear—especially sneakers. Even though tween boys still like "warm and fuzzy" ads (those featuring baby animals, animated teddy bears, and sweet sentiments), this gentle side is all but gone by their teenage years.

Girls find action and sports spots irrelevant. But girls of all ages like commercials for food and beverages, as well as those about household goods, diapers, paper towels, and carpeting, says Zandl. But their favorite commercials are for dolls and toys. "Warm and fuzzy" commercials are the most important for both tweens and teenaged girls. Kittens and animated teddy bears carry a lot of weight with young girls. Advertisements featuring "cover girl" models are also a great success among girls of all ages.

In commercials, tweens like to see children of their own age or younger in group activities. Seeing children in ads may reinforce their need to feel just like everyone else. Tweens are real conformists. They feel intense peer pressure and commitment to fads. They have "no saturation point," says Zandl. They will eat, wear, read, watch, and even sleep on Teenage Mutant Ninja Turtle products quite happily until the next fad comes along. But tweenage fads have a life expectancy of only two years.

HIGH SCHOOL
■■■■■■■■■

After more than a decade of decline, secondary-school enrollment began to rise again in 1991. This rise marked the beginning of sustained growth for high schools. By 1994, high school enrollment should reach 13.6 million, 1 million more than in 1990.

High Schoolers

Teens place a great deal of emphasis on friends and independence, says Xtreme's Irma Zandl. A good network of friends offers these young people a safe environment in which they can grow and experience life. But many of the choices that teenagers make are very different from the ones they would have made just a few years earlier.

Teenage boys are "aspirational," according to Zandl. They identify with adult male figures. They want to be thought of as older—as if they could skip the awkward adolescent years. They pay close attention to advertisements that use attractive, female spokespersons in their 20s and older. "Teenage boys do not want to identify with other teens," says Zandl. Only younger teenage girls identify with teen heart-throbs, according to Zandl. Older teenage girls look to more mature male spokespersons—especially those in the entertainment field.

Teenagers watch commercials with great interest, according to Zandl's studies. But many of their favorites advertise products not geared to them. Teenage boys say an advertisement for a medical alert device for the elderly is one of their favorite commercials. As for tweens, humorous commercials are a favorite of teens, but older boys especially like those with more risque or slapstick humor.

By age 14, boys also prefer action-packed commercials with sexy women and sports heroes. Ads for athletic equipment, like sports shoes, are especially effective in influencing shopping behavior. Most teenagers love both Nike ads and Nike running shoes, for example.

Marketing to children and teens can be challenging, and a certain amount of discretion is required. Products such as sugar-laden cereals, snacks, and drinks may

FAST CARS, SLOW MARKET

THE NEW YEAR may be three months away, but the champagne and confetti are already being opened in automobile showrooms. For auto dealers, New Year's comes in September when the new models arrive. Buying a new car is a costly experience, second only to buying a home for most people, and it can be nearly as nerve-wracking, for both buyers and sellers.

Sales of new automobiles are closely tied to the economy, but a multitude of demographic factors, including age, marital status, gender, and geography, are also important. Predicting sales is challenging and risky.

New-car sales have been slow throughout the 1980s and will continue to be sluggish until the economy picks up, but industry-specific factors must also be taken into account, says Geoffrey Greene, senior economist for DRI/McGraw-Hill in Washington, D.C. The competition between auto manufacturers has led them to depend heavily on incentives and promotions, and now few consumers will buy cars unless they get rebates or low- or no-interest loans as part of the package. General Motors, Ford, and Chrysler cannot afford to continue offering the hefty incentives that spurred their sales in 1989 and 1990, according to Greene, and this may lead to a confrontation between the big-three auto makers and their fickle public.

Only 2 percent of American households purchase new cars or trucks in a typical year, according to the 1990 Consumer Expenditure Survey (CEX) of the Bureau of Labor Statistics. That share is much higher for married couples, and it peaks among married couples with children.

U. S. consumers spent $112 billion on new vehicles in 1990, according to the CEX. Married couples with children of any age account for 43 percent of the market, even though they are just 29 percent of households. Families with older teens account for 15 percent of the total market, but just 9 percent of all households. Married couples with preschoolers are only slightly more likely than the average household to buy a new car. They are 6.5 percent of households and 7 percent of the new-car market. Couples with school-aged children (aged 6 to 17) make up 14 percent of all households and 21 percent of the new-car market.

Women On Wheels

Women are another important market for new-car sales. They bought 45 percent of new cars sold in the U.S. in 1987, up from 23 percent in 1970, and their influence is felt in 80 percent of all new-car purchases, according to studies by J.D. Power and Associates of West Lake Village, California. Targeting women is, therefore, of paramount importance, both for domestic and foreign car manufacturers.

Women car-buyers are young. Sixty-one percent of buyers under age 25 are women, and women make up 49 percent of all 25-to-44-year-old buyers. Of those aged 45 and older, only 28 percent are women, according to a 1988 Newsweek study. Within the import-car market, women are more likely than men to buy Japanese cars.

Women can present a greater challenge to local retailers than men do, according to Jayne Hamilton, author of *How to Sell Cars and Trucks to Women*. Women notice not only the car, but also the ambience of the showroom, the knowledge and attentiveness of the dealer, and the overall environment of the dealership. In order to assure a sale to a female customer, the local dealership—both the showroom personnel and the service department—must be reliable, dependable, knowledgeable, and accessible to the customer.

Since women buy cars of all categories—from economy sub-compact to luxury sedan—manufacturers must be prepared to make all types of vehicles accessible to this important market. Even one of the last bastions of male car owners—the pickup truck and van—is becoming a woman's domain. Women were responsible for 32 percent of Ford compact-van purchases in 1987, as well as 30 percent of compact utility trucks, 17 percent of utility trucks, 14 percent of full-sized vans, 12 percent of compact pickups, and 5 percent of large pickup trucks.

Luxury Sales

Sales of luxury cars depend not only on the economy, but also on the growing senior segment of the population. As the baby-boom generation becomes older and more affluent, sales in this category could increase.

Over 5 million Americans own domestic luxury cars that they bought new—including Buicks, Cadillacs, Corvettes, Chryslers, Lincolns, and Oldsmobiles—according to a 1988 study by Simmons Market Research Bureau in New York City. Luxury-car owners are twice as likely as others to have annual household incomes of $60,000 or more. Ownership peaks among people aged 55 to 64. This age group makes up only 12 percent of all adults but 23 percent of domestic luxury-car owners.

In the 1980s, domestic luxury-car sales were hurt by slow growth in the age group most likely to buy these vehicles. But between 1990 and 2000, market growth will accelerate. The number of people aged 55 to 64 will grow 13 percent, while the total adult population will increase just 9 percent.

People who now own a domestic luxury car will be the best customers for future sales. These car owners are more likely than others to make a new-car purchase every year, and their brand loyalty makes marketing relatively easy. But attracting the next generation of luxury-car buyers will be a marketing challenge. Cadillac's 1992 Eldorado and Seville models have a leaner, more "European" look than previous year's models. The redesigns were made to catch the attention of younger consumers.

But as the market for luxury grows, so will the competition. Japanese manufacturers have shown they can compete in the luxury-car category, and 8 percent of people who currently own a domestic luxury car say their next purchase will be a foreign model. A 1989 survey by the Roper Organization showed that people with higher incomes were more likely than others to think foreign cars are higher quality than American-made cars.

appeal to kids but not to their parents, and the debate about whether to direct advertising toward children or their parents has been going on for many years.

Teens and Money

Both boys and girls between the ages of 13 and 18 are most interested in products that enhance their appearance and make them more attractive to the opposite sex. Both genders spend large sums on fashion and grooming, but girls spend to excess on these two categories, says Zandl.

Money is a key issue for teenagers, many of whom live very expensive lifestyles. Teenagers are brand oriented and prioritize their spending. Many will scrimp on soda, fast foods, and snacks in order to have enough money for name-brand athletic shoes, jeans, and cosmetics.

Even while their numbers were declining in the 1980s, the spending power of teens was on the rise, according to Teenage Research Unlimited (TRU) in Northbrook, Illinois. Although the number of 12-to-19-year-olds dropped 5 percent between 1986 and 1989, their spending power rose 4 percent. Teenaged boys spent an average of nearly $49 a week in 1989, while girls spent more than $55. Teenagers spent about $79 billion in 1990, according to TRU. That's about $2,500 for each of the nation's 27 million 12-to-19-year-olds. But some of that money, $29 billion, went for family expenditures, such as groceries.

The amount of control teens have over what they buy varies by product, making it difficult to determine whether to target teens or their parents. To point marketers in the right direction, TRU developed the Teen Buying Control Index. This index is the ratio of the spending teens control to their total spending on a product. For example, the index for food bought by teenaged boys is 39—indicating that parents make most of the decisions about the food teenaged boys eat. The index for pizza from a fast-food restaurant is 62, while the index for frozen pizza is 23. Although the teenager decides what he eats after the game, mom is more likely to choose the youngster's mid-afternoon snack at home.

Both boys and girls have a lot of control over their spending on audio and video products; boys score 87 points in the purchase of prerecorded full-length audio cassettes, and girls score 71. Girls score higher than boys in clothes and shoe purchases, as well as beauty aids.

The buying control index for bubble gum is 82 for boys and 85 for girls, but the index for cold cereal is just 14 for boys and 13 for girls. Teens make the decisions when they buy posters, T-shirts, magazines, or movie tickets. But they are at the mercy of their parents when it comes to buying toothpaste, bar soap, or salad dressing.

Teens and Time

While it may appear that teenagers do little more than shop at the mall and talk on the phone, studies show they have other interests. For one thing, they sleep a lot, according to the 1985 Americans' Use of Time Project conducted by the Survey Research Center at the University of Maryland. In one week, people aged 12 to 17 spend almost 63 hours sleeping, compared with less than 56 hours for unmarried 18-to-29-year-olds.

The major difference between the time use of teenagers and young adults between the ages of 18 and 29 centers on the transition from school to work. Teenagers spend, on average, less than 3 hours a week in work-related activity, including travel to and from work. But young adults work 29 hours a week, on average. Teens, on the other hand, spend almost 24 hours a week on school-related activities, compared with only a little more than 8 hours for young adults.

What do teens do when they're goofing off? They watch almost 18 hours of television a week, compared with about 14 hours for unmarried young adults. But teenagers are also an active group—they spend more time on sports, both as participants and spectators, than young adults. They also play more card games and board games.

Contrary to popular belief, teens do not spend more time in the bathroom or kitchen than young adults. But gender differences are significant. Teenage girls spend more time than boys on grooming and personal hygiene. Girls also spend more time doing homework, while boys spend more time playing sports and pursuing hobbies. Boys and girls spend the same amount of time reading—a little more than one hour each week.

Team Spirit

Sports participation and the desire to participate in sports decline sharply and steadily between the ages of 10 and 18, according to a 1987 study sponsored by the Athletic Footwear Association. At age 10, 45 percent of young people say they participate or intend to participate on a nonschool team. This figure drops to 26 percent by age 18. How much fun young athletes are having determines whether or not they continue with a sport. When young people are bored, they drop out.

Participation in some high school sports affects the whole community. More than 30 million people attend high school football games each year, according to a 1986 survey by the National Sporting Goods Association. The survey, which included persons aged 7 and older, found that people aged 10 to 17 constitute 32 percent of the spectators—almost three times their representation in the general population. Another 25 percent of spectators are aged 35 to 54. Many of these fans are friends, siblings, and parents of the players.

One marketer, American Passage Media Corporation of Chicago, Illinois, has found a way to reach student athletes. Its product, GymBoards, is a three-paneled bulletin board placed in locker rooms. The center panel is a chalkboard that the coach can use for announcements. Another panel, called "GymShorts," is a four-color editorial panel that addresses various teen topics from teenage pregnancy and suicide to acne and school spirit. The last panel is reserved for advertising. Because the boards are hung in locker rooms, their messages can be gender-specific. The company first introduced the boards in 1987; by 1991, they were installed in more than 3,100 high schools.

THE COLLEGE YEARS
■ ■ ■ ■ ■ ■ ■ ■ ■ ■ ■ ■ ■

While high schools depend on a specific age group to make up their student body, colleges and universities market their courses to a broader audience. Overall, enrollment for many colleges in the 1980s was stable even though the supply of traditional "college-aged" young adults was dwindling.

The Student Body

In order to keep enrollment levels high, colleges have appealed to some non-traditional segments—women, older students, and part-timers—and these groups will probably help maintain or increase enrollments in the future. In 1991, 43 percent of all college students were at least 25 years old, compared with 39 percent in 1981.

The majority of mature students return to college to enhance their career opportunities, by getting a graduate or professional degree or completing the undergraduate degree they never finished. For the most part they are white women aged 25 to 34, married and working full-time, with an average family income of

$39,000 to $49,000, according to a 1988 study conducted by the Office of Adult Learning Services at the College Board in New York City.

Even though more adults are going back to school, colleges still face the challenge of recruiting high school students. Most high schoolers recognize the need for a college degree, but they are getting as deliberate about their choice of college as about their choice of career.

The price of a college education has increased steadily since the 1970s, and yearly tuition, fees, and room and board at some exclusive private institutions topped $20,000 in 1990. While these top-level colleges are looking for the best and brightest, there is a smaller pool of qualified high schoolers from which to choose, says Peggy Walbridge, associate director of admissions at Cornell University in Ithaca, New York.

Recruitment has become a major task for most colleges, from state-run institutions and small private schools to the more selective Ivy-League-type colleges as the number of qualified high school students decreased steadily throughout the 1980s, says Walbridge.

This is partly because the traditional age group attending college was declining. But it's also due to growing shares of minority youth who are less likely to go on to college, or even to graduate from high school. The share of black high school graduates who go on to college is shrinking. Hispanics and Native Americans are also underrepresented in the student body, according to Walbridge. Many minority students do not see college as a possibility. They look at the price tags and count themselves out. Other minority students are tracked into vocational streams while still in high school and are not prepared for college when they graduate.

Nevertheless, as the need for higher education becomes more apparent, the overall share of high school graduates going on to college is on the rise. Those who go on to college are very different than those who to go directly into the working world. College kids have more diverse tastes, and they are more fickle. As they come in contact with peers from different cities, countries, or religious and ethnic groups, the natural curiosity that led them to college also leads them to experiment with new products in every category, from food and clothing to entertainment and travel.

Campus Life

The favorite day-to-day activities of college kids vary greatly by gender. Young men list school, parties, hanging out, and sports as their favorite activities. Young women, on the other hand, feel that family, friends, and happiness are the most important elements of their daily life.

The 1990 college market represented about $31 billion in annual buying power, with $8.4 billion in discretionary income, according to the New York City-based Roper CollegeTrack. The average annual personal earnings of college students is nearly $4,000. Some 68 percent of college students carry credit cards—and 70 percent of these young people pay their own credit-card bills.

As college students use more of their discretionary income to buy clothes, books, and other products, they often look to print advertisements to make them aware of sales and the availability of products. College newspapers are becoming more prosperous, as advertisers use them to reach a well-defined market. More than 40 percent of college students surveyed by CollegeTrack have read all of the last five issues of their campus papers. About 2,400 college papers now reach 8 million U.S. students.

Although reaching a college newspaper reader is usually more expensive than advertising in a general daily paper on a cost-per-thousand basis, the common bonds of readers make college papers an easier sell to the advertising community, according to David Knott, coordinator of operations for the *Daily News* at Ball State University.

Sixty-four percent of all college students read their campus newspapers, according to a 1988 Roper poll. Women and freshmen are the most likely to read the campus paper—70 percent each. But the share of readers decreases as the students move through the system—only 58 percent of seniors read their paper. On-campus students (70 percent) read the paper more often than those living off-campus (61 percent) or at home (51 percent).

College students are well known for their tendencies to study hard, play hard, and eat food that makes a mother cringe. Cookies, pizza, and soda are mainstays of most dorm-room food cupboards. Students who can't bring themselves to eat at the cafeteria subsist on a diet of pasta, cereal, and any product that can be "nuked" in a microwave. Half of all students say they use a microwave oven every day, according to CollegeTrack.

The most popular food of college students is pizza—selected by more than half of students participating in a 1990 CollegeTrack study. Hamburgers came in second, chosen by 7 percent of students. Food products stored in a college student's dorm room include cookies, taco chips, Twinkies, and potato chips. Sodas are perennial favorites, and during pre-exam all-nighters, many students choose high-caffeine beverages like Mountain Dew or Jolt, a soda that claims to have twice the caffeine and all the sugar of regular Coke or Pepsi.

Seven in ten college students have televisions and six in ten have cars, according to Bickley Townsend, vice president of the Roper Organization. College students are ardent consumers of other electrical equipment, as well. "Power to the people takes on a whole new meaning when one considers that an average 2-person dorm room at UCLA requires 16 electrical outlets," says Townsend.

The average cost of tuition and fees increased nearly 10 percent for the 1991-92 school year, according to Strategic Marketing Communications' *Collegiate Trends*, published in Ridgewood, New Jersey. That's four times the annual rate of inflation for the nation as a whole. The increase was greatest in four-year public schools, 14 percent. The increase in four-year private schools was somewhat below average, at 9.7 percent. Sharp reductions in both financial aid from both federal and state agencies have driven the increases, says *Collegiate Trends*. Students will be working more, and the demand for financial aid will skyrocket.

SCHOOL TEACHERS
■■■■■■■■■■■■■

Some people are tied to the school calendar whether or not they are enrolled in school and whether or not they have children in school. Most of these people are teachers, but there are also large numbers of administrators, maintenance people, counselors, librarians, cooks, and bus drivers who depend on education for their livelihood. Almost 6 million people work as teachers, librarians, or counselers, according to the Bureau of Labor Statistics (BLS). And this number should grow to more that 7 million by 2005. Most teachers work the traditional 9-to-10-month-long school year and have a 2-to-3-month-long vacation. During their break, some may teach summer school, while others find other summer jobs, earn extra college credits, or just take a vacation.

An Apple for the Teacher

The largest share of people with education-related jobs are kindergarten and elementary-school teachers, according to the Bureau of Labor Statistics (BLS). In 1990, there were approximately 1.4 million people in these jobs; about 80 percent were employed in public schools. For the 1988-89 school year, the average salary for kindergarten and elementary-school teachers was $28,900. About 1.3 million people are secondary-school teachers; 90 percent work in public schools. During the 1988-89 school year, their average salary was $30,300. Another 275,000 Americans are special-education teachers working with mentally retarded, emotionally disturbed, learning disabled, mobility impaired, speech and hearing impaired, and gifted children. Most of these teachers work in elementary schools.

For both elementary- and secondary- school teachers, average earnings in private schools are lower than in public schools. But salaries are generally higher in the Mid-Atlantic and Western states. Employment growth for elementary- and secondary- school teachers may outpace the population growth of the children they teach as class sizes become smaller in the 1990s, according to the BLS.

College and university faculty accounted for 712,000 jobs in 1990, according to the BLS. The average faculty member who worked full-time for nine months earned $39,400 during the 1988-89 school year. But full professors earned more than $50,400, while associate professors earned about $37,500 and assistant professors earned $31,200. Teaching instructors at colleges and universities earned only about $23,700 in 1988. Little or no change is expected in total employment, says the BLS. Most job openings will arise as faculty members retire or transfer to other occupations.

Another 320,000 people are education administrators. More than 88 percent of these people work in educational services in elementary, secondary, and technical schools, and colleges and universities. The rest work for child-care facilities, religious organizations, job-training centers, state departments of education, and business and other organizations that provide training for their employees or clients. The average salary of an educational administrator was $35,000 in 1988, but salaries vary tremendously depending on the position. The average salary for an assistant principal at an elementary school is $38,500, while the average for a dean at a school of medicine is $143,200, according to the BLS. Most education administrators work year-round, although busy seasons rise and fall as students work their way through the school year.

THE MATURE MARKET

National Grandparents Day—the first Sunday after Labor Day—was legalized in 1979, and although it has not yet caught the imagination of the American public, Hallmark Cards reports steady sales of more than 4 million Grandparents Day cards annually.

Celebrating Grandparents

As the children of baby boomers become parents, watch out for an explosion of grandparents. Declining birthrates have resulted in a smaller number of grandchildren per grandparent—meaning that each grandparent has more time and money to shower on individual grandchildren. At the same time, divorces and remarriages have provided some children with more than two sets of grandparents, all vying for little Johnny's or Jennifer's attention.

While only 3 percent of 35-to-39-year-olds have grandchildren (under 18 years old), 26 percent of those between the ages of 45 and 49 do, according to Mediamark Research, Inc. of New York City. About 43 percent of people aged 50 to 54 have grandchildren, as do 55 percent of 55-to-59-year-olds and 60 percent of people in their 60s. Adults in their 70s have fewer grandchildren under 18, but more in their 20s.

By the year 2000, the oldest baby boomers will be 54. Between 1990 and the turn of the century, the number of grandparents aged 45 to 54 will probably climb from less than 9 million to nearly 13 million—a 47 percent increase.

Tapping into this grandparent market may be difficult, since recognizing the "typical" grandparent can be challenging. Many younger grandparents are happy with the title, but others feel the role has a certain stigma: bespectacled, crotchety, and old. Grandparents who live near their children may find themselves directly involved in the upbringing of their grandchildren. For some grandparents, this babysitting role may come into direct conflict with the desire to be free of responsibilities. For grandparents who live further away from their children and grandchildren, the extent of their involvement with grandchildren can range from birthday gifts in the mail to monthly visits.

No matter what the distance, grandparents express their love for grand-children with both time and money. About 61 percent of grandparents spoke with their grandchildren on the telephone in the last month, according to a Roper poll, and 52 percent had their grandchildren over for a meal. Grandparents spent an average of $250 on their grandchildren in 1990, according to the survey (although fully 25 percent of respondents didn't know how much they spent on their grandchildren).

Grandparents are heavy purchasers of toys, and the older the grandparent, the more likely he or she is to buy toys. While 14 percent of young (under 45) grandparents bought toys for their grandchildren in 1989, this number jumped to 49 percent for those aged 45 to 54, according to Simmons Market Research Bureau. Fully 62 percent of grandparents aged 55 and older bought toys for their grandchildren.

Toys are not the only things grandparents buy for their grandchildren, according to a subscriber survey conducted for *New Choices* magazine. Ninety-four percent of readers who are grandparents have purchased clothing for their grandchildren, 89 percent have purchased books, 46 percent a bicycle, 31 percent investments (stocks, bonds, U.S. savings bonds, or coins), and 25 percent entertainment equipment—a stereo, camera, or video equipment.

For the most part, grandparents make their own decisions about what to buy and how much they should spend, according to PrimeLife Marketing in Plymouth Meeting House, Pennsylvania. Important considerations in buying clothing, toys, and books include brand name, outlet, whether the item was American made or not, familiarity with the product, and price.

The largest share of grandparents (47 percent) say they learn about products from the newspaper. Another 37 percent find out about the gifts they buy by watching television, and 35 percent see them in newspaper supplements. A large share of grandparents (43 percent) say they make their decisions to buy on the spur-of-the-moment or within one week of making the purchase.

The most important occasions to give gifts are birthdays and holidays, according to grandparents. But because many grandparents give gifts for no reason at all, PrimeLife warns that its would be a mistake to think of this market as seasonal. Grandparents are likely to find any occasion suitable for giving a gift to their grandchildren, including Easter and Valentine's Day.

Even though grandparents enjoy giving to their grandchildren, they don't want to be accused of buying affection. Retailers have to walk a narrow line between what may be perceived as a genuine vehicle for a grandparent's affection and what may be interpreted as purely exploitive. They must also be careful not to stereotype grandparents.

The first step in targeting grandparents is to understand that the "little old lady" image is a thing of the past. These people cannot be reached through advertisements that insult them, play on the fears associated with growing old, or approach them in a condescending manner.

THE FIRST FROST

By November 15th, practically everyone in America is in need of an overcoat. But many need a coat in September.

(mean date of first 32° temperature in autumn)

■ Before August 1
■ August 1–September 1
■ September 1–October 1
□ October 1–November 1
□ November 1–December 1
□ After December 1

Source: National Oceanic and Atmospheric Administration

Reaching the Older Audience

Communicating with elderly adults can be effective if a number of basic principles are observed, according to Charles D. Schewe, professor of marketing at the University of Massachusetts at Amherst. Keeping the message simple is a good starting point. Older adults react more slowly and less accurately to sensory information, and if a message is overloaded, its basic premise is lost.

The message must also be familiar. Schewe points out that familiar experiences are easier for older people to process. As a message becomes more complex, this principle becomes more important. The message should also be concrete, rather than abstract. As people age, their problem-solving abilities decline. Older people also begin to lose verbal memory more quickly than visual memory. By providing concrete images, the message is more clearly remembered.

When developing a message for the elderly, Schewe suggests that it be presented point by point so that the message can be absorbed. Schewe also suggests giving preference to print media, since print media let consumers set their own pace, a characteristic not shared by radio and television advertising.

Every year, advertising campaigns miss their mark because they lack a sensible and sensitive approach to the older market. Products that provide comfort, security, and convenience can all be directed to this segment of the population. Products or services that provide elderly consumers with a sense of purpose and independence will also be well received.

September Weekends

As the green leaves of summer turn into the golds and reds of fall, many Americans are busy planning ways to get away from it all—at least for a weekend. During the six weeks when fall foliage is at its colorful peak (usually in September and October), the number of people who visit Vermont exceeds the state's population. The hues of autumn also draw tourists to the Great Smoky Mountains, Yosemite National Park, and other forested areas. Crowds gather at harvest festivals: Californians celebrate onions in Vacaville, brussels sprouts in Santa Cruz, and wine at Lake Tahoe.

To extend the summer season in Atlantic City, New Jersey, the first Miss America pageant was scheduled for September 1921. But informal autumn jaunts are becoming more popular as Americans' lifestyles change. During September, October, and November of 1990, Americans took some 164 million round trips of 100 miles or more, according to the U.S. Travel Data Center in Washington, D.C. About 111 million trips, 68 percent of fall trips, were taken for pleasure.

Fall pleasure trips in 1990 were shorter than summer trips, both in duration and distance traveled, according to the Travel Data Center. The typical autumn vacationer traveled 780 miles and spent four nights away from home. Fully 56 percent of these travelers said that visiting friends or family was their primary objective, 28 percent were looking for entertainment, and 15 percent wanted outdoor recreation. Thirty-nine percent of fall pleasure trips are taken by someone traveling alone, and 36 percent consist of two travelers. About 20 percent of fall travel parties in 1990 included children.

People who take advantage of the fall travel season are different than those who travel in summer. They are more likely than summer fun seekers to be older and retired. Almost half of the fall visitors to Great Smoky Mountains National Park in Tennessee are aged 50 or older, and 28 percent are retired.

Nationwide, 29 percent of autumn fun seekers are aged 55 or older, compared with 23 percent of summer travelers, according to the Travel Data Center. About 19 percent of fall pleasure travelers are retired, versus 17 percent of summer travelers.

In autumn, however, receipts at hotels, motels, and other lodgings are almost as high as those collected during the summer, according to Smith Travel Research in Hendersonville, Tennessee. During September, October, and November 1988, lodging receipts totaled $13.7 billion, compared with $14.4 billion during the three preceding months. Fall pleasure travelers may be older, but they can be just as profitable.

While mature adults love to travel, they present the industry with a different set of criteria than the family travel market does. Knowing how to catch their attention and how to provide for their needs is important if the travel industry is to keep up with this growing segment of the population. Older adults are particularly drawn to vacation spots that also provide educational opportunities, according to Charles Schewe. Elderhostels offer educational travel opportunities. Royal Viking Cruise Lines provides seminars on financial planning, computers, and writing for its customers. While only 17 percent of adults under age 30 look for cultural enrichment in a leisure activity, 26 percent of adults aged 45 and older do, according to Roper.

SUMMER'S END
■■■■■■■■■■■

September is frequently the beginning of the New Year for America's Jews. On the Jewish Calendar, Rosh Hashanah is celebrated on the first day of the month of the month of Tishri—sometime between September 5th and October 5th for the rest of us. Nine days after Rosh Hashanah comes Yom Kippur or the Day of Atonement, the holiest day of the Jewish year.

September is also an important time for native Americans. On the second week in September, the Navajo Nation Fair is held in Window Rock, Arizona. The Navajo Nation is the largest Indian tribe in the U. S., and its fair is the largest. The 1990 census counted 1.9 million native Americans (American Indians, Eskimos, and Aleuts), a 38 percent gain over the 1980 census count. This increase is far greater than one would expect from births alone, and many experts believe that the unexpected growth is due to an increased pride in being a native American. In other words, more people with native American ancestry decided to acknowledge that ancestry on their 1990 census forms than in 1980.

The state of Maryland celebrates Defenders' Day in September. National events include National Chicken Month, National Piano Month, National Cat Health Month, and National Courtesy Month. But it's Labor Day that marks the important transition from summer fun to business as usual. As soon as the picnic supplies are packed away, the same old routine quickly falls into place. The kids are back to school and parents are back to work.

OCTOBER WEATHER
■ ■ ■ ■ ■ ■ ■ ■ ■ ■ ■ ■ ■

By October, the 70s have given way to the 60s in many American cities. And lows in the 30s and 40s are common across the U.S.

	TEMPERATURE		PRECIPITATION	
	low	*high*	*inches*	*days*
Albuquerque, NM	43.1°F	71.7°F	0.86	5
Atlanta, GA	51.4	72.9	2.53	6
Bismarck, ND	32.8	59.3	0.81	6
Boise, ID	39.1	64.6	0.75	6
Boston, MA	47.1	62.5	3.36	9
Buffalo, NY	42.7	60.2	2.93	12
Burlington, VT	38.7	57.0	2.81	12
Charlotte, NC	49.6	71.7	2.72	7
Chicago, IL	42.9	64.1	2.28	9
Cleveland, OH	43.6	62.7	2.45	11
Dallas, TX	56.3	79.5	2.47	6
Denver, CO	36.9	66.8	0.98	5
Detroit, MI	41.2	62.5	2.12	10
Great Falls, MT	36.2	59.5	0.82	6
Honolulu, HI	72.2	86.7	1.88	9
Houston, TX	57.5	81.9	3.67	8
Indianapolis, IN	43.4	66.1	2.51	8
Jacksonville, FL	59.2	79.7	3.41	9
Juneau, AK	36.5	47.0	7.71	24
Los Angeles, CA	58.5	74.0	0.26	2
Memphis, TN	51.3	74.5	2.37	6
Miami, FL	71.6	84.2	7.14	14
Milwaukee, WI	41.9	59.9	2.25	9
Minneapolis, MN	39.4	59.7	1.85	8
Mobile, AL	57.5	79.4	2.62	6
New Orleans, LA	59.0	79.4	2.66	6
New York, NY	49.9	65.6	3.41	8
Norfolk, VA	52.8	69.8	3.41	8
Oklahoma City, OK	50.2	74.3	2.71	6
Omaha, NE	42.0	67.0	2.09	7
Philadelphia, PA	46.5	66.5	2.83	8
Phoenix, AZ	59.1	87.7	0.63	3
Portland, OR	44.6	63.9	3.05	12
Salt Lake City, UT	39.3	66.7	1.14	6
San Francisco, CA	51.2	70.0	1.06	4
Sault Ste. Marie, MI	36.9	53.6	2.89	13
Seattle, WA	45.3	59.5	3.43	13
St. Louis, MO	46.7	69.1	2.32	8
Washington, DC	49.7	68.9	2.90	7
Wichita, KS	46.9	71.2	2.47	6

Source: U.S. Department of Commerce, Bureau of the Census, Statistical Abstract of the United States 1991. Average daily minimum and maximum temperatures and average monthly precipitation were measured over a standard 30-year period.

OCTOBER

TURNING BACK THE CLOCK

The nights are cooler, and even by day, there may be a nip in the air. Red leaves, crisp apples, wool sweaters, and the fireplace's first lighting are just some of the good things that October brings. With the abundance of fresh produce, it's a wonderful time for baking. Big, bulky sweaters replace revealing summer play clothes, as hearty appetites replace summer's health kick. But the breezes of October are just the beginning of a long winter season. Homeowners must prepare for the season by putting up storm windows, caulking the cracks, and cleaning the furnace. In October, even the clock returns to its winter schedule.

While the season doesn't hit every neighborhood in America at the same time or in the same way, with few exceptions every place does experience a season that the natives call winter. Although temperatures in the 40s and 50s don't seem like much to people living in the most northern states, people living in Miami, Mobile, and Corpus Christi suffer when temperatures dip this low. It's not just that they are not used to the cold, but also that their homes are poorly insulated and their wardrobes lack winter essentials, like coats, gloves, and hats. And even though snow may not be in the forecast, chilly winds and rain give the weather person something to talk about.

Although the weather varies tremendously across the nation, there are certain fall rituals that all Americans recognize. Halloween is one of them. Another is the World Series.

OCTOBER'S BEST BUYS

(items most likely to be on sale in October)

- Camping equipment
- Floor coverings
- Hosiery
- Major appliances
- School supplies
- Silverware
- Sporting goods

Source: DOLLAR$ENSE Magazine, 1987

BASEBALL
■■■■■■■

When the kids began playing catch in the school yard, you knew it was spring. But now that the talk has turned to the World Series, you know that winter can't be far off. Officially, the baseball season opens in April and ends in October. But the serious business of baseball, including books, movies, cards, caps, and memorabilia, goes on throughout the year.

The End of the Season

No one is more interested in statistics than an avid baseball fan. But businesses should find the facts about fans more interesting than any major leaguer's earned-run average. Over 30 million adults attend baseball games each year, according to Mediamark Research in New York City. Televised weekend games regularly draw audiences of 32 million. And baseball specials like all-star games, league play-offs and the World Series average 48 million viewers.

But avid baseball fans don't just want to watch the sport on television; they want to play. Millions of Americans, both adults and children, play baseball, and the number of hard-core enthusiasts is growing, according to a survey conducted by the Sporting Goods Manufacturers Association in North Palm Beach, Florida.

Between 1988 and 1990, the number of people who play the game 52 days or more a year increased nearly 12 percent, from 3.0 million to 3.4 million. The age groups exhibiting the most growth were children aged 6 to 11 and young adults aged 18 to 34. The number of youngsters who play baseball frequently increased almost 5 percent, to 1.3 million players, and the number of young adults who were active in the sport jumped 33 percent, to 588,000.

The newcomers have enriched the game. In 1988, only 48 percent of all frequent baseball players had median incomes of more than $25,000 annually. But by 1990, nearly 66 percent did. Some of this increase is no doubt due to the rising numbers of older, more affluent athletes who enjoy the sport. "The over-30 leagues have really taken off like wildfire," says Scott Bollwage of the U.S. Baseball Federation. He credits the 1992 Olympics and baseball's full-medal status, as well as the expansion of Major League Baseball, with driving the current growth.

The only area of the country that hasn't shown an increase in the number of frequent baseball players between 1988 and 1990 is the West. The Northeast has shown a 24 percent increase, the South a 14 percent increase, and the Midwest a whopping 55 percent increase in frequent players.

Reaching the Fans

Businesses wanting to reach baseball fans shouldn't expect TV addicts. People who go to baseball games are 18 percent more likely than the average adult to be heavy magazine readers and light television viewers, according to Mediamark Research.

They are also 30 percent more likely than others to read two or more daily newspapers, and 18 percent more likely to read two or more Sunday papers.

People who attend baseball games are at least 50 percent more likely than the general public to read sports magazines like *Golf, Car and Driver, Runner's World*, or *Sports Illustrated*, according to Mediamark. But they are also at least 50 percent more likely to read *Family Computing, Modern Photography*, and *Travel & Leisure*, and they account for an above-average share of readers of *American Baby, Business Week*, and *Self*.

Fans also love to read books about their sport and its heroes. The subject matter can range from "up close and personal" biographies of current and past heroes to "bat and tell" autobiographies by notorious baseball celebrities. Perennial favorites include books of baseball trivia, baseball statistics, and reexaminations of historic moments in the sport—such as the year the Brooklyn Dodgers moved to Los Angeles or the circumstances surrounding the cancellation of the 1904 World Series. As Gene Shalit of NBC's "Today Show" points out, "Surely there are good books written about other sports, but nothing like the quantity and quality of books written about baseball."

Americans love baseball for five reasons, according to Peter Gordon, editor of *Diamonds Are Forever*, an anthology of baseball art and anecdotes published in 1989 by Chronicle Books of San Francisco. First of all, Americans relate the game to special times and places in their lives, from childhood memories of backyard games to a big-league matchup at Wrigley Field or Yankee Stadium. Fans also cherish the equipment, trophies, and memorabilia of baseball. Third, they idolize baseball heroes, thereby creating a brisk market for baseball books. Fourth, the action fascinates fans so much that they can recall the statistics and review the plays of decades past. And finally, there is a "something else" about the game that has to do with smells, sounds, and relationships between people. "Whoever wants to know the hearts and minds of America had better learn baseball," according to *Diamonds Are Forever*.

The Art of Sports

"Diamonds are Forever," an exhibition mounted to coincide with the publication of the book, toured cities across the U.S. from 1987 to 1989. In every city, museum attendance for the show was double its normal number.

American Express sponsored the show in hopes of getting more people interested in the arts. "Baseball is an American obsession. It brings people into the museum who would not ordinarily go. The subject is equally appealing to men, women, and children," according to Susan Bloom, vice president for cultural affairs at American Express in New York.

But real fans don't have to go to a museum to see baseball art. They can own it themselves. Sports art prints have been growing in popularity, according to the Stamford, Connecticut-based *Art Business News*. A limited-edition print of a Toronto Blue Jays' pitcher was 50 percent sold out within a week of its publication. "Sports fans are known for buying collectibles for significant sums, so this could be a phenomenal market," says Ted Simon, owner of Simon Art, publishers of limited edition prints. Simon suggests that galleries advertise the prints in the sports section, rather than the arts pages of magazines and newspapers.

Keepsakes

Synthetic fibers and high-tech shoes have replaced the old heavy baseball uniforms and cleats. But nostalgia is at an all-time high, and at least one old favorite has seen a resurgence in popularity. Wooden baseball bats, which had all but disappeared by 1985, are now giving the new aluminum ones a run for home plate. Some major-league players order anywhere between 100 and 1,000 wooden bats each year, which they autograph and sell.

Amateurs, especially those who are looking to a future in professional baseball, are encouraged to use wooden bats, since the wooden models are used exclusively in pro ball. The increased availability of wooden bats in discount stores has prompted parents of little leaguers to buy them for their young stars. Aluminum bats still outsell wooden ones worldwide at a ratio of about three to two, but wooden bats sell for less than half the price of aluminum ones. And anyone who grew up listening to the familiar crack of a ball against a wooden bat finds it difficult to adjust to the "ping" of ball on aluminum.

The World Series is a boom time for retailers of baseball souvenirs, books, and memorabilia. Many children, and adults for that matter, sit in front of the television for the whole series with a lucky baseball cap, glove, or bat. Team t-shirts, pennants, key rings, mugs, and mascots are in great demand during the last few weeks of the baseball season. Baseball memorabilia has even moved into the upscale auction houses. In 1988, Casey Stengel's National Baseball Hall of Fame ring sold for $17,000, and a watch fob set presented during the first World Series in 1903 fetched $4,000.

Small boys once rushed to corner stores to spend their allowances on a pack of ten cardboard baseball cards complete with a piece of cardboard-like bubble gum. Flipping, trading, hoarding, and memorizing the faces, facts, and figures of every player helped to pass the afternoon. But starting in the 1980s, baseball-card collecting suddenly became big business. Just as some of the innocence of the game was lost when Shoeless Joe and his cronies were caught, so too was there a certain loss of naivete when a 1910 Honus Wagner card sold at auction for $451,000 in 1991. On average, baseball-card collectors realized a 25 percent annual rate of return on their investment during the 1980s, according to *Money* magazine.

Baseball souvenirs don't have to be antiques to capture the attention of sports fans. Starting in 1985, the Major League began discovering just how profitable licensed merchandise sales can be, according to an October 1991 article in *Forbes* magazine. Back then, the total retail sales of licensed merchandise was only about $200 million, far below the take for the National Football League. In 1991, total retail sales topped $1.8 billion, far above the $1 billion in sales brought in by the NFL.

The credit for the increased profitability of baseball's licensed merchandise goes to smart marketing, according to the *Forbes* article. Licenses are going to higher-quality products aimed at middle-aged fans "whose allegiance to the teams they grew up with runs as deep as their grownup pockets." Products include everything from designer fashions and leather jackets to replicas of historic caps and jerseys.

Baseball fans are truly major league—they're better educated and have higher-than-average incomes. Advertisers and promoters who take advantage of baseball's image won't strike out.

WINTERIZING
■ ■ ■ ■ ■ ■ ■ ■ ■

October is a great month for sports because fans can enjoy both summer and winter activities. Football and basketball are in full swing. And as the baseball season winds down, hockey season is picking up—just one more symbolic shift from the warm days of summer to the chilly days ahead.

But the first cold morning of October is probably the first morning that most people think seriously about the things that must be done before winter arrives. From buying warm sweaters and snow boots to upgrading a home's heating system, the tasks to be performed are both important and time-consuming.

The Beginning of a New Season
Two "winter zones" cover most of the United States, according to the National Climatic Data Center in Asheville, North Carolina. The inner zone, which includes such cities as New York, Boise, Minneapolis, Chicago, Denver, and Boston, normally has below-freezing temperatures in January. The outer, fringe zone extends as far south as parts of Arizona, Texas, New Mexico, and Nevada. Average January temperatures range between 32 and 40 degrees Fahrenheit in the fringe zone.

About 111 million Americans live in the inner zone, which encompasses all or part of 27 states. Even though migration has shifted much of the population southward over the last few decades, inner-zone cities are densely populated and account for the majority of the country's buying power. An additional 49 million people live in the fringe zone of winter weather. Altogether, about 150 million Americans live in places that have "real" winters.

Since the energy crisis of the 1970s, Americans have been aware of the need to economize on fuel, both for their cars and in their homes. Prices of home-heating oil, natural gas, and electricity fluctuate wildly from one season to the next, and even from one month to the next. Conservation has become the watch-word of the 1990s.

Home improvements to ward off winter chills can range from major renovations—upgrading a heating system, installing thermal windows, or blowing insulation into the attic—to more mundane and inexpensive tasks like putting weather-stripping around windows and doorways or covering windows with thermal blinds or a layer of plastic. No matter what renovations one undertakes, every little bit helps. Even something as simple as taking down screens, repairing the windows, and putting up storms can save as much as 15 to 30 percent of the average fuel dollar, according to June Fitzgerald, executive secretary of the Chicago-based Screen Manufacturers Association.

Over a two-year period ending in 1989, 15 percent of homeowners repaired or replaced roofs, 14 percent bought and installed storm doors or windows, and 8 percent added insulation, according to the Department of Commerce's *Current Construction Reports*. The work was mostly done by others, according to almost three-quarters (73 percent) of the homeowners who repaired their roofs. However, just 52 percent of those who installed storm windows or doors and just 42 percent of those who added insulation required any substantial assistance.

Winter Woolens

Clothing-related items account for an overall average of 6 percent of consumer spending, but the apparel industry is extremely sensitive to climate. Unseasonably warm or cold weather, rain or snow, can send markets soaring or plunging. It is difficult to estimate the impact of winter on clothing sales, but its influence is surely enormous.

Spending on coats, jackets, sweaters, and vests reached almost $14 billion in 1990, according to the Bureau of Labor Statistics. Women's clothing represented fully half of these expenditures, men's clothing represented 33 percent, and children's and infants' wear were 17 percent of the total. But the market grows slowly because few people buy new outerwear garments every year. If current trends continue until the year 2000, sales will increase 1.4 percent annually after adjusting for inflation, according to *Consumer Power: How Americans Spend Their Money*, by Margaret Ambry.

New technology could get consumers to consider a new winter coat or parka. Such innovations include Gore-Tex®, a fabric that traps heat while allowing moisture to escape from the body, and Thinsulate®, a lightweight synthetic inter-lining material that has the same insulating properties as the more bulky fiberfill or down feathers used in the past. These technological advances allow designers to create more flattering winter outerwear fashions that keep people warm and dry without making them look like walking marshmallows. Manufacturers hope that an increasing emphasis on warmth and fashion will also increase sales.

"The young, affluent consumers of today are narcissistic," says Sebastien de Diesbach, president of the Paris-based Promostyl. "They take pains to keep their bodies in shape, and they want it shown. . . . Winter clothes must appeal to this narcissism."

Mark Blumes, the owner of Mark's Work Wearhouse in Calgary, Alberta, takes a more pragmatic approach to winter fashion. "If it's functional, it's fashionable," says Blumes. "A worker on an oil rig wearing an aluminum hard hat is fashionable." Heavy, functional clothing in winter climates is as essential as food, Blumes points out.

Growth in winter-clothing sales will come through specialization, says Blumes.

Athletes will need clothing tailored specifically to their needs—skiers have different priorities than hunters or ice skaters, for example. And the winter-clothing industry must also take into account the needs of other groups, including pregnant women, the elderly, and workers whose jobs take place outdoors.

Welcoming Winter

In October, even the most northerly of states can expect a few days of Indian summer, but snow flurries are equally plausible. Some people experience anger, depression, or hostility when the weather turns cold. But when the public feels good about winter, it can greatly enhance sales. Retailers can work together with local government and consumers to actively promote the season.

Rather than hiding from winter, cities should be designed in harmony with the season, says William Rogers, a University of Minnesota professor who published The Winter City Book in 1979. Rogers advocates such measures as winter landscaping, stylish and brightly colored buildings, mass transit, and public shelters in the urban core. Distinctive urban styles create positive attitudes, according to Rogers.

If winter is approached with a cheerful and creative attitude, it can boost the spirits of locals and even draw out-of-towners to join in the fun. Winter festivals are popping up like icicles throughout the country. Planners may have taken a lesson from the City of Quebec, which began an annual winter carnival in 1954 to boost its stagnant winter economy. The Carnivale du Quebec is now that city's third-largest industry, generating revenues of some $30 million per year.

The St. Paul, Minnesota, winter carnival, first held in 1886, is America's oldest. Usually lasting ten days, from the end of January to the beginning of February, the carnival has as its centerpiece a huge ice palace, and also features concerts, sleigh rides, and even a softball tournament on ice.

Other cities that have jumped on the festival bandwagon include Boston, which hosts a First Night celebration featuring concerts, costumes, parades, and a fireworks finale on the Common. In Anchorage, Alaska, where temperatures can easily stay below zero for weeks, the annual Fur Rendezvous produces revenues estimated at $20 million. This "if you can't beat it, join it" attitude is, for many Americans, the best way to get through the winter season.

Moving Indoors

Another way to handle winter is to shut it out by building climate-controlled shopping malls. One of the first enclosed, winter-friendly shopping centers was built in Edina, Minnesota, more than 30 years ago. By 1988, America had more than 3,000 enclosed shopping malls. But none of them can yet compare with the world's biggest mall in the Canadian city of Edmonton, Alberta. It covers 110 acres and has 800 shops, 11 department stores, 100 restaurants, 20 theaters, an 18-hole miniature golf course, a 10-acre water park, a tanning center, amusement rides, and a hotel.

The biggest mall in America is the 4.2 million-square-foot Mall of America, opening in 1992 in Bloomington, Minnesota. No doubt the city fathers of Bloomington hope their mall will meet with the success that Edmonton's has. Seventy percent of the Edmonton mall's shoppers come from outside the city, including a host of charter-flight passengers from Japan and Australia, and visitors spend an average of $250 each.

But bigger malls and other retail outlets may not necessarily be better. For millions of disabled and activity-limited shoppers, these large stores may be totally inaccessible. For some people, even short walks are exhausting. And for others, lifting a heavy shopping bag is out of the question.

The Americans with Disabilities Act, recently passed by Congress, requires retailers to make their establishments accessible to people with disabilities. But some retailers are going beyond the law to ensure that their stores are not only accessible, but convenient and manageable for those with limited mobility or capabilities.

The Kmart Corporation is one such retailer. In 1990, it began a $2.3 billion renovation program in which 2,410 stores were revamped. They now provide wider aisles and electronic doors. In 672 new or enlarged Kmarts of more than 86,000 square feet in size, electric carts are standard equipment and store maps help customers plan their shopping trips.

Malls in general are losing popularity as consumers become disenchanted with their confusing signs, lack of amenities, dearth of variety, and general lack of character. In order to be successful, the Mall of America will have to offer a lot more than just retail outlets. Its 18 theaters, 1,000 hotel rooms, more than 400 specialty stores, amusement park, and water rides will certainly provide a wide variety of diversions for consumers who prefer to shop indoors during all seasons.

WINTER APPETITES

Cool weather brings out robust appetites. But not everyone has the time or inclination to bake up a batch of cookies from scratch, and few people can spend the better part of a morning making yeast breads, danishes, or rolls. Even so, Americans love to eat these goodies, so they buy plenty of premade bakery goods at the store.

The Flavor of Autumn

Consumption of bread increased 1.5 percent in 1990—to almost 50 pounds per person, according to the 1991 U.S. Industrial Outlook. White pan bread accounted for fully 56 percent of consumption. Consumption of rolls and sweet goods each rose 2.6 percent. Americans consume nearly 23 pounds of rolls and over 4 pounds of sweet yeast goods, including doughnuts, each year.

But the cookie monster was the real winner in 1990. Consumption of cookies increased 3.8 percent, to almost 14 pounds per person. No matter how much

Americans try to eat healthy and balanced diets, cookies—especially chocolate-chip cookies—will always be part of their psyche. Chocolate-chip cookies accounted for some $1 billion in sales in 1990, according to the *U.S. Industrial Outlook*.

Cookie consumption is especially high for households with children, according to Mediamark's 1990 survey. Seven in ten householders buy ready-to-eat cookies on occasion, and 20 percent are heavy purchasers, making three or more purchases monthly. But homemakers with children are 30 percent more likely than others to be frequent purchasers, and those with teenagers are 47 percent more likely to be frequent purchasers.

Home-Baked Goodies

More than 300 new baking-ingredient products were introduced in 1990, compared with just 137 in 1986, according to Gorman's *New Product News*. With that many choices, manufacturers hope people will be anxious to get into the kitchen and bake up a storm.

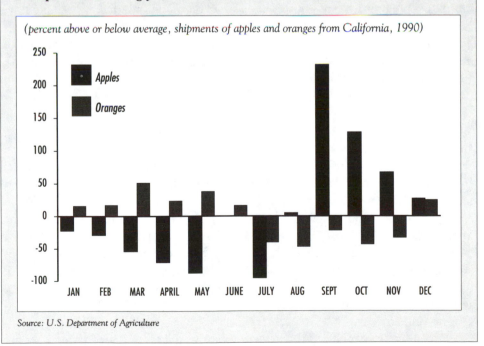

CALIFORNIA APPLES AND ORANGES

California's apple growers reap their greatest profits between September and December. But orange growers find their best pickings between December and June. Knowing the factors that drive the local economies in your marketing area can be important to serving your customers.

(percent above or below average, shipments of apples and oranges from California, 1990)

■ Apples
■ Oranges

Source: U.S. Department of Agriculture

Even though some people prefer home-baked goodies to store-bought, many are simply too busy to devote much time to the kitchen. Mixes must not only taste good, they must be convenient and include simple, effective instructions for consumers who may not have cooking experience, according to *Milling & Baking News* in Kansas City, Missouri.

One in three homemakers purchases brownie and cookie mixes from time to time, but less than 4 percent are heavy users who make more than two purchases each month, according to Mediamark's 1990 survey. The presence of children in the household sends mothers to the store much more frequently. When their children are aged 6 to 11, homemakers are 47 percent more likely than average to be frequent purchasers. And when there are children aged 12 to 17 in the household, homemakers are 81 percent more likely to be frequent purchasers.

At least six in ten homemakers purchase cake mixes occasionally, according to Mediamark. Ten percent are heavy users, making three or more purchases during the month. Heavy users are likely to be single parents and have an average household income between $10,000 and $19,999. As income increases, the share of frequent purchasers declines.

The majority of householders own a microwave oven, and 3 percent bought one in the last 12 months, according to Mediamark's 1990 survey. Manufacturers have responded by producing a variety of easy-to-bake microwave cakes and other baked goods. One new product, a 4-inch microwaveable cake that bakes in 15 seconds, appeals to a broad range of demographic groups—college students, children, senior citizens, people living alone—who want a small piece of home-baked cake quickly.

Microwaveable cake mixes, conventional cake mixes, and canned frostings have all helped boost grocery store sales in baking needs, according to *Progressive Grocer* magazine. The product category increased 5.7 percent from 1989 to 1990. The top three products—frosting and cake decorations, cake frosting, and cake mixes—showed double-digit gains.

Who Enjoys Cooking?

Three out of five working adults cook more on weekends than on weekdays, according to a survey conducted in the mid-1980s by General Mills of Minneapolis, Minnesota. These recreational bakers are anxious to try out new recipes, bake from scratch, and host dinner guests on weekends.

Home baking and cooking take on a whole new meaning among affluent Americans. People whose annual household income is between $50,000 and $74,999 are 21 percent more likely than the average person to pursue gourmet cooking as a hobby. And people whose average household income tops $100,000 are 87 percent more likely to indulge in fancy cooking, according to a 1991 survey by the Lifestyle Market Analyst reported in the Long Island City, New York-based *Affluent Markets Alert*.

Affluent cooks can afford the newest cooking gadgets designed to make home

THE HARVEST PEOPLE

N O BUSINESS is more seasonal than farming, and people who want to do business with farmers need to know how the seasons influence their income and spending. A farmer's cash outlays for farm supplies and equipment may be heaviest in the spring, but farmers wait until the fall harvest to spend money on themselves.

"A farmer is going to begin to borrow money early in the spring if he is a corn or soybean producer," says Richard Fenwick, the corporate economist for the National Bank for Co-ops in Denver. "Winter wheat is planted in the fall, so these farmers have debt requirements in September." For most other crops, including cotton, grains, and vegetables, farmers borrow in early spring and harvest in the fall. After their crop is harvested, they have money to pay off their debts. With the exception of hogs and poultry, which produce commodities several times a year, the same pattern holds true for livestock, according to Fenwick.

It takes a great deal of planning to manage agricultural cash flows. "When the cash goes out and when it comes back will be different," says Jim Putnam, the Director of the Research Department of Farm Credit Bank in Springfield, Massachusetts. Spending is heaviest from April through September, but the returns don't come in until September, October, or even November.

Farmers borrow money to buy fertilizer and chemicals. They need to meet payrolls and fuel their equipment. There are also costs associated with planting, harvesting, and storing the crop. During the time that spending for these essentials is heaviest, farm families may not have the cash to spend on luxuries for themselves, says Sharon O'Malley, editor of the Rural Electronic News Service. But farmers and their families will be ready to buy personal items once the harvest is in.

The Family Farm

In 1989, 4.8 million Americans, less than 2 percent of all U.S. residents, lived on farms. Their numbers are rapidly declining. In 1980, over 6 million Americans, nearly 3 percent of the population, lived on farms. One hundred years earlier, 22 million people lived on farms, almost 44 percent of all Americans.

Farm populations may be shrinking, but they still significantly influence spending in the rural heartland in which they are concentrated. Just 5 percent of the farm population live in the Northeast, 15 percent in the West, and almost 30 percent in the South. But over half live in the Midwest, making up almost 4 percent of the population there.

Ninety-two percent of farmers live in married-couple families, compared with 79 percent of nonfarm residents. An almost equal share of both farm (21 percent) and nonfarm (22 percent) residents are under age 15. Even so, the median age of farm residents is 38, more than five years older than the general U.S. population.

Almost 70 percent of farm residents aged 15 and older are in the labor force, but not all of these people are employed on the farm. Only 47 percent of employed farm residents say their primary work is in agriculture. The off-farm work they do varies. Among those whose main source of employment is not agriculture, almost 20 percent say they work in manufacturing. Another 16 percent are employed in retail trade, but no other industry captures more than 10 percent of these workers. The median household income of farm residents was $24,000 in 1989, compared with $27,000 for nonfarm residents. The poverty rate for farm residents is not significantly different from the rate for nonfarm residents.

The farm population is based on place of residence, but an increasing number of farmers live off the farm, according to Calvin Beale of the U. S. Department of Agriculture. In 1987, 23 percent of farm operators did not live on the site of the farm. In 1950, the share that lived off the farm was only 5 percent.

"A higher percent don't have animals, and that means they don't have to be there," says Beale. In many cases, a working spouse may need to live in town or the family may decide that the educational facilities for their children are better there. More farmers are commuting to work, according to Beale. Relocation is one of the many reasons for the declining farm population.

Whether they live on the farm or in town, farmers have become sophisticated consumers and a challenge for retailers. With only a few basic categories directly involved with the agricultural market—seed, feed, animal health, equipment, and crop chemicals—companies are looking for new ways to advertise to their limited, but profitable customers.

Retailers and manufacturers that are strictly agricultural may find it useful to see what agricultural marketers are doing to reach their audience, in order to get farmers thinking about treating themselves and their families to a few luxuries as this October's bumper crop rolls in.

preparation of food easier and more fun. While microwave ovens are now within the reach of most households, only a few may have the discretionary funds or inclination to buy a bread machine that mixes and kneads dough, allots the rising time, and bakes the loaf—all in the same unit. These items retailed for $150 to $400 in 1991.

Mail-order catalogs and upscale cooking-equipment stores that cater to the affluent market also display top-of-the-line electric mixers retailing for up to $355. They carry heavy-duty toasters with price tags of $195 and such gourmet standbys as pasta machines and Euro-style cookware.

Finding the right way to market ingredients for scratch baking as well as ready-to-microwave and ready-to-eat bakery products can be challenging, but important. By running commercials only on programs with a large concentration of scratch bakers, the marketer improves the efficiency of television advertising. Magazines targeted at people who cook, like *Cooking Light* and *Gourmet*, will also affectively reach this market.

Many retailers have found that providing in-store samples is an effective marketing tool. Giving shoppers a taste of any product—from fresh fruits or vegetables to seafood, baked goods, or deli offerings—has been gaining steadily in popularity. Some stores use sampling only when introducing a new product item, while others promote weekly specials in this way. Until there is a way to bottle the smells of grandma's kitchen on a crisp October morning, in-store sampling may be the best way to inspire home cooks to take advantage of the season.

Healthy Appetites

Americans' concerns with health and nutrition affect all aspects of baking, from fresh items to mixes and even the specific ingredients used in scratch baking. Companies are producing low-fat and low-cholesterol alternatives to coconut and palm oil, and the demand for less-refined sugar and processed flour is driving other product innovations. Many packaged cookies targeted at the health-conscious consumer now contain honey and fruit juices, soybean or canola oil, and even whole-wheat flour.

The manufacturers of cake and muffin mixes have followed suit with an array of fat-free and low-calorie mixes. Some wholesalers have expressed skepticism, pointing out that many people who consume these products aren't counting calories in the first place. But manufacturers feel it is worth the risk. More low-fat and no-cholesterol mixes are being introduced each year, and many regular mixes now include instructions for preparing a "lighter" version of the product.

In 1990, General Mills introduced a 96 percent fat-free, no-cholesterol brownie mix. This mix joins seven other products in the Betty Crocker dessert line. "Consumers want healthy products that taste as good as full-calorie versions and are a good value," according to Pam Becker, manager of public relations for General Mills. "We are trying to fulfill all those consumer desires."

The trend towards healthy eating has also affected cooking oils, with new products like canola oil hitting grocery-store shelves. But the health claims of many new products have been met with everything from skepticism to legal battles. In 1987, the Food and Drug Administration (FDA) began allowing health claims to be used on food labels. Such phrases as "high-fiber" and "low-sodium" became commonplace, and sales in many categories of packaged foods increased greatly. But health claims soon became exaggerated, so much so that consumer groups and the FDA lobbied the government to restrict or control package labeling. In November 1990, President Bush signed the Nutritional Labeling and Education Act into law. This law makes labeling mandatory for all processed foods and calls for voluntary labeling of seafood and commonly consumed fruits and vegetables.

Seventy-two percent of Americans always read labels to check the product's expiration dates, according to the Food Marketing Institute's (FMI) 1990 Trends survey. But only 36 percent always read ingredient or nutritional information. More than 80 percent of shoppers say food information on food labels influences their purchases in some way, according to the National Food Processors Association.

While 38 percent of women in the FMI survey check food labels for nutritional information, only 29 percent of men do. Full-time homemakers are the most likely to read the ingredients (48 percent) and check the nutritional information (41 percent) on labels. Only 31 percent of adults between the ages of 18 and 24 read food labels, compared with 48 percent of those aged 50 or older.

Providing nutritional information on product labels is an important step toward helping people eat well. But many Americans still put convenience and taste ahead of good nutrition. Foods that can be prepared and consumed quickly are often purchased over those that may provide better nutrition but require more preparation time. The conflict between what foods people need to maintain a healthy diet and those that fit into their busy lifestyles have created a new niche for manufacturers—foods that provide consumers with both.

New products that boast convenience and nutrition can be found in almost every supermarket department—from leaner cuts of meat already prepared for stir-frying to cholesterol- and fat-free frozen desserts and microwaveable entrees. Even fast-food restaurants have jumped on the health-food bandwagon by offering a wider variety of products, including salads and fresh fruits, and reformulating some old favorites to be lower in salt, fat, and cholesterol.

Harvest Time

The flavors of autumn include apple, pumpkin, and pecan—and fresh produce of many varieties. A "fall in love with apples" campaign can garner increased sales for supermarkets, according to Murray and Neil Raphel, marketing consultants based in Atlantic City, New Jersey. To get people into the mood for fall baking, they also suggest such themes as pumpkin recipe contests, Halloween parades for tiny tots, and cooking demonstrations.

AMERICA'S FARMS

Every state in the Union has farms. But the type of farms and their business cycles vary tremendously by region.
(location of U.S. farms, 1987, with each dot representing 250 farms)

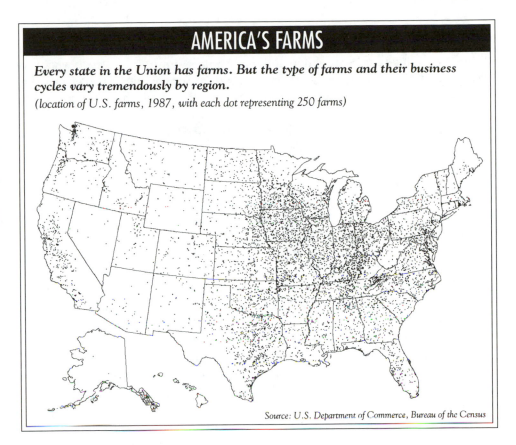

Source: U.S. Department of Commerce, Bureau of the Census

In the autumn, the lure of freshly harvested fruits and vegetables often gets people out of the grocery stores and into the country—to farm stands and farmers' markets. Eighty percent of people in the Northeast shop at roadside stands at some time, and 14 percent do so an average of once a week or more, according to a 1987 "Fresh Trends" survey conducted by Market Facts Inc. and Vance Research Services for *The Packer* magazine. On the other hand, 66 percent of Midwesterners shop at roadside stands, and only 6 percent do so once a week or more. Less than 1 percent of Westerners frequent roadside stands once a week or more.

Northeasterners are also most likely to shop at local farmers' markets—69 percent did so during the year preceding the survey, and almost 16 percent shopped at farmers' markets once a week or more. But only 59 percent of Westerners ever shop at a farmers' market, and only 4 percent do so once a week or more.

Whether consumers buy their fresh produce at the farm or in the supermarket, they still look for produce that is flavorful, ripe, clean, and appealing. Organically grown fruits and vegetables are also becoming more important to the restaurant business, according to *Restaurants USA*, a publication of the National Restaurant Association. Vegetarian plates are in demand—and not just by vegetarians.

Many consumers choose vegetarian plates for health reasons or just because they like them. Fully 20 percent of adults say they look for restaurants that serve vegetarian dishes, according to a 1991 Gallup poll. Fully 88 percent of the patrons who want vegetarian dishes say they choose them for health reasons, while 86 percent say they order vegetarian foods because they like the way they taste. Just 39 percent cite ethical considerations as a motivator, and only 22 percent cite religious reasons.

The preference for vegetarian dishes is distributed fairly equally across the U.S., but Southerners are the most likely to want this option by a slight margin. Interest is highest among women aged 35 and older and peaks among respondents over age 65. Fully 46 percent of respondents say they enjoy main-dish fruit salads, another 43 percent want main-dish salads with vegetables and grains, and 41 percent look for stir-fried vegetable dishes. Meatless pasta dishes rank fourth, with 32 percent of respondents citing this preference.

Sweet Profits

For candy merchants, the holidays begin with Halloween. Their most profitable time of the year is from the end of October until Christmas. But with over 1,000 companies, the competition is stiff.

The average American bought 10.4 pounds of chocolate candy and 8.8 pounds of nonchocolate candy in 1990. Between 1980 and 1989, per capita consumption of all types of candy rose 2.3 percent annually, according to the 1991 *U.S. Industrial Outlook.* Per capita consumption of these products topped 20 pounds in 1991.

Ninety-one percent of households with children under age 12 have chocolate stashed away, according to the Chocolate Manufacturers Association, as do 93 percent of households with teenagers. Fully 78 percent of households without children have a chocolate supply at home.

The kinds of sweet things that appeal the most to young people vary by sex. Boys prefer candy with a sweet fruit orientation, says Irma Zandl, president of Xtreme, Inc. in New York City. The craving for sweetness may be tied to their active participation in sports. Only 32 percent of preteen boys prefer chocolate.

Girls are less brand oriented than boys in their candy choices. Like boys, they prefer strong fruit flavors. But Zandl sees a connection between puberty among girls and their increasing desire for chocolate. Only 31 percent of preteen girls select chocolate as their favorite candy, but this share grows as they age.

The subject of girls and candy is one aspect of a much more complex subject— girls and food. It concerns not only girls' perceptions of themselves, but also boys and their perceptions of girls, says Zandl. Many boys consider a healthy appetite to be unfeminine. Girls, worried about their acceptance among peers, are likely to be obsessed with food and eating (or not eating). From the preteen years on, young women are loathe to admit that they even eat such things as candy, much less that they have a favorite one.

During this season, many manufacturers capitalize on consumers' festive moods with special holiday packaging. But candy makers also recognize that their primary market, children and teenagers, is stagnating, and that the adult market must be tapped if they hope to maintain their high sales figures.

Mars, Inc. and Hershey Foods Corporation share over half of the American candy market. In the 1970s, lifestyle marketing dominated the industry, according to Packaged Facts of New York City. Mars ads featured young, attractive athletes, and its candy sales soared. Hershey ads focused on the quality of its products, and sales slumped. But because mature adults are more quality-conscious than young people, the emphasis today is shifting to quality, and this shift may be to Hershey's advantage.

Candy marketing is following the European model. As the U.S. population ages, it will more closely resemble the population of western Europe—the oldest market in the world, according to Packaged Facts. Nestlé of Switzerland recently introduced upscale, bite-sized, foil-wrapped candies to the American market. The candies, packaged in paper bags with old-fashioned labels, capitalize on the company's European heritage.

In the U.S., superpremium chocolates are dominated by Godiva Chocolatier of New York, a subsidiary of the Campbell Soup Company. Godiva's products retail for about $21 a pound and are sold in more than 1,000 outlets nationwide.

Another trend that targets the adult candy consumer is liquor-filled chocolates. Federal regulations that once put a damper on these products have been relaxed. While some states still control their distribution, the determined shopper can now find chocolates filled with everything from strawberry margaritas to Smirnoff vodka.

Sugar-free candies, breath mints, and miniatures are also increasingly popular with adults. The most likely consumer of sugar-free candies is a suburban woman aged 35 to 44 who has attended college and has an annual household income exceeding $60,000. Miniatures and snack-sized candy bars are eaten most frequently by people aged 35 to 44; these consumers are most likely to be low-income rural residents.

More than half of all adults surveyed by the National Confectioners Association indulge their sweet tooth once a week, including 60 percent of people aged 18 to 34. But only 6 percent of people aged 35 to 54 eat candy at least once a week. With the aging of America, candy manufacturers must look for new treats to appeal to older Americans.

A GREAT TIME FOR FAMILIES
■■■■■■■■■■■■■■■■■■

Columbus Day is a national holiday, celebrated on the second Monday of the month, and October 1992 marks the 500th anniversary of Columbus's landing. As an historical event, the day is not without controversy. Debates rage over Columbus' motivations, his treatment of Native Americans, his religious convictions, and even his appearance. Nevertheless, the holiday is celebrated throughout the country with parades, parties, and Columbus Day sales.

From baseball to cooking to Halloween parties, October is a great month for families to do things together. It's Family History Awareness Month, National Adopt-a-Dog Month, National Pizza Month, National Popcorn Poppin' Month, and National Seafood Month. Alaska and Nevada have both declared state holidays in October to celebrate state pride. National Boss Day is held every October 16, except when that day falls on a weekend. Then it is held on the preceding Friday. In 1958, this holiday was first observed to improve relationships between workers and their bosses. And believe it or not, more than 1 million people today care enough to send their best on this obscure holiday, according to Hallmark cards.

There is something about October that brings out America's sweet tooth. Sweetest Day, held on the third Saturday in October, reminds us to make someone happy. The holiday was invented by a Cleveland candy merchant, and among its first events was a big candy give-away. Today, Hallmark distributes about 2 million Sweetest Day cards, many in the Ohio-Pennsylvania area.

But many more cards and tons more candy are distributed on October's most popular holiday, Halloween. Halloween is not just candy. It's also ghosts, goblins, scary creatures, and costumes. And while the majority of trick-or-treaters are children, there is a growing move afoot to get adults into the act. About three in ten adults will attend a Halloween party this year, according to The Crown Royal Report on America Entertaining as cited in *The Lifestyle Odyssey* from the editors of *Research Alert*.

PART 2

THE
HOLIDAYS

The holidays are the most important time of year for many marketers. So, even though a few shoppers are slow about getting into the spirit, business can't be.

NOVEMBER WEATHER
■■■■■■■■■■■■■■■

For many people, the chill in the air in November reminds them that the holidays are on the way.

	TEMPERATURE		PRECIPITATION	
	low	high	inches	days
Albuquerque, NM	30.7°F	57.2°F	0.38	3
Atlanta, GA	41.3	62.6	3.43	9
Bismarck, ND	17.7	39.4	0.51	6
Boise, ID	30.5	49.0	1.29	10
Boston, MA	38.7	51.6	4.21	11
Buffalo, NY	33.6	47.0	3.62	16
Burlington, VT	29.6	43.6	2.80	14
Charlotte, NC	39.7	61.7	2.86	8
Chicago, IL	31.4	48.2	2.06	11
Cleveland, OH	34.3	49.3	2.76	15
Dallas, TX	44.9	66.2	1.76	6
Denver, CO	25.1	52.4	0.82	5
Detroit, MI	31.4	47.6	2.33	12
Great Falls, MT	24.5	43.5	0.74	7
Honolulu, HI	69.2	83.9	3.22	9
Houston, TX	48.6	71.6	3.38	9
Indianapolis, IN	32.8	50.8	3.04	10
Jacksonville, FL	49.2	72.4	1.94	6
Juneau, AK	28.0	37.5	5.15	20
Los Angeles, CA	52.1	70.3	1.52	4
Memphis, TN	41.1	61.4	4.17	9
Miami, FL	65.8	79.8	2.71	8
Milwaukee, WI	29.9	44.7	1.98	10
Minneapolis, MN	25.3	41.1	1.29	8
Mobile, AL	47.9	69.3	3.67	8
New Orleans, LA	49.9	70.1	4.06	7
New York, NY	40.8	53.6	4.14	9
Norfolk, VA	43.0	60.8	2.88	8
Oklahoma City, OK	37.6	59.9	1.53	5
Omaha, NE	28.6	50.3	1.32	6
Philadelphia, PA	37.1	54.5	3.32	10
Phoenix, AZ	46.9	74.3	0.54	3
Portland, OR	38.6	52.3	5.17	18
Salt Lake City, UT	29.2	50.2	1.22	8
San Francisco, CA	46.3	62.7	2.35	7
Sault Ste. Marie, MI	26.4	39.0	3.20	18
Seattle, WA	39.3	50.3	5.60	18
St. Louis, MO	35.1	54.0	2.53	9
Washington, DC	39.9	57.4	2.82	8
Wichita, KS	33.5	55.1	1.47	5

Source: U.S. Department of Commerce, Bureau of the Census, Statistical Abstract of the United States 1991. Average daily minimum and maximum temperatures and average monthly precipitation were measured over a standard 30-year period.

NOVEMBER

TIMING IS EVERYTHING

There are two kinds of customers in November: those who can't wait for the holidays to begin and those who can. Even the most enthusiastic shopper can be offended when promotions come too early or the messages are too commercialized. But when so much of their income is dependent on how well they do over the next two months, retailers can't afford to be shy. The most profitable businesses will forget about pleasing everyone and focus on what their customers want.

"The 1990s are going to be the decade of the customer," says Russell Vernon, president of the West Point Market in Akron, Ohio. Writing in the July 1991 *Retailing Issues Letter*, a bi-monthly essay co-published by Arthur Andersen & Company and Texas A&M's Center for Retailing Studies, Vernon says, "The competition in retailing has never been as fierce as it is today, and this will continue throughout the coming decade. In the 1990s, the smart retailers, large and small, will keep the focus on the real reason they come to work every day—the customer."

It's especially important to keep the customer in mind during the important Christmas season. Three-quarters of all shoppers would make purchases in the first store they stopped in if they were treated right, according to the American Research Group. Catering to customers goes beyond the basic, common-sense principles of being polite, friendly, and accessible. Retail sales staff must also be encouraging and creative, and they must speedily complete the customers' transactions. When extra staff is brought on to help during the busy holiday season, it is important to let these new salespeople know that these qualities are essential.

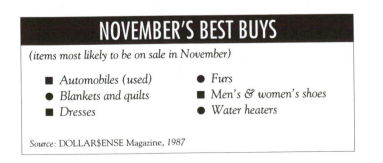

NOVEMBER'S BEST BUYS

(items most likely to be on sale in November)

- Automobiles (used)
- Blankets and quilts
- Dresses
- Furs
- Men's & women's shoes
- Water heaters

Source: DOLLAR$ENSE Magazine, *1987*

Make the customers feel wanted, says Lynda Paulson, president of Success Strategies in Napa, California. A store that caters to young customers should turn down its loud rock music around the busy Christmas season, when older people—parents or grandparents—may be in the store to buy gifts for the kids. Offering free samples of food, beverages, or even perfume can also encourage sales. Any way to make Christmas shopping easier will appeal to almost every customer. Some malls produce video merchandising magazines to sell their products and services.

It's important for retailers to be sensitive to different cultures and traditions. The Jewish Festival of Lights, Hanukkah, is celebrated around the same time as Christmas (beginning in November or December). In areas with Jewish populations, many malls are decorated both with symbols of Christmas and Hanukkah, and mall-based community events pay attention to both traditions. In ethnically diverse areas, retailers can celebrate the different traditions of Christmas with decorations and events that cater to a multicultural clientele.

HOLIDAY SHOPPERS

The day after Thanksgiving is traditionally the busiest shopping day of the year. But some shoppers begin their holiday spree much earlier—whenever they find bargains throughout the year. Yet many Americans complain about the ever-longer holiday selling season. Christmas is a high-stakes game, with some merchants claiming to make 80 percent of their profits from mid-November through January. Retailers must be ready for all types of shoppers, from early-bird bargain hunters to convenience-oriented mail-order shoppers and last-minute treasure seekers.

The Holiday Countdown

Holiday gift catalogs are almost useless unless they are in the customers' hands by early October. But few retail shoppers begin their holiday spending before mid-November, according to Francesca Turchiano, president of InFact, a New York City consulting firm. Just one in five Americans starts shopping for next Christmas before this year's decorations come down, according to the Roper Organization in New York City. But only 7 percent finish their holiday shopping before Thanksgiving, while another 8 percent finish soon after.

Women are more likely than men to finish their holiday shopping by mid-December (40 percent of women versus 31 percent of men). Full-time homemakers are more likely to shop early than are those employed outside of the home. But Americans aged 60 or older are the most likely to finish their Christmas shopping early. One-tenth of older shoppers finish before Thanksgiving, and almost half finish within the first two weeks of December. "Older people and people who don't work shop early, but many working people also shop early to avoid stress," says Turchiano. One-third of all Americans finish their holiday shopping within the first two weeks of December, according to Roper. But most adults don't finish shopping until a week before Christmas.

Last-minute shoppers are most likely to be under the age of 30, according to Roper. One in four adults under age 30 doesn't finish shopping until Christmas Eve, compared with 9 percent of people aged 60 or older. Three percent don't finish until after Christmas Day. Turchiano says that many young adults wait until the last minute for pragmatic reasons: "They have lower incomes, so they live in smaller dwellings and have less storage space." Also, friendships and relationships are less predictable. A present purchased for a boyfriend in June could be useless by December.

Catching the Christmas spirit is costly: even though half of all Americans begin their holiday shopping with a budget in mind, only one-quarter stick to it. Budget-minded shoppers spent the least: during the 1988 holiday season, their median expenditure for holiday gifts was $429. People who shopped without a budget spent $489. Those who started out with a budget, but then gave it up, spent the most ($570).

The average American household spent $474 for holiday gifts in 1988, according to Roper. Households headed by people aged 60 or older and those under age 30 spent less. People aged 30 to 44 spent the most ($621). One in five people aged 30 to 44 spent $1,000 or more. The median amount of holiday spending for households with incomes of $50,000 or more was nearly $900, and 37 percent of these affluent shoppers spent more than $1,000.

The economic climate can have a great impact on people's holiday spending patterns. As of mid-November 1990, more than 40 percent of consumers were still undecided on how much they would spend on holiday gifts, according to Maritz Marketing Research of Fenton, Missouri. This was a significantly higher proportion than found in similar surveys conducted in the free-spending 1980s.

Stretching the Season

If kids had their way, holiday shopping would begin right after summer vacation. But most parents aren't ready to hit the stores quite that early. How can retailers keep parents happy, while at the same time catering to the enthusiasm of kids? Jan Luttrell, marketing manager at the Aventura Mall in Miami, developed a plan that works for everyone. Her idea was first instituted at the Gwinnett Place Mall in Norcross, Georgia. The mall runs a program of children's events that begins with pre-registration advertising in mid-October and continues with games, crafts, magicians, and storytellers on consecutive Saturdays in November. The program is designed to give the kids something to do while their parents shop—alone.

By providing safe, supervised activities for the kids on a weekly basis, the program encourages parents to shop at the mall more than once. Parents feel confident about leaving their children in a mall setting, because they are required to "check in" their kids and must present a claim check to get their children back.

Luttrell's program has borne fruit. Some 300 to 400 children participated each week, and the response of both parents and mall merchants was excellent. The mall now offers Saturday workshops at other times of the year as well—Easter, the Fourth of July, and Halloween. By anticipating the day-care needs of busy shoppers, Luttrell has managed to tap into an important market segment—dual-earner parents.

Families with two working spouses have higher incomes than those with a single earner. In 1990, the median income of dual-earner parents was $45,000, compared with $36,000 for couples with children and only one spouse working outside the home. Studies also show that busy dual-earners are among the least likely to enjoy shopping. Saturday programs for kids establish customer loyalty early in the season, accelerate morning traffic and Saturday buying, and they promote the mall's family-oriented image, according to Luttrell. They extend the season without offending the group that says Christmas should not start until after Thanksgiving Day.

Other retailers have also come up with innovative children's programs. The "Kids Clubhouse"—a child-care facility that provides games, toys, stories, and movies—was developed at the Los Cerritos Center in Cerritos, California, in 1990. "The Kids Clubhouse officially opened during a fall promotion, the Monday Night Football Widow's Club. The service was so successful that we decided to include it in our 1990 holiday plans," says Nora Levy, marketing director of Los Cerritos Center.

Knowing that the 1991 recession could ruin their holiday season, retailers pulled out the stops to attract earlybird shoppers, USA Today reported. Financially stressed Macy's Department Store offered its customers pre-Thanksgiving savings during its "Customer Appreciation Days." Sears' Sunday flier promised "no lower prices before Christmas." And Kmart lured customers in with chances to win a Disney vacation and other prizes.

Almost 80 percent of shoppers say that holiday decorations don't affect the date they start gift shopping at all, according to Maritz Marketing Research. But retailers can do a lot more than just trim the window to entice earlybird shoppers. Sales, promotions, and special services are three incentives retailers can use to get the market moving.

On Donner, On Blitzen, On Federal Express

When Santa can't keep up, who does he call? The Postal Service, Federal Express, United Parcel Service, or any local delivery service that can get the job done. The increased volume of packages and letters at this time of year can put a damper on the holiday spirit, and consumers are reminded to plan ahead, especially when packages must be sent across the country or overseas.

Each year, the United States Postal Service asks Americans to get their cards and packages in the mail early and avoid the holiday rush. But private delivery services are not as restrictive. While Federal Express handles some 15 to 20 percent more packages in the final few weeks before Christmas, it guarantees next-day delivery right up to Christmas Day, when the company is closed.

Although most gifts are given within a household, one gift in three is for someone outside the giver's household, according to a recent study by Thesia Garner of the Bureau of Labor Statistics and Janet Wagner of the University of Maryland. Garner and Wagner analyzed data from the 1984 and 1985 Consumer Expenditure Surveys. After income, household type is the most important indicator of how much people spend on gifts.

About 90 percent of households give gifts to people in other households. During the year, they spent an average of $850, or about 3 percent of all their expenditures on these gifts. The most likely gifts are clothes, jewelry, flowers, appliances, and toys. People with higher incomes are more likely than those with lower incomes to give a gift to someone in another household. As family size increases, the probability of giving gifts to people in other households goes down.

Spending on gifts also changes with the life cycle of the family. Householders who are single, childless, and under age 35 spend more on gifts for members of other households than do young childless couples or couples with infants. For young childless single people, gift giving is often an important aspect of their social life.

Among all household types, retired couples are most likely to give gifts to people in other households. "Because retired people have discarded their employment roles, one might expect the number of gift-giving opportunities to decrease," say the researchers. "However, the results of this study suggest that the number of gift-giving opportunities may increase with retirement." Grandchildren, in particular, are on the receiving end of many retirees' gifts.

Married couples aged 35 or older and retired householders (regardless of marital status or age) spend the most on gifts for people in other households. As families age, gift-giving networks expand. Parents whose children and grandchildren live elsewhere often try to fortify their long-distance relationships with gifts.

Residence is also related to a person's pattern of gift giving. Suburban residents are more likely to give gifts to people in other households than either city or rural dwellers. And while suburban and rural householders spend the same amount on gifts, urban householders spend less. Differences in gift giving between urban, rural, and suburban residents may be related to the nature of relationships in those areas. "Social networks may be smaller in rural areas, limiting the number of gift-giving opportunities," write Garner and Wagner. City dwellers may live in a more impersonal environment, which may reduce their incentive to give gifts.

Sending greeting cards is another way people share the holiday spirit with people in other households. But even this small token can be subjected to holiday economics. Fifteen percent of Americans planned to mail fewer greeting cards in 1990 than they did in 1989, according to the Maritz AmeriPoll. The decline is offset somewhat, but not completely, by the 9 percent who planned to send more cards. Sixty-five percent of people planned to mail the same number of cards as usual.

Only 12 percent of Americans planned to send more than 50 Christmas cards. Twenty-four percent planned to mail between 26 and 50 cards, and 26 percent planned to send between 11 and 25. Another 12 percent planned to send 10 or fewer cards, and 11 percent didn't plan to send any Christmas cards.

CREDIT CARDS
■■■■■■■■■■

As pre-Christmas shopping intensifies in November, consumers rely more on their credit cards for purchases. "Credit-card usage is definitely higher in the fourth quarter of the year," says economist Charlie Luckett of the Federal Reserve Board in Washington, D.C. "And the recession doesn't seem to be having any great effect on the use of credit cards." The level of outstanding consumer credit is still going up, but not as rapidly as it has in the past, says Luckett. The typical American credit-card customer carries nine different cards, according to the Federal Reserve Board. But the more credit cards consumers have, the more difficult it is for any one card company to capture their attention.

The Importance of Plastic

In 1990, Americans charged $480 billion on credit cards. Visa is the biggest issuer, with 257 million cards in circulation worldwide. MasterCard is the second largest credit-card company, with 163 million cards worldwide, followed by the Discover Card (38 million), American Express (37 million), and Diners Club (7 million). There are now some 6,000 financial institutions that issue credit cards. New credit-card issuers want to profit from Americans' urge to charge, but in order to be competitive, they must provide lower interest rates, fee waivers, and a variety of incentives.

Sears' Discover Card is an example of how a nonbank card can challenge the industry. The Discover card signed up 12 million members in its first year of business in 1986. Sears charges no annual fee and offers refunds as much as 1.5 percent of all annual charges. Despite the recession, Discover's profits were up 50 percent during the first six months of 1991. Even though the card's interest rate of 19.8 percent was among the highest in the industry, the money-back concept was especially attractive to many blue-collar clients. Discover Card customers are younger, less affluent, and more likely to live in large families than other cardholders.

AT&T also joined the credit wars in 1990. Its Universal card gives 10 percent discounts on long-distance calls. Other companies, including Ford and Chrysler, are offering no-fee credit cards as well. Affinity cards, those that are linked to special causes or interest groups, have become commonplace as banks strive to take advantage of market segmentation. The most popular affinity cards are those linked to environmental groups, says Brad Hennig, spokesman for Visa U.S.A. in San Francisco. Among the many large and small organizations currently profiting from affinity cards are the Sierra Club, the Wisconsin Humane Society, Friends of the Earth, the Audubon Zoo, the Foundation for North American Wild Sheep, and the World Wildlife Fund.

Dollar Dry Dock Savings Bank in New York began issuing a special bank card in 1987 designed to raise funds for a nonprofit organization, the Vietnam Veterans of America (VVA). At that time, the card paid $6 to a local chapter of the VVA for every new account, rebated $4 to the national organization on every membership renewal, and made a donation to the VVA every time the card was used. These benefits attracted new cardholders and acted as incentives for people to use the cards.

Sun Bank of Orlando, Florida, issues another program card, aimed at Florida's aging population. The cardholders receive price breaks on health-care items, prescription drugs, and emergency-room services. Florida Hospital in Orlando expedites admittance procedures for cardholders. Sun Bank also gives money to the hospital when people use the card.

Mellon Bank's "Lifestyle Cards" are a spin-off of the affinity card, designed to attract sports fans. Using the lifestyle card does not raise funds for nonprofit organizations, but it gives users certain "value-added services." Cardholders have access to a toll-free number to get information about their favorite sport. Skiers call their number to find out about the conditions on the slopes. Golfers can find a course designed by their favorite architect. Sports equipment discounts are available to cardholders, who also get access to a free video-lending library.

Another bank card for sports buffs emerged when the National Football League teamed up with Citibank of New York. The card features NFL helmets in its design and offers discounts on football merchandise. Airline affinity cards, like the American Airline Citibank Card, offer frequent-flyer points for every card dollar charged.

A new service offered by some credit-card companies is "price protection." Citibank refunds the difference if the cardholder charges an item and later finds it costs less elsewhere. Credit-card companies also offer warranties on purchases, as well as theft-protection plans and discounted automobile and life insurance. Other incentives to use credit cards include Citibank's free gifts program, in which customers are rewarded for using their cards by receiving a free gift—a stereo, microwave, or cellular phone, for example—based on the dollar amount of purchases charged in a five-month period.

While it may be difficult to find a retail store that doesn't accept credit cards, analysts estimate that only 13.5 percent of U.S. consumer spending is paid for with plastic. And since people who pay with plastic are less reserved about spending than those carrying cash, new venues in which they can spend are opening all the time. Supermarkets and fast-food restaurants are two areas in which credit cards are becoming a more common sights. New ways for credit-card companies to persuade consumers to use plastic are emerging almost daily.

During the 1991 holiday season, store cards were part of retailers' overall marketing strategy, reports the *Wall Street Journal*. In October, J.C. Penney launched a drive to sign up new store-card customers. As an incentive, the new customers were given a 15 percent discount on certain items. Penney's deferred-payment program began three weeks earlier than in the previous year. Saks Fifth Avenue also used discounts to lure new charge-card customers in October. Then, Saks gave "holiday gift checks" to customers who charged at least $750 between November 15th and

SEASONAL WORK TRENDS

Mens' labor force participation rates peak in the summer when seasonal work, including construction jobs, is greatest. But women's rates don't begin rising until after school starts and they remain high until the Christmas shopping season.

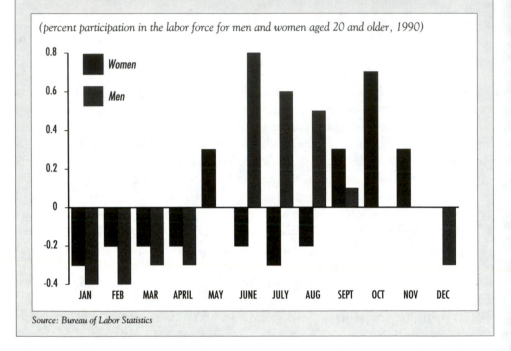

(percent participation in the labor force for men and women aged 20 and older, 1990)

Source: Bureau of Labor Statistics

December 15th. The checks were good for discounts on purchases made between February and April. This strategy not only encouraged early shopping, but extended after-holiday buying.

Cash vs. Cards

In a typical week, 29 percent of Americans use their credit cards, according to a 1991 survey by the Roper Organization of New York City. Usage is greatest among people aged 30 to 54. About 34 percent of these adults use a credit card during the week. Usage increases substantially among people with higher incomes. Only 8 percent of people in households with annual incomes of less than $15,000 use a credit card during the week, compared with 49 percent of those with household incomes of $50,000 or more.

Three in four adults say a major reason they have a credit card is because it's good for emergencies, according to Roper. But this reason becomes less important as people age. While 79 percent of people aged 18 to 29 say they have credit cards for emergency purposes, this share drops to 68 percent for those aged 60 or older.

Convenience is the second most popular reason for having a credit card, according to 71 percent of respondents in the Roper survey. The importance of convenience increases as people age. Less than 70 percent of adults under age 45 say they have a credit card because it is convenient; among those aged 45 and older, the share rises to nearly 75 percent.

Almost half of credit-card holders say they use credit cards because they are safer than cash transactions. Older Americans are more likely than others to appreciate the safety benefits of credit cards. While only 40 percent of adults under age 30 depend on the safety of plastic, 56 percent of people aged 60 or older feel this way.

Only 40 percent of Americans admit they have credit cards so that they can extend their payments. Yet, just 27 percent of Americans have no outstanding consumer debt. Twenty-one percent of those surveyed had less than $1,000 outstanding. Thirteen percent owed between $1,000 and $2,500, 6 percent owed between $2,500 and $5,000, and 3 percent owed $5,000 or more. Older people are less likely than others to owe money on credit cards. While 46 percent of people aged 60 or older reported having no outstanding credit-card balances, this figure was 24 percent for adults aged 30 to 59 and only 19 percent for adults under age 30.

Thirty-seven percent of Americans admit they have a credit card because it allows them to buy things they don't have money for. While this feature appeals especially to those between the ages of 18 and 29 (48 percent), it is cited as a good reason by only 24 percent of those over age 60. People also like credit cards because they provide a good system for recordkeeping; because they provide protection from loss, theft, or damage; and because they provide one month of interest-free credit. Only 9 percent of those surveyed thought that credit cards carried any prestige.

The Youthful Card Holder

College students are a growing new market for credit-card companies. As credit cards reach saturation levels in every other market segment, card-issuing companies are reaching out to this last untapped niche. There were almost 7 million college students using credit cards for major purchases in 1990, according to *Credit Card News*. These credit-card customers brought the companies some $3.5 billion in income. Although this figure accounts for only a small share of all credit-card sales in 1990, it represents an important investment in the future of the industry. College students have great potential for becoming high earners.

Credit-card companies work hard to solicit students. It is not unusual for them to waive such requirements as previous credit histories, income requirements, and parental co-signatures. Some companies offer incentives like free dictionaries, while others offer more than one card for a single application.

Credit-card companies are anxious to sign up students. "We've found that they are somewhat more responsible than our other customers. Student delinquency rates are less than those of the general population," says Susan Weeks, a spokesperson for Citicorp, the largest credit-card issuer in the U.S.

THE GREAT AMERICAN SMOKEOUT
■■■■■■■■■■■■■■■■■■■■■■■■■

"No problem," say the Wrigley's Spearmint Gum ads and commercials. "When you can't smoke, enjoy pure chewing satisfaction." These commercials address one of the most important sources of tension for Americans today: the conflict between smokers rights and the rights of those who don't smoke. The commercials focus on various situations that most smokers can relate to: when the in-laws are visiting, when the kids are in the car, and when office policy says no.

No Smoking, Please

Since 1977, the Great American Smokeout has been held each year on the third Thursday of November. This national event, instituted by the American Cancer Society, challenges cigarette, cigar and pipe smokers to kick the habit. Today, the effort is changing consumer behavior all over the country. "A Gallup poll revealed that 38 percent of the nation's 50 million smokers participated in the 1990 Smokeout. More than 7 million of these smokers were able to stay off cigarettes for 24 hours, with nearly 5 million still not smoking one to three days later," says Walter Lawrence, president of the American Cancer Society.

Self-help books and stop-smoking clinics profit from the great numbers of people trying to kick the habit. But even though smokers are an ever-decreasing share of the population, the conflict between smokers and nonsmokers is one that every business must be aware of. Nonsmoking sections are no longer limited to the last five rows of transcontinental flights. There is a growing demand for smoke-free environments in restaurants, hotels, and shopping areas, and there is a growing need for retailers to be sensitive to the desires of their customers, both smokers and nonsmokers.

In 1987, 29 percent of adults smoked cigarettes, according to a report from the National Center for Health Statistics (NCHS) in Hyattsville, Maryland. Another 23 percent were former smokers. Men were more likely to be currently smoking than women, 32 percent versus 27 percent. The share of smokers peaks among people aged 25 to 44. Almost 36 percent of men and 31 percent of women in this age group are current cigarette smokers. By age 75, only 11 percent of men and 8 percent of women still smoke.

Fully 88 percent of nonsmokers find cigarette smoke annoying, according to the NCHS survey. While the share declines for former smokers and current smokers, it is interesting to note that about one-third of current smokers are also annoyed by cigarette smoke. When bothered by cigarette smoke in public places, only a small share of adults (4 percent) ask the smoker to stop. The majority (52 percent) simply move away. And 40 percent do nothing.

Almost half of all cigarette smokers have been told by a doctor they need to quit, according to the 1987 NCHS survey. The most popular method of quitting is to stop

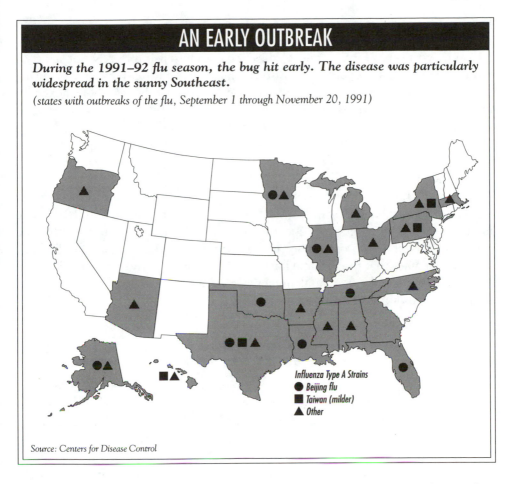

AN EARLY OUTBREAK

During the 1991–92 flu season, the bug hit early. The disease was particularly widespread in the sunny Southeast.

(states with outbreaks of the flu, September 1 through November 20, 1991)

Influenza Type A Strains
● Beijing flu
■ Taiwan (milder)
▲ Other

Source: Centers for Disease Control

"cold turkey." This method has been tried by 85 percent of current smokers and 84 percent of former smokers. But over 30 percent of former smokers said they tried more than one method before they finally quit.

Facing a declining domestic market, tobacco manufacturers hope to expand into international markets. Meanwhile, segmenting markets, targeting women, and offering lower-priced generic cigarettes have helped manufacturers maintain profits. Although Americans in general are smoking less, some segments of the population are still hooked. Teens and preteens, minorities, women, and blue-collar workers are picking up the habit faster than college-educated people, men, and white-collar workers.

Even so, the cumulative effects of the Surgeon General's warnings, increased taxation on tobacco products, a proliferation of local, state, and federal bans on smoking in public places, and changing public opinion have earned impressive results. Less than 30 percent of adults smoked in 1990, compared with 40 percent in 1964.

The Surgeon General's health warnings—pointing out that smoking causes lung cancer, heart disease, emphysema, and other health problems—are required on all cigarette packages and advertisements. But other factions point out that there are two sides to every story. While studies show that self-interest is not a prime motivator for people supporting many social causes, like affirmative action or raising the legal drinking age, smokers are significantly more likely than nonsmokers to oppose public restrictions on smoking and increased tobacco sales taxes. The *Smokers' Advocate*, a monthly newsletter published in Washington, D.C., keeps smokers up to date on all the current issues. *Philip Morris* magazine, a quarterly with features on a broad range of topics from entertainment to ecology, devotes its "forum" section to news of interest to smokers.

Wrigley's has positioned itself to please both sides of the issue. Today, many nonsmokers probably keep candy dishes filled with spearmint gum on their coffee tables for their smoking guests. Other products, from room fresheners to toothpaste, can create similar niches for themselves. Traditionally smoke-filled places, like bars, should remember that the demand for fresh air is growing. And retailers who must keep their shops smoke-free should remember to say please when they ask defensive smokers to put out their cigarettes.

THANKSGIVING

What is it that families celebrate when they sit down to Thanksgiving dinner, the day before the biggest shopping day of the year? Is it a simple harvest festival, as it was for American Indians before the Pilgrims landed? Is its significance primarily religious, as it was until the mid-19th century? Or is it a patriotic holiday, as President Lincoln intended when he declared it a national holiday at the time of the Civil War. Today's celebration has some of all these qualities. But in modern America, Thanksgiving has become a day when families celebrate abundance, according to the paper "Domestic Consumption Rituals and the Reproduction of American Households: U.S. Thanksgiving Day," by Eric Arnould of California State University at Long Beach and Melanie Wallendorf of the University of Arizona at Tucson. Americans also celebrate the wholeness of their families, whether or not this image is accurate.

Giving Thanks

Thanksgiving is remarkable because of the incredible consistency with which it is celebrated. Ask someone what they are doing on New Year's Eve, and chances are they won't have a clue. But almost everyone has plans for Thanksgiving—right down to the stuffing and cranberry sauce.

The essence of the Thanksgiving Day celebration is a mid-afternoon feast. Over 90 percent of hosts serve turkey for Thanksgiving, according to Arnould and Wallendorf. The meal is very likely to be bracketed by television viewing—parades in the morning and football in the afternoon. The ritual remains largely the same among Americans from different backgrounds. Even recent immigrants celebrate Thanksgiving in much the same way as other Americans, he says. Asians may substitute rice for mashed potatoes, but the turkey is sacred.

While the overall picture is one of a day of rest, the researchers explain that the distribution of work is gender-specific: "Thanksgiving Day feasts ritually confirm women as custodians of the familial shrine—the home." Women traditionally prepare the meal, often starting the elaborate preparations early in the day. They are also responsible for the festive aspects of the holiday, such as setting the table, usually with heirloom china, linen, and glassware that are carefully stored during the rest of the year.

Men, on the other hand, are excused from all but token tasks like carving the turkey, making the gravy, or clearing the table. Over their years of studies, including surveys, unstructured interviews, and scientific observations, Arnould and Wallendorf found relatively few instances of men actually involved in meal preparation. Instead, they often spend the day eating, drinking, chatting, reading, and watching sports on television.

The traditional aspect of the holiday is reflected in the choice of menu. The food is simple, but abundant, and regional preferences are clear—oyster stuffing in Louisiana or cornbread in Tennessee, for example. Roast turkey, stuffing, and cranberry sauce, the foods most clearly associated with Thanksgiving, are rarely eaten at other times of the year.

With the emphasis on home and hearth during this holiday, homemade dishes are particularly important. Almost every cook has a "secret family recipe" for a dish that is only prepared on Thanksgiving.

A Time for Family

The perfect Thanksgiving gathering includes people from outside the nuclear family. Three-quarters of respondents in one survey said their ideal celebration included seven or more people, according to researchers Arnould and Wallendorf. On average, gatherings are larger in owner-occupied dwellings than in rentals. "A stable home environment, namely that of a married couple who own a single-family dwelling, is the prevalent site for the Thanksgiving Day feast," say the researchers.

Holiday hosting is nearly always the responsibility of middle-aged couples. Thanksgiving celebrations symbolically pass the role of provider from the oldest to the succeeding generation. Younger participants are rarely expected to contribute anything, except their presence, while older generations bring dishes—hors d'oeuvres or desserts. And while the younger generations may take up their positions on the couch before and after the meal, older family members, especially women, pitch in to help the female head of the house with her duties.

Thanksgiving is a day for families, and in this era of extended and blended families, younger married couples may find themselves feasting at more than one table. Tensions can run high when children of divorced parents are forced to choose one parent's home over the other as a site for their Thanksgiving day celebration.

In October 1991, a survey by D.K. Shifflet and Associates (DKS&A) found that one in five householders planned to travel over the Thanksgiving holiday. This share is about the same as it was in the previous year. But travel patterns were substantially different than they were in the year before the recession, according to DKS&A. Only 19 percent of householders with children planned to make a holiday trip, compared with 23 percent in 1990. This decline was offset by an increase in the share of childless householders who would be on the road—25 percent versus 19 percent the year before. Over 40 percent of the respondents in the survey said that the cost of travel most influenced their travel plans.

Even family members who cannot make a trip to see their loved ones keep in touch on Thanksgiving Day. The family nature of the holiday makes it an important one for long-distance telephone calling. In 1990, more than 50 million long-distance calls crossed the AT&T network, making it the fifth most popular holiday for telephone calls.

The holiday is also one in which nonfamily members are included in festivities. Thanksgiving may be a good time to introduce a serious boyfriend or girlfriend to the family. For the recently widowed or divorced, a Thanksgiving celebration with close friends may provide a continuing sense of family. The holiday also easily accommodates those who "don't have anywhere else to go," according to Arnould and Wallendorf.

The religious aspect of Thanksgiving has not disappeared, but for many, "Thanksgiving Day prayer is celebrated at home, rather than publicly in a church service," say Arnould and Wallendorf. The blessing may be traditional memorized religious verses or secular expressions of love. It may even be as simple as a toast of good cheer, according to the researchers. Whatever the tradition, the messages consistently praise the gift of family.

Thanksgiving is a way of demonstrating that a family has won the war on poverty for another year. But perhaps equally important, Thanksgiving is a way of transmitting family rituals and traditions from one generation to the next. The family china is used, family stories are retold, and family recipes are passed on. As American families grow farther apart, both geographically and emotionally, carrying on traditions becomes more important than ever.

A Bird for All Seasons

When a product is too seasonal, it can be a problem. But turkey producers are changing the way consumers behave, with a combination of new products and consumer education. Turkey, the Thanksgiving mainstay, is quickly gaining popularity at other times of the year. Consumers are looking for good-tasting nutritious foods, and low-fat low-calorie low-cholesterol turkey fills the bill. The average American ate more than 18 pounds of turkey in 1990, compared with just a little

WELCOME HOME, SOLDIER

A 1991 ABC television drama entry, "Homefront," depicted America at the end of World War II. It was a time when Americans were taking pride in their victory and veterans enjoyed their fellow citizens' respect and admiration. While an antiwar series like "M.A.S.H." was a huge success in the aftermath of Vietnam, "Homefront" is perfect for today's audiences. The recent victory in the Persian Gulf has revitalized America's interest in its veterans. This concern extends not only to veterans of the recent war, but also to veterans of past wars, including the Korean and Vietnam conflicts. Today, Americans are experiencing a surge of patriotism that hasn't been seen in nearly 50 years.

Further bolstering this feeling of pride in our military is a series of anniversaries. The golden anniversary of American involvement in World War II began with the 50th anniversary of the attack on Pearl Harbor— December 7, 1991. But other important World War II battles—Midway Island (1992), D-Day (1994), and Hiroshima and Nagasaki (1995)—will be commemorated before the end of the century. The year 2000 will mark the 25th anniversary of the end of the Vietnam conflict.

November 11, Veteran's Day, marks the signing of the Armistice between the Allies and Germany that ended World War I. It has subsequently become a day to honor veterans of all conflicts, from the Great War to the Gulf War, with parades, religious services, and moments of quiet reflection.

As of March 31, 1991, the Department of Veterans Affairs (VA) estimated that there were 27 million veterans in the U.S.—and that more than 20 million of these men and women were war-time veterans. Categories overlap, but more than 8 million veterans served during the Vietnam era, almost 5 million were part of the Korean conflict, and almost 9 million were involved in World War II. Only 72,000 veterans from World War I were still alive in 1991. The median age was 44 for Vietnam veterans, 60 for Korean conflict veterans, 70 for World War II vets, and 91 for World War I vets. Only 1.2 million veterans were women—263,000 were Vietnam era vets, 109,000 were Korean conflict vets, and 324,000 served during World War II.

California, with some 2.8 million vets, has the largest veteran population of any state, according to 1991 figures. New York and Texas are each home to

1.7 million veterans. Other states with veteran populations exceeding 1 million are Florida, Ohio, Pennsylvania, and Illinois. When Michigan, with 997,000 veterans, and New Jersey, with 850,000 veterans, are added in, these nine states account for more than half of the veteran population.

Assuming no new major conflicts involving large numbers of military personnel, the number of veterans is expected to decrease to 24 million by 2000, according to VA projections. However, the number of veterans aged 65 and older is expected to increase, from less than 7 million in 1989 to a peak of 9 million by 2000—growing from less than 25 percent to 37 percent of all veterans.

A second peak of 8.6 million veterans aged 65 and older is projected in the year 2015, as a result of the aging of Vietnam veterans, combined with the remaining World War II and Korean conflict veterans. Veterans aged 65 and older will comprise almost 52 percent of veterans by 2015.

While the total number of female veterans will increase only slightly during the 1990s, the percentage of women in the veteran population is expected to more than double—from just 4 percent in 1989 to 11 percent by 2040. Female veterans are younger than their male counterparts—their median age in 1989 was 50, compared with almost 55 for men.

The share of female veterans aged 65 and older will not increase significantly over the 1989 level of 31 percent until female Vietnam-era and post-Vietnam-era vets begin to reach age 65. Between 2020 and 2040, the proportion of female veterans aged 65 years and older will increase from 28 percent to 37 percent.

more than 10 pounds in 1980 and slightly more than 6 pounds in 1960, according to the Reston, Virginia-based National Turkey Federation. The federation predicts that Americans will eat 30 pounds of turkey per capita by 1993.

Although the traditional 25-pound stuffed bird is still the turkey of choice for Thanksgiving, it is not the prime mover in the market. While whole-bird sales rose 41 percent between 1982 and 1987, the sale of turkey parts grew 85 percent, and processed meats gained 65 percent, according to the National Turkey Federation. Forty percent of turkey meat is processed into hot dogs, ground meat, turkey hams, sausages, and cold cuts. Turkey parts account for one-third of turkey consumption, and about one-quarter is sold whole.

The growing popularity of turkey has increased competition in the marketplace. The industry leaders, Swift-Eckrich and Louis Rich, each process about 400 million pounds of turkey a year. But smaller companies with clearly defined market niches are not intimidated.

The reasons for turkey's growing popularity are health-related, says Rick Chenoweth, sales director for Shady Brook Farms in Harrisonburg, Virginia. He admits that smart marketing has also done a lot to increase sales. A variety of new turkey products have been introduced in the past few years, and consumers have learned how to use them.

When Shady Brook Farms first introduced turkey parts, its advertising showed consumers what they could not do with the whole bird. "You can't barbecue or deep fry a whole turkey, but you can do these things with turkey parts," explains Chenoweth. "Shady Brook did a tremendous amount of research to find out what the consumer wanted. We found that they wanted a fresh and natural product."

Since 1985, Shady Brook has been producing fresh all-natural turkey products for the northeastern corridor—from New England to Washington, D.C. Besides its now commonplace turkey franks, the company has been experimenting with more upscale turkey products. Its new line, Limited Edition turkey, costs more than other brands, but contains 10 percent more white meat. Chenoweth explains: "It's part of the overall trend toward upscale products, like bottled water."

Shelton's Poultry of Pomona, California, specializes in chickens and turkeys that have been raised without antibiotics or stimulants and contain no preservatives or curing agents. Although natural or organic turkey accounts for only a tiny segment of the industry, sales have been increasing every year. Shelton's Gary Flanagan says his sales rose 15 to 30 percent every year for a five-year period. Every time meat and poultry products are attacked for their chemical additives, Flanagan's business surges.

The increasing variety of turkey products has spread demand for the meat throughout the year. From 1982 to 1987, the growth rate in turkey consumption remained the same in all months. That kept turkey consumption seasonally stable, at 17 percent in the first quarter of the year, 20 percent in the second quarter, 24 percent in the third quarter, and 40 percent in the fourth quarter. The first shift occurred in 1988. Consumption jumped more than 20 percent in the first and second quarters. The third-quarter increase was just 11 percent, and the fourth-quarter share fell slightly. The growing variety and healthy reputation of turkey products will ensure that turkey is not just for Thanksgiving anymore.

WILDLIFE ENTHUSIASTS
■ ■ ■ ■ ■ ■ ■ ■ ■ ■ ■ ■ ■ ■ ■

Some outdoor lovers thrive in the chilling temperatures of November—among them are birdwatchers, hikers, and hunters. With the opening of the hunting seasons for duck, goose, pheasant, turkey, and big game, November is the peak month for hunting in New England and much of the northern half of the United States. Nearly 17 million Americans aged 16 or older hunted in 1985, according to a survey by the Fish and Wildlife Service (FWS) of U.S. Department of the Interior.*

*A new survey with 1991 data is due to be published in the spring of 1993; until then, 1985 data are the most recent available.

A-Hunting We Will Go

Big-game hunting—for deer, elk, bear, moose, and other large mammals—is the most popular type of hunting, enjoyed by some 12.5 million Americans. Small-game hunting, practiced by close to 11 million hunters, ranks second, followed by migratory-bird hunting (5 million), and hunting for other animals such as coyote, crows, fox, raccoon, and woodchuck (nearly 3 million). Of course, many participants enjoy more than one type of hunting.

Americans spent more than $10 billion hunting in 1985, of which 37 percent was trip-related, according to FWS. This boost to local economies included $1.9 billion in spending for food and lodging and $1.6 billion for transportation. Other trip costs, such as guide fees and equipment rentals, accounted for another $218 million. Spending for equipment totaled $4.9 billion in 1985. The lion's share ($2.8 billion) went for hunting equipment. Another $1.5 billion was spent on special equipment used primarily for hunting like vans and campers. And $688 million went for tents, backpacking gear, and other auxiliary equipment. Hunters spent $65 million on magazine subscriptions, membership dues, and contributions in 1985. They also spent $911 million to own or lease land for hunting, and $435 million for licenses, stamps, tags, and permits.

In 1990, 95 percent of frequent hunters (those who hunt 25 days or more annually) were men, according to American Sports Data, Inc. of Hartsdale, New York. More than half of frequent hunters are aged 25 to 44. Only 22 percent of frequent hunters are aged 45 or older.

Lower-income people are more likely than those in high-income brackets to be frequent hunters. Less than 1 percent of people with 1990 annual incomes of $50,000 or more hunt frequently, compared with 2 percent of the population in general. The share increases to nearly 3 percent for adults with incomes between $15,000 and $25,000, then it declines slightly—to 2.2 percent—for those with incomes below $15,000.

Forty-eight percent of hunters live in the South. Another 25 percent live in the Midwest, and 19 percent live in the Northeast. Just slightly more than 8 percent of hunters are from the West. People in nonmetropolitan areas are almost four times as likely to be hunters as those living in metropolitan areas.

In general, hunting is losing popularity, according to data from the National Opinion Reseach Center of Chicago. In 1977, 17 percent of people hunted. This share decreased to 12 percent in 1989. But among some age groups, hunting's popularity is increasing. Eighteen percent of people aged 30 to 35 hunted in 1989, compared with 11 percent in 1987. Hunting has also become more popular among those aged 48 to 53, jumping to 15 percent in 1989 from 8 percent in 1988.

Wildlife Art

Although hunting may be losing popularity, capturing wildlife on canvas has become a popular sport for America's art collectors. Annual sales of wildlife art reached more than $200 million in 1988. Women are often the buyers of wildlife art, but many are buying the prints as gifts for men.

The location of wildlife-art galleries indicates that their target is the affluent market. And wildlife-art prints are not only destined for the den or home office. Corporations with art collections are also big customers, according to Byron Webster, former director of retail galleries for Wild Wings in Lake City, Minnesota.

In 1934, the federal government began issuing duck stamps as a way to raise money for the preservation of waterfowl. But its appeal for art collectors accelerated after 1949, when the design for the stamp was first determined by an annual competition. Limited-edition prints of the artwork are sold by the winning artist, and picture framers frequently frame the stamp along with the print. Today, the federal government sells more than 2 million duck stamps annually at a cost of $15 each. Winners of the federal duck stamp competition typically earn over $1 million in commissions and sales. A total of 43 states also hold competitions for wildlife stamps, and these stamps are also popular among collectors.

Wildlife art is popular throughout the U.S., but some of the biggest fans are in Minnesota. One entrepreneurial Minnesotan turned his hobby into a career. William Webster, founder of Wild Wings, began as a dealer in the late 1960s. He realized that all the prints he bought were made in England. In 1971, Webster's company produced the first American-made prints.

Today, Wild Wings is one of the biggest wildlife-art dealers in the country. It is the only publisher that sells wholesale to independent galleries, retail through 25 galleries of its own, and direct to consumers through the mail. Wild Wings sent its catalog to just 6,000 households in 1970. Today, it reaches over 3 million.

Wildlife Art News boasts a circulation of over 40,000. In 1988, more than 60 percent of subscribers were men whose median household income exceeded $40,000. Their average age was late 40s. Like hunters, the greatest markets for *Wildlife Art News* are in rural areas.

WRAPPING UP NOVEMBER
■ ■ ■ ■ ■ ■ ■ ■ ■ ■ ■ ■ ■ ■ ■ ■ ■

As the holidays approach, the retailing pace begins to pick up in November. Pre-Christmas promotions are well underway before Thanksgiving. But even though retailers must be ready for holiday shoppers as soon as the spirit hits them, many customers do not wish to be rushed into the holiday mood.

November can be a politically active month, with campaigns and elections on many different levels. Veterans' Day—always a somber occasion—has taken on a new significance in the aftermath of the Gulf War and the golden anniversary of World War II. November is also time to remember the children. It marks Child Safety and Protection Month, as well as International Creative Child and Adult Month. Alabama celebrates Robert E. Lee Day in November.

DECEMBER WEATHER
■■■■■■■■■■■■■

While most Americans are wishing for a white Christmas, above-freezing tempera-tures in most of the nation limit the possibility.

	TEMPERATURE		PRECIPITATION	
	low	*high*	*inches*	*days*
Albuquerque, NM	23.2°F	48.0°F	0.52	4
Atlanta, GA	34.8	54.1	4.23	10
Bismarck, ND	4.8	25.9	0.51	8
Boise, ID	24.6	39.3	1.34	11
Boston, MA	27.1	40.3	4.48	12
Buffalo, NY	22.5	35.0	3.42	20
Burlington, VT	14.9	30.3	2.43	15
Charlotte, NC	32.6	52.6	3.40	9
Chicago, IL	20.3	35.0	2.10	11
Cleveland, OH	24.6	37.5	2.75	16
Dallas, TX	37.4	58.1	1.67	6
Denver, CO	18.9	46.1	0.55	5
Detroit, MI	21.6	35.4	2.52	14
Great Falls, MT	16.6	34.7	0.80	8
Honolulu, HI	66.5	81.4	3.43	10
Houston, TX	42.7	65.2	3.66	9
Indianapolis, IN	23.7	39.2	3.00	12
Jacksonville, FL	43.2	66.3	2.59	8
Juneau, AK	22.1	31.5	4.66	21
Los Angeles, CA	47.8	66.1	1.62	5
Memphis, TN	34.3	52.3	4.85	10
Miami, FL	60.8	76.2	1.86	6
Milwaukee, WI	18.2	32.0	2.03	11
Minneapolis, MN	11.7	26.7	0.87	9
Mobile, AL	42.9	63.1	5.44	10
New Orleans, LA	44.8	64.4	5.27	10
New York, NY	30.3	42.1	3.81	10
Norfolk, VA	35.0	51.9	3.17	9
Oklahoma City, OK	29.1	50.7	1.20	5
Omaha, NE	17.4	36.9	0.77	6
Philadelphia, PA	28.0	43.0	3.45	10
Phoenix, AZ	40.2	66.4	0.83	4
Portland, OR	35.4	46.4	6.41	19
Salt Lake City, UT	21.6	38.9	1.37	9
San Francisco, CA	42.2	56.3	3.55	10
Sault Ste. Marie, MI	12.7	26.6	2.57	20
Seattle, WA	36.3	45.6	6.33	19
St. Louis, MO	25.7	42.6	2.22	9
Washington, DC	31.2	46.6	3.18	9
Wichita, KS	24.2	44.6	0.99	6

Source: U.S. Department of Commerce, Bureau of the Census, Statistical Abstract of the United States 1991. Average daily minimum and maximum temperatures and average monthly precipitation were measured over a standard 30-year period.

DECEMBER
··········
JOYOUS NOEL

By early December, all but the most determined Scrooges have succumbed to the spirit of Christmas yet to come. From the decorations in shop windows to the street-corner Santa Clauses, the holiday reminders are everywhere. Christmas trees spring up in grocery stores, offices, restaurants, and airports. Almost every television show has its holiday special, and almost every commercial has its holiday message. Traditional holiday carols and rock 'n' roll Christmas tunes fill the air in homes, shopping centers, and elevators. Almost 80 percent of Americans say they are happier during the holidays than at other times of the year, according to Maritz Marketing Research in Fenton, Missouri.

The holidays have an enormous impact on both children and adults. Where people go, what they wear, and what they eat are all influenced by the holiday season. It is a time to get together with friends and family, to share gifts and experiences. The holidays are the busiest, most exciting time of the year for both consumers and marketers.

New Orleans celebrates Creole Christmas in the French Quarter, and Biloxi, Mississippi, marks the month with a display of ethnic Christmas trees. A Territorial Christmas Celebration is held in Guthrie, Oklahoma, complete with parades, concerts, and turn-of-the-century decorations. And Jews all over America and the world celebrate the eight days of Hanukkah. From December 26 to January 1, millions of blacks celebrate their African heritage during Kawanzaa. For everyone, the holidays end with the New Year's Eve celebration.

DECEMBER'S BEST BUYS
(items most likely to be on sale in December)

- ■ *Automobiles (used)*
- ● *Greeting cards*
- ■ *Hats*
- ● *Infants' needs*

- ■ *Party items*
- ● *Shoes*
- ■ *Toys*

Source: DOLLAR$ENSE Magazine, 1987

While Christmas lasts just one day, the holiday season stretches from early November to January. For many retailers, the decorations, symbols, and sentiments of Christmas are a year-round industry, with a sales value of more than $37 billion in gift-giving alone. But December leads the year in retail sales totals for almost every category.

In 1990, December sales in department stores, food stores, and clothing stores were way above monthly averages for the year as a whole. So were sales in household-appliance stores, bookstores, and sporting-goods stores. Jewelry stores, which averaged $1.2 billion in monthly sales during the year, saw sales of $3 billion in December. December retail sales totaled nearly $180 billion, compared with the monthly average of $151 billion.

Christmas spending goes beyond just gifts. Americans purchase more gift wrap, cards, and decorations during December than any other month. During the year, people spend over $450 million in gift wrap. For some, business slows down during the holidays. People entertain more and eat out less in December. They also spend less than average on building supplies, floor coverings, and automobiles.

GIFTS FOR CHILDREN
■■■■■■■■■■■■■■

Parents think their children stop believing in Santa Claus much sooner than they actually do. Only 10 percent of parents think their first grader firmly believes in Santa Claus, but 70 percent of first graders say they believe, according to Cynthia Scheibe, assistant professor of psychology at Ithaca College, and John Condry, professor of human development at Cornell University. Parents think their children find out Santa's secret from a brother, a sister, or a friend. But the researchers report that children initially react with disbelief when they are told. On Christmas morning, they weigh the evidence and decide for themselves.

Santa's Coming

Children look forward to finding plenty of toys underneath the tree. But marketers shouldn't mistake toys for simple playthings. Millions of parents see toys as basic learning tools, teaching their children everything from mathematics to social behavior and sexual identity. Parents also depend on toys to be trusted playmates.

Sales of toys follow demographics fairly closely, according to statistics from Mediamark Research in New York City. Parents with children under age 2 are more than three times as likely as other adults to buy infant toys. Parents of children between the ages of 2 and 5 are more than twice as likely as others to buy toys designed for preschoolers. Parents with children aged 2 to 11 are twice as likely as the population in general to spend $200 or more each year for children's toys and games.

Demographics may be working against the toy industry. Between 1990 and 2000, the number of children aged 2 to 11 could decline 1.5 percent—to 36 million.

Even so, Judith Corea of the Commerce Department's Office of Consumer Goods sees other trends that are countering the decline in population. "Couples today have smaller families than their counterparts of a generation ago. As a result, more dollars are spent on each child," she points out.

"Working parents have more money, as well as a guilt factor from being away from home more," says Frank Reysen, editor of *Playthings*, a trade magazine for the toy industry. Other demographic trends favor the toy industry, too, according to Reysen. "Up until recently, the influence of grandparents has been negligible," he says. But because grandparents are now living longer, "they are more likely to be around to spoil the kids."

Grandparents are less likely than parents to be swayed by television in making their toy selections. They are likely to buy the same type of toys for their grandchildren that they bought for their own children. This trend is contributing to the strength of basic and traditional toys, according to Reysen.

Parents can be hostile to advertising targeted at their children. Many feel that advertising exploits children by convincing them to buy things that are bad for them or things they don't need. Fully 78 percent of parents feel that advertisements often put undue pressure on kids (and, consequently, on them), according to a 1991 Roper Organization survey.

What Parents Want

Although demand among older children has shifted away from traditional toys to video games and other contemporary items, the parents of young children are interested in "more basic and traditional toys that are safe and have more educational and play value," says the Commerce Department's Corea.

But in this era of Nintendo computer games and high-tech building kits, finding traditional toys can be difficult. Some mail-order houses, like Back to Basics Toys, Games & Hobbies in Silver Spring, Maryland, specialize in the toys that have been favorites for generations. Many of the toys featured in the catalog, like the classic Flexible Flyer sled or the full-sized 027-gauge Lionel train set, look the same as the ones many parents had when they were children. The only change is the price. The Flexible Flyer now retails for $50; a Lionel train set will cost Mom and Dad $120.

Because parents today are more educated, they want more educational value from the toys they buy their children, says Reysen. "But in an economic pinch, they don't want to spend a lot of money on toys that can wear out quickly. The arrival of video games has broken traditional price barriers for toys. We have talking dolls that cost $60 and more."

Safety concerns parents most. For over 15 years, federal law has enforced standards for small parts, breakability, paint, and other safety features for toys. "The toy industry is fully aware of these standards, and we have good compliance," says Ken Giles of the Consumer Product Safety Commission in Bethesda, Maryland.

"Noncomplying toys are usually imports, and we work with the customs services so they never get into distribution."

The standards have been very effective in reducing deaths and injury. But the big problem begins when toys intended for older siblings get into the hands of children under age 3. The Consumer Product Safety Commission currently publishes two booklets about the best toys for children of different ages, and it is proposing mandatory labeling of toys for age appropriateness.

"Safety is built into the toy. It is the first consideration in the design stage. But there have been a number of toy-related incidences, and they are highly publicized. Toy recalls are also highly publicized. And the influence of consumer groups has made consumers extremely aware of product safety," says Reysen. More than 40 percent of parents feel children's toys should be regulated more tightly, finds the Roper Organization.

A Fickle Market

Demographic trends are not the only problem that toy manufacturers face. The industry hasn't had a hit toy since the Cabbage Patch Dolls of the mid-1980s. Corea points out that a hit toy can benefit more than just one manufacturer. A hit toy gets people into the stores and in a shopping mood. Spin-offs can also mean big business.

"Teenage Mutant Ninja Turtles have been top sellers—also Nintendo games," says Reysen. "What these toys don't have is the traffic-pulling power that a Cabbage Patch Doll had. That product carried the whole industry." Reysen adds that the toy industry is completely unpredictable. In the summer of 1991, people were spending up to $30 on water guns.

But high-priced water pistols will someday go the way of hula hoops, pet rocks, and even the highly profitable Cabbage Patch Kids. In 1985, the winsome Cabbage Patch dolls were the rage, and their manufacturer, Coleco Industries, was at the top in the world of toys. The dolls' popularity peaked that year, with $600 million in sales. Then sales plummeted to $230 million in 1986, and the toy company suffered major losses. In 1989, Coleco sold most of its assets to one of its chief competitors, Hasbro Industries.

Profits in the toy world, even in the biggest companies, depend on the passing whims of children. Success means producing a variety of toys so that a company is not at the mercy of fads. Cabbage Patch dolls were a fad, and in 1985, they accounted for fully 85 percent of Coleco's profits.

Other companies may have learned by Coleco's mistake. In 1987, the Tonka Corporation expanded its toy line by acquiring Kenner Parker Toys, maker of Monopoly, Play-Doh, and Nerf balls. This move reduced Tonka's dependence on its most profitable item, Pound Puppies plush animals. Stephen G. Shank, chairman of Tonka, hoped to break the boom-and-bust cycle by planning ahead for the demise of Pound Puppies.

It's not just the little ones who are picky about which toys they love. The whims

OPEN ME FIRST

"DECEMBER is the peak month for taking pictures, processing film, and buying cameras," according to Bill Lewis of the Photo Marketing Association International of Jackson, Michigan. Family get-togethers are always perfect occasions for taking pictures. More than 60 percent of households purchase or process film during an average quarter, according to the Photo Marketing Association International. But when there are three or more members in a household, the likelihood that this household will be actively involved in photography is above 70 percent.

The presence of children in a household really inspires picture taking—the younger the child, the better. Seventy percent of households with young people aged 12 to 21 purchase or process film, as do three-quarters of households with 3-to-11-year-olds. When there is at least one child under age 2 in the family, the share of photo-active households is over 80 percent. Only 55 percent of childless households are active picture-takers.

Other factors that send householders running to the store for more film are pets, motor homes, and VCRs. Black householders are less likely than whites or Hispanics to be photographers, but Asians are much more likely to get out the camera. The urge to take photos falls off after age 65.

The photography industry has generated sales in other categories as well. Some picture-taking buffs are sure to find a fancy photo frame under their tree at Christmas. But frames are only part of the associated merchandise that photo retailers now carry. Photo files—boxes in which the avid photographer can file away snapshots—come in a number of different varieties. Digital and electronic photography are changing the industry. The techniques—cropping, blowing up images, combining images, and changing colors—were until recently only used by skilled darkroom technicians. But with the advent of computer-based digitizing, amateurs and hobbyists can perform these operations. The newest technology allows consumers to edit a snapshot of Aunt Jane into the family Christmas photo.

Not all amateur photographers are ready for such sophisticated equipment. The key to retailing cameras, photo supplies, and accessories is to know the audience. Eckerd Corporation of Clearwater, Florida, targets new mothers.

"When a new mother is discharged from the hospital, she receives a bag of products from Gift-Pax. In the Gift-Pax bag, we have an invitation for her to join the Eckerd BabyCare Club. Once she joins the club, she receives our quarterly newsletter. We always have a photo article featuring ancillary items like photo stickers or our big picture packages," says Linda Angelacci, Eckerd's marketing communications manager.

of teenagers are also difficult to predict. "Recreational fads have about a three-year life cycle," says Irma Zandl, president of Xtreme in New York City. "It takes one year for the activity to get going, one year to become mainstream, and one year for the people who buy the product on sale at Kmart to finally catch on."

The fickleness of youngsters, combined with their parents' reluctance to spend big dollars on toys during times of recession, has added up to great difficulties for toy manufacturers. While the Christmas season is the biggest time for toy sales, toy makers must come up with products that both catch kids' imagination and fit their parents' budgets. During the Christmas 1990 season, manufacturers were unable to come up with new best-sellers. The three biggest sellers—Nintendo video games, Barbie dolls and accessories, and Teenage Mutant Ninja Turtle characters—were the same top three as the year before.

Although it would seem to be the easiest thing in the world to sell toys to children, retailers often find it a nightmare. Children are sensory creatures who are not satisfied simply with looking at products. They want to open up packages, touch the toys, and play with them. But that does not necessarily mean that the kids or their parents will buy the toys they have taken apart and strewn all over the toystore.

Creating a kid-friendly children's department is the first step in successful children's product retailing, according to Don Boyer, a consultant and writer in Nashville, Tennessee. Writing in the *Bookstore Journal*, he suggests giving kids' products the space they deserve, displaying the products effectively, grouping kids' items by age or grade level, using music and videos in the children's department, and actively promoting children's products. One retailer Boyer interviewed said he makes samples of products available for children to pick up and play with. When breakage occurs, the retailer just chalks it up to advertising.

Different Kids, Different Toys

Recognizing that 31 percent of children belong to minority groups, ethnic toys were hot at the 1991 American International Toy Fair in New York City. California's Hamilton Toys introduced Candy Girls, fashion dolls that come in black, Latina, Asian, and Caucasian versions. Mattel unveiled Shani, a black doll with authentic-looking hair and features that comes in a variety of shades.

Gender-based toys—dolls for girls and trucks for boys—are another issue with which manufacturers must come to terms. Two of the top three toys in America—Nintendo games and Teenage Mutant Ninja Turtle action figures—are aimed primarily at boys. But manufacturers are now realizing that they are missing half the potential market. "Girls have been largely ignored in the industry," says Bill Pearse of the toy magazine *Playthings*. "What you're seeing now for the first time are games geared specifically to attract them." Girls' video games are being designed to coincide with the latest trends in the media. There are currently at least three Little Mermaid video games and one Barbie video game.

Gender roles are channeled through the toys children receive from their elders, according to Cynthia L. Steinkamp and Melanie Wallendorf of the Department of Marketing, University of Arizona in Tucson, in their recent study, "Beyond Wrapping Paper: The Roles of Gift Receipt in Constituting Household Production, Pooling and Redistribution, Transmission, and Reproduction." Steinkamp and Wallendorf maintain that boys receive toys that foster activity and competition, such as cars, blocks, sports equipment, guns, and action figures. Girls receive toys that foster domesticity and concern with appearance, such as dolls, books, makeup, dishes, and pots and pans.

Gender-stereotyped toys given as gifts to children can be viewed as an attempt to reproduce the gender-based division of labor within the household, according to Steinkamp and Wallendorf. Sixty-three percent of parents surveyed by the researchers said that gender influenced their choice of toys for their children a great deal. Twenty-two percent said that gender was a moderate influence in the selections they made. The most frequently mentioned birthday gifts for 10-year-old boys were Nintendo or other computer games, selected by 30 percent of parents. Sports equipment, chosen by 22 percent, was the second most popular. For 10-year-old girls, however, 52 percent of parents selected clothes. The second most popular choice was a new bicycle, favored by 11 percent of parents.

The toy industry is also sensitive to the strong division in gender roles. Many major toy manufacturers have separate vice presidents in charge of boys' and girls' toys, according to Sydney Stern and Ted Schoenhaus in their 1990 book *Toyland*, published by Contemporary Books of Chicago. Manufacturers have made an effort to design toys that reflect contemporary society's changing gender roles. Mattel's Barbie now has a computer and a business suit, but as Stern and Schoenhaus point out, "Her bridal gowns always outsell her suits."

Many parents want to break the gender-based stereotypes when they choose toys for their children, and manufacturers try to follow suit. In one toy catalog, a child's tool chest is monogrammed with a girl's name and a little boy is shown "cooking" in a make-believe kitchen. But "little girls want to be like other little girls, and boys want to be like boys," according to Melanie Wallendorf. Toy companies respond to this sentiment as well. One company markets dress-up kits for little girls, containing hats, dresses, beads, and bangles, as well as a booklet of "fashion tips."

The same company sells a dress-up kit for boys, with the props they need to be detectives, explorers, and doctors.

He-man, She-ra, and other action figures are aimed at children's competitive nature. Even board games like Monopoly and Candyland have winners and losers. But some parents want to teach their children the benefits of cooperation and noncompetitive play. In a world of Teenage Mutant Ninja Turtles and Nintendo, it seems almost impossible to find a nonaggressive gift to put under the tree.

But Animal Town, a mail-order toy company based in Healdsburg, California, has been selling noncompetitive toys and games for over 14 years. The company maintains that games that "emphasize cooperation, fairness, nonviolence and foster an appreciation of nature are very beneficial to families." Its line of nature books, crafts projects, and cooperative board games provides an alternative for parents who seek a change from Masters of the Universe.

GIFTS FOR ADULTS

How many years in a row can a wife give her husband ties, socks, and the current hardbound best-seller? And how many wives can still smile after they've gotten another new robe and the wrong perfume? The challenge for retailers is to market products that will be put under the tree and not returned as soon as the stores open after Christmas.

I Won't Grow Up

Many adults will admit to buying a few puzzles, games, toys, and stuffed animals for themselves. During a typical year, 28 percent of adults spend up to $50 on toys and games for adults, and another 17 percent spend $50 or more, according to a 1990 survey conducted by New York City's Mediamark Research. Adults under age 45 enjoy toys more than older adults. This group is fully 30 percent more likely than average to make purchases of $50 or more during the year. College graduates are 41 percent more likely than average to be big spenders on toys for adults, and professional, executive, administrative, and managerial workers are also more likely to enjoy toys and games than others. Heavy purchasers are most likely to be people in households with incomes of $50,000 or more, and parents are more likely than childless adults to buy toys for themselves.

In 1990, nearly 30 percent of home-video-game players were over the age of 25. But adults are somewhat leery about admitting it, says Paul Samulski, chief of product development for Acclaim, a video-game software maker. While most home video games are aimed at young boys, some are geared toward adults. Sports video games are favorites for boys of all ages. Adults also prefer "shooters," blasting away at enemy starships; and "role players," sorting out clues to a puzzle or mystery.

Just as video games that aim primarily at young boys find a secondary market in their fathers, the doll industry has found a new grownup niche with expensive limited-edition collectors' dolls. These carefully rendered, hand-painted china dolls are not the playthings of little girls. They are destined for high shelves and glass-fronted cabinets. Collectors' dolls can retail for well over $200, and the industry has expanded to include magazines, do-it-yourself kits for craftspeople, and even a doll-makers' organization.

Some toys are aimed strictly at adults and their high-stress lifestyles. The Mini-Ma, an hourglass-shaped wooden roller that reduces back, shoulder, and back tension, sells for $15. Magic Moonballs and Sqwish Balls are toys that let people clench their fists in rage. Each sells for about $20. A toy that helps people vent pent-up hostilities is the Stressball, which retails for $25. This foam-covered, battery-operated ball makes the sound of shattering glass when flung against a wall.

For decades, whoopee cushions and rubber chickens have been profit centers for Spencer Gifts, a retail chain that specializes in unique and humorous products. New products in the 1990s include dancing beer cans and Bart Simpson boxer shorts. Although Spencer has traditionally targeted teenagers and young adults, older adults are becoming increasingly important customers. Gifts that make fun of the mid-life crisis have been big sellers since 1987, the year the oldest baby boomers turned 41. Retirement gag gifts are also hot.

Executive toys—puzzles and little games made of good-quality wood and brass—are popular items, according to Beth Schlansky of Spencer Gifts in New York City. Since 1968, Spencer's annual sales have grown from $22 million to $300 million. "Gag gifts comfortably sell for up to $30. Unique contemporary items sell for $100 to $200. They have a perceived value," says Schlansky.

Five Golden Rings

The holidays are for lovers. During this season, many romantics express their feelings with gifts of gold and silver. Jewelry stores can more than triple their monthly sales in December.

December is a peak month for engagements. During the 1970s and 1980s, young people became increasingly likely to postpone marriage until they were sure they were emotionally and financially ready. Over that same time period, however, that shining symbol of everlasting love, the diamond engagement ring, became more popular. Seventy-five percent of brides received diamond engagement rings in 1987, compared with only 68 percent in 1968, according to the 1989 *American Diamond Industry Association Newsletter*.

How much someone is willing to spend greatly depends on their age and income, says a 1988 survey conducted by Bruskin Goldring Research in Edison, New Jersey. In 1988, half of Americans believed that a diamond engagement ring should cost from $250 to $1,000. The amount people are willing to spend increases with age, but peaks among people aged 35 to 49. About 6 percent of all adults think even $3,000 isn't enough for this token of their affection.

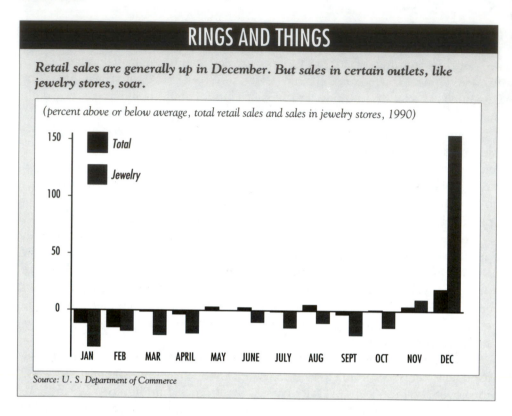

RINGS AND THINGS

Retail sales are generally up in December. But sales in certain outlets, like jewelry stores, soar.

(percent above or below average, total retail sales and sales in jewelry stores, 1990)

■ Total

■ Jewelry

JAN FEB MAR APRIL MAY JUNE JULY AUG SEPT OCT NOV DEC

Source: U. S. Department of Commerce

Although the jewelry business has been sluggish in general, America's aging population should give the industry a boost in the 1990s. The increased number of women in the labor force is another force driving sales. Shipments by costume-jewelry manufacturers reached $2.2 billion in 1990 and are expected to hit $2.8 billion by 1995, according to Packaged Facts of New York City. Costume jewelry is frequently an impulse purchase. The buyer is most likely to be a middle-aged woman who has attended college and has a part-time sales or clerical job. Women willing to pay $50 or more for individual pieces are college graduates, aged 45 and older with full-time careers and household incomes of $50,000 to $60,000. About 73 percent of women bought at least one piece of costume jewelry in 1988, but only 27 percent of men are buyers.

Religious Sentiments

The December holidays of Christmas and Hanukkah are sacred to Christians and Jews, but marketing religious products is a delicate task. Even so, the number of religious bookstores in the U.S. is growing rapidly—from 1,700 in 1972 to more than 4,100 in 1984. Sales increased at a compound annual rate of nearly 13 percent between 1975 and 1985, to more than $2.3 billion, according to a study led by the Evangelical Christian Publishers Association (ECPA) in Tucson, Arizona. The

ECPA predicts that sales will continue to grow 8 or 9 percent a year until 2000, when they are expected to reach $8.7 billion.

Christian bookstores sold $609 million worth of books in 1985, according to the ECPA survey. They also sold music ($484 million); curriculum materials ($432 million); Bibles ($337 million); church supplies ($208 million); gifts, toys, cards, and other items ($183 million); electronic products such as computer software ($65 million); and other publications ($35 million). Although the total of $2.3 billion may seem large, the sales of religious books amounted to only $4.76 for every U.S. church member in 1986, and sales growth has leveled off since then.

The challenge is for religious stores to attract new customers. "They're hitting the same people over and over," says George Bama, an evangelical consultant. He points out that the stores must find a way to attract the 75 percent of Christians who have never shopped in a religious book and gift store.

One way to attract new customers is to offer a new twist on an old item. In 1988, *The Book*, the latest, most modern version of the Bible, was the favorite translation of nonchurchgoers, according to a survey conducted for the Christian Broadcasting Network (CBN). *The Book* (also called *The Living Bible*) was the product of extensive research by CBN and Tyndale Publishing. Marketers took surveys to find out the type of Bible consumers wanted. The result was a paraphrase of the King James version, written in colloquial English and packaged as a paperback that sold for less than $10.

The Book's marketing plan moved the Bible into new territory. Endorsements came from celebrities like Bubba Smith, Nell Carter, and Dick Butkus. Unlike other versions of the Bible, *The Book* sold in grocery stores and discount centers. An estimated 2 million copies of *The Book* were sold in the first few years of production. Before sales started to slack off, the company expanded into cassette tapes, children's versions, and a chronological version called *The Story: From Adam to Armageddon*.

"Most Bible marketing today is done through denominational magazines," explains Bob Schwalb, a Nashville-based consultant to Christian booksellers. That may be preaching to the choir, but marginal profits prohibit religious publishers from advertising in periodicals like *Reader's Digest* or *Prevention* where they could reach many potential buyers.

Regular Bible readers are more likely than the general population to be aged 55 and older, according to the Standard Rate and Data Service of Wilmette, Illinois. They are most likely to live in a single-income married-couple household. The 1987 median household income of Bible readers was $21,500, compared with $26,000 for the nation that year. Between 1982 and 1986, people who read the Bible at least once a day dropped from 15 percent of all adults to 11 percent, according to Gallup surveys. However, the percentage of adults who never read the Bible declined, while the percentage reading weekly or monthly grew.

It's expensive to market to borderline prospects, according to Jeannette Eberhart, director of operations and marketing for Zondervan's Bible Division in Grand Rapids, Michigan. But there are newly emerging trends in Bible marketing. "There is much more niche marketing. There's the *Concordia Study Bible* for Lutherans and the *Disciple Study Bible* that's mainly for Southern Baptists. The choice of colors is revolutionary. In the past, there were only black, brown, burgundy, and white. Now we have rose, teal, navy, and mauve," says Eberhart.

In 1988, Zondervan celebrated the tenth anniversary of its leading seller, *The New International Version*. The *NIV* is a translation of original Hebrew and Greek manuscripts. Studies indicate that sales of the *NIV* have steadily increased since its release. Today, it's challenging the perennially popular King James version for the number-one spot. Eberhart says that marketing helps sell the *NIV*, but sales growth results from the high quality of the product. When asked why *NIV* took ten years to seriously threaten the King James version, Eberhart replies, "With the Bible, it takes a while for people to get used to change."

CHARITABLE ACTIVITIES

The holiday message "Peace on Earth, Goodwill toward Men" inspires Americans to help the less fortunate. On street corners throughout the country, the Salvation Army's bell ringers collect spare change. Religious organizations, charitable concerns, medical research hospitals, and even animal shelters use this time of year to ask people to donate money, food, clothing, and their time to help those in need. Toys for tots and some mall-based programs address the special problem of needy children.

The Giving Season
Over the years, per capita donations to charitable organizations have increased. But charitable donations as a share of the Gross National Product have remained around 2 percent since 1960, reports *The American Enterprise*. During the year, the typical American household gives $316 to churches, $15 to educational organizations, and $81 to charities, according to the 1990 Consumer Expenditure Survey (CEX) conducted by the Bureau of Labor Statistics. Donations generally increase with age.

Young adults give the least to charity. Householders under age 25 give an average of only $10 annually to charitable organizations like the Red Cross or the United Way. They give an additional $48 to their church and just $2.50 to educational organizations. Householders between the ages of 25 and 34 make annual contributions to charity of $51, on average. They contribute $195 to their churches and only $4 a year to educational institutions. Householders aged 35 to 44 make annual charitable contributions of about $84, and they give $339 to their churches. These Americans give $19 to educational organizations.

The large generation of baby boomers is moving into the age groups where charitable giving is the greatest, and this could give a real boost to nonprofit organizations. Householders aged 45 to 54 give $113 annually to charity and contribute $439 to churches. Their contributions to educational organizations amount to $18 per year. Householders aged 55 to 64 also give a lot to charity. These Americans make annual contributions of $91 to charitable organizations. They also give $349 to churches and $25 to educational organizations, according to the CEX.

Elderly householders aged 65 and older give $106 to charitable concerns during the year. Their donations to churches average $410, and their contributions to educational organizations amount to $19 per year. Between 1989 and 1990, per capita charitable contributions showed some decline. But it's interesting to note that as the recession approached, contributions from elderly donors held strong and even grew in some categories.

Religious organizations are by far the greatest recipients of cash contributions, receiving financial contributions from about 65 percent of the population, according to the Independent Sector, a national association of philanthropic and voluntary organizations in Washington, D.C. Human services and education are tied for second place, with 8 percent, followed by health (6 percent), youth development (4 percent), the arts (3 percent), organizations for the public or societal benefit and environmental causes (2 percent each), and international and recreational concerns (1 percent each).

Religious attendance is a major factor in determining who gives. Fully 88 percent of people who go to religious services about once a week make monetary contributions, according to the Independent Sector, compared with 58 percent of people who never go. People who attend religious services are also more likely than others to volunteer their time. About 71 percent of regular attendees volunteer, compared with 40 percent of those who never go.

The Bell Ringers

About 38 million Americans did some volunteer work in 1989, according to Howard Hayghe of the Bureau of Labor Statistics (BLS). That's just one in five persons aged 16 and older in the the civilian noninstitutionalized population. Attracting volunteers has become increasingly difficult. In the past, full-time homemakers were the main source of volunteer workers. But women have been joining the work force in record numbers, and the amount of time they have to devote to charitable service is shrinking.

Because women are slightly more likely than men to volunteer and because they outnumber men in the general population, women account for 56 percent of all volunteers, says Hayghe. In 1974, 43 percent of women who volunteered were employed, 2 percent were unemployed, and 54 percent were not in the labor force. Eighty-two percent of men who volunteered were employed, 2 percent were unemployed, and 16 percent were not in the labor force. A similar survey conducted in 1989 showed that 59 percent of women who volunteered were employed, while the figures for men remained about the same. When the average female volunteer was a full-time homemaker, she could be more flexible about choosing the hours for which she volunteered. Now that the majority of female volunteers are employed, the hours they can donate are restricted.

The increasing number of divorced and widowed Americans has also changed the volunteer pool. The share of volunteers who were single (never married, divorced, or widowed) was 31 percent in 1989. But nearly half of these volunteers were widowed or divorced. And many of these volunteers had other obligations vying for their time—children and grandchildren, for example.

Many organizations are changing their focus when searching for volunteers. A delicate balance exists between the desire to volunteer and the amount of time volunteers can spare. Some organizations are creating volunteer positions that have very tangible goals—renovating a home for a low-income family or getting parents together to build a playground. Other organizations are arranging for volunteers to work in their homes rather than in an office or corporate headquarters.

Churches and other religious organizations capture the lion's share of volunteer workers, 37 percent. As people grow older, they are more likely to do volunteer work for this type of organization, according to BLS data. Almost 46 percent of people aged 55 to 64 do unpaid work for churches and other religious organizations during a typical year. After age 65, the share drops only slightly, to 43 percent.

Schools and other educational institutions get the next largest share of volunteers, 15 percent. People under age 45 are the most likely to volunteer for this type of organization. Civic and political organizations are in third place (13 percent), followed by hospitals or other health organizations (11 percent). Trailing are social and welfare organizations (10 percent) and sports and recreational organizations (8 percent).

The jobs most commonly done by volunteers include assisting a paid employee (8 percent), aiding the elderly or handicapped (7 percent), assisting the clergy (7 percent), driving (4 percent), and sitting on a committee (4 percent). Babysitting, leading a youth group, serving as a parish visitor or missionary, doing telephone work, and teaching each accounted for about 3 percent of volunteer commitments, according to a Gallup poll conducted for the Independent Sector.

Most people (62 percent) volunteer because they want to do something useful, according to the Independent Sector. Other reasons include enjoyment of volunteer work (34 percent), benefitting a family member or friend (29 percent), religious concerns (26 percent), a surplus of free time for volunteering (10 percent), and seeking fulfillment absent in the volunteer's regular job (8 percent).

Who are the people most likely to do volunteer work? Volunteerism peaks among adults aged 35 to 44, according to the BLS. Fully 31 percent of people in this age group do some volunteer work during the year. Whites are almost twice as likely as members of minority groups to volunteer. Married people are much more likely than others to volunteer. Education is also a very important factor. Among adults over age 25, 41 percent of people with 16 or more years of schooling volunteer during the year, compared with only 9 percent of those with less than 12 years of education.

Older volunteers are a rapidly growing pool. The Retired Senior Volunteer Program (RSVP) has tapped this rich resource by sponsoring chapters nationwide. The share of volunteers over the age of 65 increased to nearly 13 percent in 1989, from 8 percent in 1974. These volunteers, many of whom can work during the daytime, bring with them a variety of talents. RSVP strives to take advantage of their abilities by giving them volunteer assignments that match their skills. A retired accountant may volunteer his time to help prepare income-tax forms for welfare recipients, while a former secretary may do some typing or office jobs.

The picture may actually be somewhat brighter than the one painted by the BLS numbers. A 1990 Gallup survey found 54 percent of adults did some volunteer work over the year. The BLS survey included people under age 18, which lowered the overall rate. Also, in the BLS study, respondents were asked about the volunteer activities of others in the household, while in the Gallup study, people were only expected to answer for themselves. A lack of information on others in the household might have resulted in underreporting in the BLS study.

Corporate Giving

Corporate charitable gifts reached nearly $5.9 billion in 1990, or just under 2 percent of pretax profits. This money is not just given away indiscriminately. Instead, many companies now practice what is called "strategic philanthropy" or targeted giving. In this way, corporations can focus their philanthropic efforts to maximize returns. They can also see that the charities they support meld with the company's overall corporate goals. In 1988, 71 percent of chief executive officers described themselves as being "highly involved" in corporate giving, according to the Council on Foundations.

Federated plans, like United Way, contribute to a diverse group of programs, but they may not fit the company's philanthropic goals. Companies are targeting local concerns to make streets safer, have better schools, and eliminate drug and alcohol abuse. Corporations give first to education (38 percent of corporate donations), followed by health and human services (34 percent), according to *Giving USA*, an annual publication of the American Association of Fund-Raising Council Trust for Philanthropy in New York City. The fastest-growing area is primary and secondary education, with 10 percent of corporate giving targeted to this one area.

Corporations don't give to charity solely for altruistic reasons. They do it to build public awareness and loyalty by supporting their customers' or employees' favorite issues. Americans feel strongly that corporations should support causes that bear directly on local issues. Older people are most likely to say it is very important for a company to have good relations with its home community. Slightly more than 50 percent of people aged 60 and older feel that good community relations are important, according to a 1989 poll conducted by Opinion Research Corporation in Princeton, New Jersey. Forty-six percent of people aged 40 to 59 feel the same way,

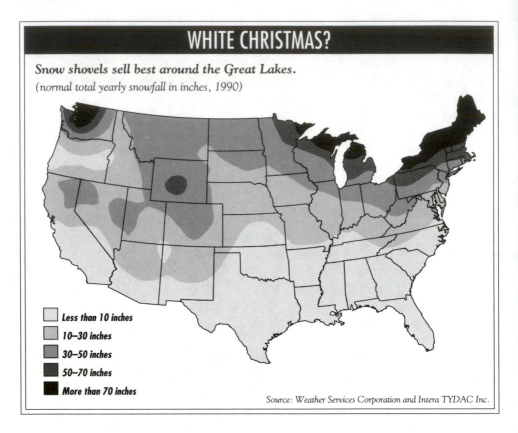

WHITE CHRISTMAS?

Snow shovels sell best around the Great Lakes.
(normal total yearly snowfall in inches, 1990)

Less than 10 inches
10–30 inches
30–50 inches
50–70 inches
More than 70 inches

Source: *Weather Services Corporation and Intera TYDAC Inc.*

as do 45 percent of those aged 30 to 39, while only 40 percent of adults under the age of 30 feel that good community relations are important.

On the other hand, somewhat more than 55 percent of people under the age of 30 feel that a company's responsiveness to community needs is important. This percentage decreases to about 48 percent for people aged 60 and older.

Older people are more likely to purchase the products of a company involved in charitable work. Only 11 percent of older consumers considered a 10 percent discount a good reason to rent a car from the Thrifty car rental company. But when the company offered to donate a portion of rental charges to a fund that buys vans for senior citizens' centers, more than 40 percent of mature customers saw this as a prime incentive for using Thrifty, according to David Wolfe, a consultant who specializes in mature markets.

Giving to charitable concerns is an important part of the image a company presents. Women are more likely than men to value a company's support of cultural activities and obligations to society. More than 50 percent of women consider a company's efforts to meet the needs of society as an important factor in forming an opinion about that company, according to a 1989 Opinion Research Corporation survey. Some 45 percent of men feel the same way.

David Lewin, director of the Institute of Industrial Relations at the University of California at Los Angeles has found a positive correlation between companies' involvement in their community and their return on investment. Employee morale is also high when community involvement is high. Building good relations between the community and corporations is beneficial to everyone.

WINTER TRAVELERS
■ ■ ■ ■ ■ ■ ■ ■ ■ ■ ■ ■ ■ ■

The holiday season is a time for families to get together. The primary purpose of 34 percent of winter trips is to visit friends and relatives, according to the U.S. Travel Data Center in Washington, D.C. Travel has increased every winter since 1983, according to the Travel Data Center. From December 1989 through February 1990, Americans made nearly 137 million round-trips of 100 miles or more, or 39 percent more trips than they made just six years earlier. The number of trips taken by air increased 20 percent. Trips taken by car, truck, or RV (the most frequently used modes of transportation) grew 44 percent. Between 1983 and 1989, winter business and convention trips increased 35 percent. Pleasure trips went up 36 percent.

Home for the Holidays
Growth in both supply and demand fueled the travel industry in the 1980s, according to Suzanne Cook, executive director of the center. The number of hotel rooms in the U.S. increased 40 percent during the decade, while the average budget of state travel offices nearly tripled. Air passengers increased 43 percent, and cruise passengers more than doubled in number.

Older people, who are more willing to travel at all times of the year, have smoothed out seasonal differences in the travel industry. But most of the industry's growth came in the second half of the 1980s, after the country emerged from a severe recession. When the economy is sluggish, off-season profits suffer.

Many Americans travel in winter to get away from the cold. The most popular destinations are the South Atlantic states, which capture 25 percent of all adult travelers. But people also travel to enjoy the snow: 3 percent go to New England and 11 percent head for the Mountain states.

Home Hospitality
Florida is a favorite winter destination. Floridians play host to friends and family members more often than the residents of any other state, according to a 1987 study by Market Facts of Washington, D.C. Their hospitality doesn't help the state's hotels, but it is an opportunity for marketers in other industries.

The money spent by visiting friends and relatives has a powerful effect on the state. It is spread around more areas of Florida than the money spent by hotel and motel travelers, who concentrate around Miami and Orlando. Furthermore, the spending of guests is amplified by the spending of Florida's hosts. The average Florida host spends an extra $200 when friends and family members come to visit. Groceries and gasoline are a big part of this, but so is entertainment. Almost 90 percent of hosts accompany their guests to restaurants, over 80 percent shop with them, and almost as many take them to live performances, sporting events, historic sites, and scenic areas. Over 40 percent accompany their guests to attractions like Disney World, Sea World, and Spaceport U.S.A.

Florida's residents are its best promoters. Even among people who always stay at hotels and motels, 43 percent get advice on things to do and see from people they know who live in Florida. Visiting friends and relatives are even more dependent: only 16 percent read travel articles about the state, compared with 45 percent of hotel and motel travelers. Reaching out-of-state houseguests with conventional advertising is extremely difficult. They are less likely than others to see travel brochures or watch television ads about Florida.

Serving Florida's hosts may be an effective way to reach tourists, according to the Florida Commerce Department's Division of Tourism, which sponsored the study. Most hosts want to take advantage of tourist-assistance programs: 85 percent say that resident and guest discounts at major Florida attractions are useful, and 70 percent find coupon books for local restaurants helpful.

In a fast-growing state like Florida, the spending associated with houseguests should grow in the years ahead. But in any state where tourism contributes to the economy, home hospitality should not be overlooked by marketers.

HOLIDAY ACTIVITIES
■■■■■■■■■■■■■

The Norman Rockwell image of the happy family group going out to cut down a special Christmas tree is not a thing of the past. Cut-your-own Christmas tree operations doubled between 1975 and 1987, to 5,000. But the traditional trek to the neighborhood street-corner lot to pick out a tree is on the decline. Moving up in popularity are mail-order, rented, and ready-to-plant trees.

Trimming the Tree
Mail-order trees appeal to customers without cars, especially city dwellers, and families shipping to service men and women overseas. The venerable L.L. Bean Company in Freeport, Maine, will send a 5- to 6-foot-tall balsam fir tree anywhere in the U.S. except Hawaii or Alaska for about $52.

Rooted trees are aimed at environmentally aware customers who want to plant the trees rather than throw them out. In another environmentally motivated move, a home-furnishing store at Plymouth Meeting, Pennsylvania, rents Canadian balsams for $10 plus a $10 deposit. When they are returned, the trees are ground up into garden mulch.

The Night Before Christmas

Christmas Eve and Christmas Day are times for traditions. People usually spend these important hours with family and friends, doing the same things they have done for years.

Forty percent of Americans opened presents on Christmas Eve, according to a 1989 survey by the Roper Organization in New York City. But 68 percent say they opened presents on Christmas Day—indicating that many people are spreading this Christmas tradition over the two-day period. Christmas lists must have been well-written, because 56 percent of those surveyed reported getting a gift they really liked. Only 6 percent didn't get the gift they most wanted.

Sixty-one percent of Americans spent Christmas Eve or Christmas Day with friends or family. Seventeen percent had family or friends visit overnight. Only 2 percent were alone for the holidays. Young adults were the most likely to go somewhere to visit overnight, while older people were the most likely to host guests.

Television was an important part of the holiday for many people. While 39 percent watched a Christmas special on television, 31 percent watched a football game, 12 percent watched a church service, and 31 percent watched something else, according to Roper. In 1989, 39 percent of Americans went to church either on Christmas Eve or Christmas Day. Married couples, older adults, and upper-income householders are the most likely to attend Christmas church services.

Among the most sacred of holiday traditions is the Christmas meal. Sixty-three percent of Americans ate turkey, and 51 percent ate ham. Obviously, many people got to eat both these holiday favorites. Thirteen percent ate roast beef, and 12 percent opted for chicken, according to Roper. America's cooks must feel the big holiday meal is not a good time for experimentation. Only 11 percent cooked something special that they had never cooked before. Fully 59 percent of adult women participated in preparing the Christmas meal, but only 22 percent of men did.

Blockbuster Movies

The holiday season is a busy one for movie houses. Many studios aim for blockbusters at this time of year, when people are looking for indoor activities. Movies that appeal to kids are especially popular with parents who must find ways to fill up vacation time.

Christmas releases generally open in hundreds of theaters simultaneously, but they frequently have a relatively short run. For these reasons, movie companies want to get as much attention for their films as quickly as possible. There are a number of ways of doing this.

Tie-in promotions with fast-food restaurants and retailers, spin-off toys, dolls, clothes, and free give-aways are a few of the ways movie-makers get the word out to kids. Television advertising, soundtrack recordings, and "teasers" —trailers that advertise the film before another feature in a theater—are also popular devices.

The Walt Disney Company is well known for its systematic tie-ins with sponsors for its films and associated products. The studio has long-term tie-in deals with

McDonald's and Sears, Roebuck & Company. The McDonald's link began with the 1986 reissue of *Snow White*. The deal with Sears began in conjunction with the 1988 reissue of *Bambi*.

Movie-makers target the Christmas season for adult films as well. The Oscar-award-winning *Dances with Wolves* made its debut in November 1990. It was followed by such big films as *The Godfather Part III*, *Look Who's Talking Too*, *Awakenings*, and *Russia House*. But cross-promotions between movie marketers and other advertisers for adult films have been decreasing as the economy gets tighter. "There's less money [for potential promotional partners] to take risks with," says one studio executive. While *Russia House* prompted a tie-in agreement between the film maker MGM/UA and PepsiCo's Stolichnaya vodka, the tie-in trend is not recession-proof. But tie-ins are still the trend for kids' films. Tri-Star Picture's *Hook*, a 1991 holiday sequel to *Peter Pan*, has tie-ins with Mattel. A line of action figures debuted along with the film.

So many new films are launched during the holiday season that films must compete for high box-office figures. And even though people still enjoy going to the movies, watching films on the home VCR has become more popular. Although this could indicate a drop-off in revenues at the theater, the profits to be gained in video royalties more than make up for it. Fifty-eight percent of people enjoy going to the movies, and 71 percent enjoy watching a movie or entertainment show on television or VCR, according to a 1991 survey conducted by the Roper Organization.

More women (62 percent) than men (54 percent) think that going to the movies is fun, according to Roper. The popularity of movie-going decreases with age. Fully 73 percent of young adults aged 18 to 29 like going to the movies, but only 34 percent of adults aged 60 and older feel the same way.

People with lower incomes enjoy going out to the movies less than those with high incomes. While only 48 percent of people with annual household incomes under $15,000 feel that seeing a movie in a theater is fun, 69 percent of people with annual household incomes of $50,000 or more think the movies are great entertainment.

In single-income families, 53 percent of adults enjoy going to the movies, compared with 64 percent of dual-income married people. Sixty-nine percent of dual-income parents like to go to the movies, compared with 66 percent of parents in single-income households, according to Roper.

Staying home and watching the VCR is popular in every demographic group. Men and women enjoy it almost equally (71 percent of men and 72 percent of women). Seventy-six percent of young people aged 18 to 29 enjoy staying home with the VCR, as do 62 percent of adults over age 60.

Video viewing is also slightly more popular with lower-income people than among those with higher incomes. Seventy-six percent of people whose annual household income is under $15,000 like to watch the VCR, while 72 percent of those with annual household incomes over $50,000 find it enjoyable. Three-quarters of dual-income couples enjoy watching a movie at home, as do 77 percent of dual-income parents with children under 17, reports Roper. Unmarried people under age 45 also find watching the VCR enjoyable (74 percent), but single people aged 45 and older are less interested in videos (63 percent).

Nearly two-thirds of VCR owners like to rent comedy videos, according to Roper. Young adults are especially interested in the comedy format, and high-income people are more likely than people with low incomes to pick a comedy video.

It's Party Time

The holiday season is also party time. People celebrate at home and in the office. There are big formal events and small quiet family get-togethers. The biggest party of the year—New Year's Eve—caps off the month and brings in the new year.

For the majority of Americans (53 percent), home entertainment is a monthly event, according to *The Lifestyle Odyssey: 2,001 Ways Americans' Lives Are Changing*, a publication by the editors of *Research Alert*. Most Americans (55 percent) are guests at a friend's gathering during a typical month. Almost everyone (82 percent) enjoys hosting an affair in their home. And even more people (90 percent) enjoy going to someone else's home.

American parties are usually casual, according to the *Research Alert* editors. Almost half of Americans say their own parties are more informal today than they were five years ago. They say the type of food as well as the style of dress is less formal. The selection of guests is not as rigid, and parties are more likely to include children. Most Americans (81 percent) prefer small gatherings with friends over large parties, according to *The Lifestyle Odyssey*.

Still, the sit-down dinner remains popular. Half of adults choose this way to entertain more than half of the time. Only 29 percent serve buffet-style dinners more than half of the time. However it's served, fully 84 percent of adults say that good food is the number-one ingredient for entertaining success.

Office parties are very popular among owners of mid-sized companies. Almost eight out of every ten owners provide for an office party at Christmas, according to a 1990 survey by BDO Seidman, an accounting and consulting firm based in New York City. Close to 70 percent of these businesses distribute employee bonuses at Christmas. And just over half of the owners give gifts to employees.

Only 76 percent of family businesses are likely to have an office party, compared with 84 percent of nonfamily-owned businesses. Holiday parties are especially popular among service-industry businesses, with 88 percent reporting that they give office parties each year. Among companies with over $80 million in revenues, 92 percent celebrate with an annual office party.

Christmas bonuses depend on company size. More than 80 percent of companies with fewer than 20 employees distribute bonuses, compared with 53 percent of companies with over 500 employees. While 73 percent of family business owners prefer to give bonuses, only 63 percent of nonfamily businesses reward their employees with a big holiday check. Gift-giving is the least favored holiday perk among mid-sized businesses. Only half of those surveyed by BDO Seidman distribute gifts to employees. Manufacturers are the most likely to distribute gifts—56 percent reward employees at Christmas with presents.

The New Year's Bash

While noisemakers, party hats, and champagne are the usual props for New Year's Eve, many Americans spend this traditional party night at home, according to Roper.

When Roper polled Americans to find out what they did on New Year's Eve in 1989, the largest share—45 percent—said they celebrated quietly in their own home or in the home of a friend or relative. Twenty-eight percent stayed at home and did nothing special at all. Older folks are more likely to take it easy than young people: nearly half of adults aged 60 or older spent the evening at home, compared with only 14 percent of those under age 30.

Just 25 percent of Americans partied on New Year's Eve. Three percent hosted a party in their home, while 12 percent went to a party at a friend's or relative's house. Ten percent went to a club or restaurant for a special New Year's Eve celebration, but only 2 percent put on formal evening attire.

Young adults are most likely to go to a party. One in five adults under age 30 spent New Year's Eve at a friend's or relative's party, compared with 1 in 10 people aged 30 to 59 and just 1 in 25 aged 60 or older. Young adults are twice as likely as the average adult to throw a party in their own home, and they are 80 percent more likely to go to a club or restaurant. As income rises, so does the propensity to party.

If most people don't party on New Year's Eve, what do they do? Almost half of adults watched television, according to Roper. Another 10 percent rented a movie for their VCR. Twenty-three percent went to bed before midnight.

Toasting the New Year

More Americans buy beer than champagne to toast the New Year, according to the Roper study. Beer is the New Year's drink of choice for 13 percent of Americans. Eight percent buy domestic champagne, while 4 percent buy the imported product. Other wines are the choice of 7 percent of adults, while 3 percent select wine coolers. Nine percent buy hard liquor such as whiskey, vodka, or gin.

In general, people under age 30 are more likely than older adults to buy alcoholic beverages for New Year's Eve. The exceptions are domestic champagne and other wines, for which purchases peak among people aged 30 to 44. Men are twice as likely as women to buy beer or hard liquor for the celebration.

During the 1980s, per capita consumption of alcoholic beverages declined, according to the 1989 Industrial Outlook from the U.S. Department of Commerce. Changing attitudes, tastes, and preferences are partly responsible. But more important is the alcoholic-beverage industry's heavy dependence on young adults, a shrinking segment of the total population.

While the share of people who go to parties on New Year's Eve has not declined over the past few years, according to Roper, a smaller share of party goers buy alcohol. Between January 1986 and January 1989, the proportion of people who bought beer for New Year's Eve fell from 18 percent to 13 percent. The proportions buying hard liquor and wine dropped by 3 percentage points each. And the share buying domestic champagne slipped 2 percentage points. However, the share buying imported champagne held steady.

"Drinking is down across all ages," says Beth Nieman, research manager at Maritz Marketing Research. "In fact, after reaching age 26, there is a trend toward not drinking at all. Seventeen percent of 26-to-34-year-olds don't drink—which increases to 24 percent of those 35 to 44, 33 percent of those 45 to 54, 49 percent of those 55 to 64, and a whopping 65 percent of people 65 and older."

As taxes, import duties, and tariffs take their toll on the liquor, beer, and wine industry, health and safety issues are also coming to the forefront. State laws have come down hard on drinking and driving, and 56 percent of Americans would like to see alcohol advertising banned, according to a 1989 poll conducted by the Roper Organization. Thirty-one percent think this is an "excellent" idea, and a majority of almost every population segment favors the idea.

The alcohol industry can improve its image by sponsoring advertisements that encourage responsible drinking. Eighty-one percent of Americans think that there should be more ads that encourage responsible drinking habits.

BAH, HUMBUG

Even with all the good cheer in the world, some people cannot get into the Christmas spirit. One in five Americans does not believe that the effort involved with Christmas is worth even a single day of enjoyment. On average, these Scrooges take less time shopping and spend less money on the gifts they do buy, according to a 1990 survey conducted by the New York City-based Warwick Baker & Fiore, Inc.

Eighty-one percent of these new-wave Scrooges are over age 35, and 58 percent have less than a high school education. But the vast majority of Americans revel in the holiday spirit and don't let the party-poopers get them down. Still, retailers should be aware that some crimes, especially shoplifting, peak around the holiday season.

PART 3

TIME FOR

A SALE

After the holidays,
the weather is bad and
consumers are spent. But
the right promotion may
just have the power to pull
consumers away from
their television sets and
back into the stores.

JANUARY WEATHER
■■■■■■■■■■■■

In January, just about everyone knows it's winter. While temperatures in the 40s and 50s may not seem so cold to people who live in the North, people in Miami, Mobile, and Los Angeles suffer when the temperatures get this low.

	TEMPERATURE		PRECIPITATION	
	low	*high*	*inches*	*days*
Albuquerque, NM	22.3°F	47.2°F	0.41	4
Atlanta, GA	32.6	51.2	4.91	11
Bismarck, ND	- 4.2	17.5	0.51	8
Boise, ID	22.6	37.1	1.64	12
Boston, MA	22.8	36.4	3.99	11
Buffalo, NY	17.0	30.0	3.02	20
Burlington, VT	7.7	25.4	1.85	14
Charlotte, NC	30.7	50.3	3.80	10
Chicago, IL	13.6	29.2	1.60	11
Cleveland, OH	18.5	32.5	2.47	16
Dallas, TX	33.9	54.0	1.65	7
Denver, CO	15.9	43.1	0.51	6
Detroit, MI	16.1	30.6	1.86	13
Great Falls, MT	9.2	28.2	1.00	9
Honolulu, HI	65.3	79.9	3.79	10
Houston, TX	40.8	61.9	3.21	10
Indianapolis, IN	17.8	34.2	2.65	12
Jacksonville, FL	41.7	64.6	3.07	8
Juneau, AK	16.1	27.4	3.69	18
Los Angeles, CA	47.3	64.6	3.06	6
Memphis, TN	30.9	48.3	4.61	10
Miami, FL	59.2	75.0	2.08	7
Milwaukee, WI	11.3	26.0	1.64	11
Minneapolis, MN	2.4	19.9	0.82	9
Mobile, AL	40.9	60.6	4.59	11
New Orleans, LA	43.0	61.8	4.97	10
New York, NY	25.6	38.0	3.21	11
Norfolk, VA	31.7	48.1	3.72	10
Oklahoma City, OK	25.2	46.6	0.96	5
Omaha, NE	10.2	30.2	0.77	6
Philadelphia, PA	23.8	38.6	3.18	11
Phoenix, AZ	39.4	65.2	0.73	4
Portland, OR	33.5	44.3	6.16	18
Salt Lake City, UT	19.7	37.4	1.35	10
San Francisco, CA	41.5	55.5	4.65	11
Sault Ste. Marie, MI	5.4	21.2	2.20	19
Seattle, WA	34.3	43.9	6.04	19
St. Louis, MO	19.9	37.6	1.72	8
Washington, DC	27.5	42.9	2.76	10
Wichita, KS	19.4	39.8	0.68	5

Source: U.S. Department of Commerce, Bureau of the Census, Statistical Abstract of the United States 1991. Average daily minimum and maximum temperatures and average monthly precipitation were measured over a standard 30-year period.

JANUARY
TIME FOR A CHANGE

Many Americans feel that the New Year is a good time for self-evaluation and change. After the overindulgence of the holidays, some resolve to lose the weight they began gaining around Halloween. Others decide to stop smoking or drinking. And many vow to save more money, make better investments, and spend more wisely.

If the holiday season was good, merchants want to keep the momentum going with a post-season sale. If, on the other hand, the Christmas season was a disappointment, then merchants must cut their losses with post-season bargains. No matter what the motivation, the outcome is predictable. Shoppers are burned out, but the tug of a great bargain can get them out of their houses and back into the stores. Bargain-hunters look forward to sales, and people whose New Year's resolutions include spending more wisely can justify saving money on sale items.

POST-HOLIDAY SALES

Consumers have come to expect January sales, and they plan their spending patterns accordingly. Although January has always been associated with "white sales"—markdowns on bedding, linens, and towels—people are looking for other bargains as well. Cosmetics, home furnishings, radios, small appliances, stationery, and women's clothing are all great bargains at this time of year.

JANUARY'S BEST BUYS

(items most likely to be on sale in January)

- Bedding
- Cosmetics
- Home furnishings
- Radios
- Small appliances
- Stationery
- White goods
- Women's clothing

Source: DOLLAR$ENSE Magazine, 1987

The Bargain Hunters

The sense of prosperity experienced by so many Americans in the 1980s has given way to a feeling of postponement. Consumers in the 1990s feel their prospects are more limited, and that they can have some of the things they want only some of the time, says Judith Langer, president of Langer Associates Inc., a New York firm specializing in focus group research. Uncertainty about the economy and how it directly affects them is part of the fear many consumers face.

This "New Realism," as Langer calls it, can manifest itself in many ways. It has a direct bearing on shopping and spending patterns. More people today are shopping carefully, watching prices, and trying to get the most for every dollar. A growing number of shoppers vow to buy what they need instead of what they want.

Sales and low prices are two of the strongest triggers for impulse purchases. In contrast to the 1980s, when people boasted about how much money they were making, people now talk about how much money they are saving by being careful shoppers. Twenty years ago, Langer says, focus group respondents were reluctant to admit that their purchase decisions were based on price. Today, price is of paramount importance.

Langer calls another concept "Classics;" people want to buy things that will last. It's a constant sum game. Some consumers admit to spending the same amount of money, but they are spending it in a different way. These shoppers are trying to make sure that everything they buy is a bargain. In spite of time pressures, they go from store to store comparing prices. They read *Consumer Reports*, and they feel more powerful as shoppers, knowing they can wait for retailers to hold a sale.

Another trend during times of recession is trading down, says Langer. People don't give up their pleasures, but they find less costly ways of enjoying themselves.

Consumers are changing their entire approach to shopping. Today's shoppers are purposeful, says Langer. They are shopping to buy a necessity, not to spend a few hours looking in store windows. They are also constantly looking for ways to save money. In the 1980s, there was a definite schism between premium shoppers (the "high-end" shopper who frequented only the most upscale stores) and price shoppers (those who sought competitive prices from low-end stores). But in the 1990s, the same person is often both, buying a high-quality item from an upscale store and coordinating it with low-end accessories. Retailers have responded to the dual nature of shoppers. Many off-price stores have become more upscale and offer more services in order to accommodate the diverse customer base. Proprietors of upscale shops, who used to hide price tags, are now boasting about the great "values" consumers can find in their stores.

More for Less

Looking for high-quality merchandise at discount prices has become almost an obsession with shoppers. For that reason, the factory outlet industry has flourished in recent years.

Factory outlets started as just that—a few square feet in the corner of a factory where seconds and overruns could be sold at reduced rates. Intrepid shoppers often found out about these bargains by word of mouth, and many were put off by the distances they needed to travel to get to the factory as well as the uncertainty about the quality and quantity of stock on hand at any given time.

Today, factory outlets are often located in areas with prime tourist attractions. "Shopping is usually second on the tourist's list [of things to do] after the primary tourist activity," says Rex Burgher, vice president of development for the Buffalo, New York-based Benderson Development Company. Benderson has operated a successful outlet center in Niagara Falls, New York, since 1982. The 400,000-square-foot center has been expanded eight times and now houses 100 outlet stores.

The outlet malls of the 1990s are upgraded in design and quality. "When the industry first started, you wanted to emphasize the fact the consumer was saving money, so you gave them concrete floors. But now, the consumers are too smart for that. If you give them a bad-looking store, they will feel the quality of the merchandise is not as good," says Amy Smith, corporate marketing director for Company Stores Development Corporation, a Brentwood, Tennessee-based outlet center developer.

Not only do outlet centers spring up in tourist areas, they often become tourist attractions in their own right. Take the northeastern Alabama town of Boaz, for example. Boaz, located 40 miles from the nearest metropolitan area on secondary roads, has fewer than 8,000 permanent residents. But it has become one of the state's biggest tourist attractions. Every day, about 15,000 shoppers come to Boaz to scour the 700,000 square feet of retail space looking for bargains. Sales-tax receipts in the town rose from $665,000 in 1981 to an estimated $4 million in 1989. On peak days, Boaz plays host to 75,000 shoppers and up to 135 tour buses.

Downscale Shoppers

While bargain hunting is a recreational activity for some Americans, it is a necessity for others. Almost half of American households had an annual income of less than $25,000 in 1989. Members of this "downscale market" are usually young people who are struggling against the odds or older people whose spending is determined by their fixed incomes. The younger half of the downscale market goes for the low-priced version of the American Dream, like wood-veneer cabinets and imitations of expensive perfumes. The older half has less energy, fewer options, and a greater need for security. Many of their purchases are dictated by need or controlled by insurance or government programs.

Low-income families are more likely than the general population to be black or Hispanic, but whites still make up 81 percent of the total. Sixteen percent of downscale householders are black, and 9 percent are Hispanic.* About 11 percent of all households are black, and 6 percent are Hispanic.

*The figures do not add to 100 percent because Hispanics can be of any race.

The strongest predictor of a low income is education, or the lack of it. Fewer than one in ten downscale householders has a college degree, and almost 40 percent never finished high school.

Twenty-nine percent of downscale households have children at home, compared with 36 percent of all households. Fully 18 percent of downscale households are headed by single women, double the share among middle-income households and four times the rate among upscale households. Just 16 percent of downscale households contain four or more people, compared with 30 percent of midscale and 40 percent of upscale households.

The poorest Americans earn only about 20 percent of what the average American makes. But they spend a significantly greater share of their income on education, including child-care and day-care tuition. Because many of them are older, they spend comparatively more on prescription drugs and medical supplies. While downscale households have little to spend on discretionary items, tobacco and smoking supplies rank high. But the bulk of lower-income Americans' money goes to rent and heat.

Downscale households spend less per person than upscale consumers. But because there are so many of them, they spend billions of dollars annually. Department and variety-store operators like Wal-Mart that have focused on this market have flourished. Targeting downscale shoppers can be a challenge. "There is a tendency, when marketers address this segment, to talk down to it," says Ken Smikle, publisher of *Target Market News* in Chicago. He feels that the problem stems from the number of marketers with upscale backgrounds. "There is a real arrogance among some marketers. It is as though they are saying 'You want to be like me.'" Smikle recommends bringing in people who have experience outside the upper class.

Marketers tend to stereotype downscale shoppers. "The most dangerous thing you can do is lump everybody together in the $25,000-or-under category," says Robert Pitts, professor and chairman of De Paul University's Kellstadt Center for Marketing Analysis. Ken Smikle prefers the term "average" to "downscale." "That large a segment of the population has earned the right to be called average. They are part of the norm," he says.

Women in Search of a Bargain

Three out of four women buy most of their clothes on sale. Half will wait for a sale before buying, according to a 1991 study conducted for *Glamour* magazine. Only 22 percent of women aged 18 to 55 usually pay full price for clothes. And just 8 percent of women buy whatever clothes they want, whenever they want, without waiting for a sale.

The typical woman spends 27 percent of her annual clothing budget on career or work clothes, 24 percent on weekend or leisure clothes, 18 percent on shoes, 12 percent on evening wear, 11 percent on accessories, and 8 percent on lingerie.

Work clothes are the first priority of 56 percent of women. Everyday clothes are cited as a top priority by 35 percent of women. Just 16 percent rank leisure clothes first, and only 8 percent rank party clothes as the main clothing-budget priority. (Some women in the survey chose two categories as their top priority.)

Seventy-five percent of the women surveyed said that needing an outfit for a special occasion was a prime shopping motivation. The other factors that get women to buy clothes are sales (69 percent) and replacing old or worn-out clothes (60 percent). Eighty-one percent of women buy their clothes from department stores, 70 percent frequent discount stores, and 68 percent shop in local specialty stores and boutiques. Catalog shopping attracts 64 percent of women.

Supermarket Specials

Food is bought more frequently than clothing. The average household spent 15 percent of its money on food in 1990, compared with just 6 percent on apparel, according to the government's Consumer Expenditure Survey.

The majority of grocery shoppers economize, according to a 1991 survey conducted by the Food Marketing Institute (FMI) in Washington, D.C. But only 18 percent could be defined as "heavy economizers"—those who use five or more economizing measures when they shop. The person most likely to be a heavy economizer is a married woman aged 18 to 24, who does not work outside of the home, and who lives in a household with three or more people. The heavy economizer has young children (especially between the ages of 2 and 6), and her annual household income is between $35,000 and $50,000.

Heavy economizers spend an average of $80 a week on groceries, about the same as any other shopper, according to FMI. But heavy economizers spend less per person than all shoppers do. While the average shopper spends $32 per person per week on groceries, heavy economizers spend only $29 per person per week. Among cost-cutting measures, the most popular is price-off coupons. Other measures include doing more with leftovers, buying fewer luxury or gourmet items, eating out less often, buying fewer convenience foods, doing more meal planning, and buying only what is on the grocery list.

Weekly family expenditures for food rose to $79 in 1991, from $74 in 1989 and 1990, according to the FMI survey. Despite this rise, the average consumer bargain hunted less frequently. In 1982, one in two food shoppers looked for specials in the newspaper, and one in three comparison shopped among grocery stores. But in 1991, only one in three shoppers checked newspaper ads, and just one in five comparison shopped between grocery stores. Busy lifestyles may keep many shoppers from taking the time needed for these cost-cutting measures.

Women who do not work outside of the home and shoppers from large households tend to economize most frequently. Men, employed women, and shoppers from small households economize less frequently, according to the FMI survey. While only 44 percent of men use coupons, fully 63 percent of women do. But 53 percent of men and 56 percent of women shy away from gourmet items.

Since the pool of grocery shoppers who economize heavily is relatively small, food retailers may be better off with attractive initial pricing, important to 71 percent of all shoppers, rather than newspaper-advertised specials. In-store specials, important to 88 percent of all shoppers, can also be effective, especially if retailers are targeting young, single shoppers, says FMI.

POST-HOLIDAY DIETING

About 17 percent of Americans make a New Year's resolution each year, according to the Roper Organization in New York City. While no information is available on just how they intend to change their lives, it's a good bet that many of them are planning to lose some weight. In January 1991, the Calorie Control Council in Atlanta estimated that about 5 million Americans were dieting because of the weight they gained during the holiday season.

The Diet Craze

Americans give a number of reasons for dieting. Only about half of dieters say they want to lose weight; the rest want to stay healthy and attractive. A significant share want to reduce cholesterol levels, salt intake, or blood sugar by dieting. One of the major factors driving people to diets is the media barrage promoting them. "Hardly a magazine directed to women does not feature on its cover at least one article describing a diet, the importance of proper nutrition, or other weight-related matters. Month after month, one survey or another stresses how unhealthy it is to be overweight," says Packaged Facts' 1991 report on *The Diet Aids Market.*

The calorie-conscious market has been credited with bolstering the sales of soft drinks, salad dressings, and beer. Each year, the total diet market, including health clubs, artificial sweeteners, appetite suppressants, diet books, and diet sodas, produces over $33 billion in sales. But it is easier to add up the revenues they generate than to estimate the number of people currently on a diet.

Some sources estimate the number of dieters as high as 65 million, says Packaged Facts of New York City. Others place the total as low as 40 million. Certainly, the number of dieters exceeds the number of Americans who are obese. About 20 percent of adults (34 million Americans) are overweight, according to the National Center for Health Statistics. But 36 percent of men and 54 percent of women consider themselves overweight. Another survey of women aged 18 to 34 found that 75 percent thought they could stand to lose at least some weight, says Packaged Facts.

The Americans who choose to diet may not be the ones who need it most. Among Americans who planned to lose weight in 1991, 40 percent of men and 50 percent of women wanted to lose 10 pounds or less, according to a survey by Maritz Marketing Research of Fenton, Missouri.

A significant majority of Americans—77 percent—are generally pleased with

BIRTHS AND DEATHS

The death rate is above average after the holidays, but the peak season for births is from May to September.

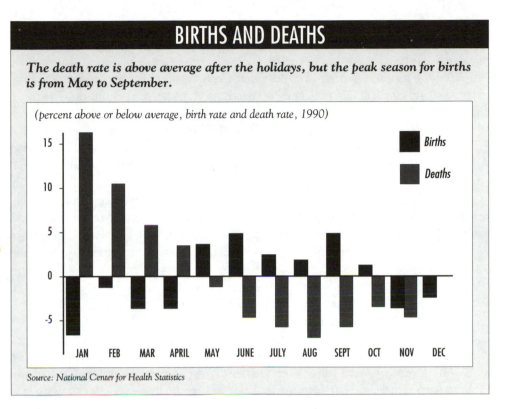

(percent above or below average, birth rate and death rate, 1990)

Source: National Center for Health Statistics

the way their bodies look. Just 15 percent of men and 36 percent of women are unhappy with their bodies. But weight plays an important role in how satisfied people are with themselves. Only 19 percent of those who classify themselves as very overweight say they are pleased with their bodies, but 92 percent of those who think they are about the right weight are pleased with their body's appearance.

In 1990, the average American woman was 5 feet, 4 inches tall and weighed 142 pounds. The average American man was 5 feet, 10 inches tall and weighed 180 pounds. But American women would like to be 5 feet, 6 inches tall and weigh 129 pounds, while men want to be 5 feet, 11 inches tall and weigh 171 pounds, according to Gallup.

Fads and Fat

The diet business frequently rises and falls with current fads. Diet crazes range from the Drinking Man's Diet, Metrecal, and starch blocks to the Grapefruit Diet and so-called "miracle diets" and "miracle drugs," says Packaged Facts. The profitability of diet products can vary tremendously. Between 1988 and 1990, the sales of all diet aids grew 72 percent, but the sales of diet replacements swelled 197 percent, while sales of appetite suppressants shrank 25 percent. Negative publicity associated with Cal-Ban 3000, a diet pill linked to several deaths, was just one of the factors hurting sales in the late 1980s. Even though her trim figure lasted only a short time, Oprah Winfrey's dramatic weight loss of 67 pounds with a meal-replacement diet gave the market a real boost.

Appetite suppressants are one of the least commonly used diet aids. According to the Calorie Control Council, they are used by only 4 percent of dieters. "Miracle diet pills" and "magic diet pills," nonprescription diet aids that promise rapid and easy weight loss without the need for exercise or dieting, have created a bad image for the appetite-suppressant industry. But recent rulings by the Food and Drug Administration (FDA) have begun to put controls on the wild claims made by many companies.

Young people, especially teenaged girls, account for a disproportionately large share of people who misuse appetite suppressants. Too many youngsters think of appetite suppressants as a standard method of dieting, says Packaged Facts. Hospitals and clinics report that the majority of patients they treat for anorexia and bulimia routinely misuse diet pills, diuretics, and laxatives. Although the number of teenagers who abuse diet suppressants has declined in recent years, 22 percent of high school seniors still use them, according to the National Institute on Drug Abuse.

The number of dieters in the U.S. is actually stable, according to the Calorie Control Center. But the center reports that the nature of dieting is changing. "Staying in good health is the number-one reason why people consume low-calorie foods and beverages," says Julie Wilgus of the Calorie Control Center. "People are looking for balance in their diet, rather than following on-again, off-again diets," she says.

Jill Melton, a registered dietician with Cooking Light magazine, says that even though her publication features low-fat recipes, the periodical is designed for "the healthy person who is trying to stay healthy" rather than someone who needs to diet. She says that Americans' eating habits have become healthier. In the average American's diet, the proportion of calories that come from fat has dropped below 40 percent. While consumption of certain high-fat gourmet foods, like Haagen Daaz ice cream, has gone up, people are cutting back on other things so they can afford those high-fat desserts.

During the holidays, Cooking Light tries to offer its readers mainstream traditional holiday menus. In November 1991, for example, Cooking Light's cover featured a turkey roasted with its skin on to retain moisture and tenderness. Readers were told that cooking a turkey with its skin on doesn't hurt its healthy qualities, but they were also told not to eat the skin because it contains a lot of fat.

Unlike other publications targeted at women, Cooking Light doesn't feature a special quick-weight-loss diet after the holidays. "In January, we emphasize simple cooking. [Our readers] have been entertaining; now they want to unwind and take it easy," says Melton. Cooking Light's message is that healthy eating should be part of people's lifestyle throughout the year. Many people are getting this message, and it is changing the way diet products and services are marketed.

Between 1986 and 1990, sales of healthy prepared foods doubled. Between 1990 and 1995, they are expected to double again, according to FIND/SVP of New York City. These healthy products include low-fat and low-cholesterol foods, reduced-fat and reduced-calorie foods, high-fiber foods, and low-sodium foods, but do not include diet soft drinks. In 1990, the healthy-foods market had $14 billion in sales. "In contrast to diet foods, healthy foods are targeted at that large and growing portion of the population that is trying to eat more healthfully in the long run, rather than as a part of a short-term effort to lose weight," says FIND/SVP's vice president of marketing research reports, Peter Allen.

Still, seasonal dieters are a fact of life. During the holiday season, enrollment in Weight Watchers classes is lower than normal. But in January, the number of people enrolling in classes almost doubles, according to chief executive Charles Berger.

THE SUPER BOWL

January is a big football month. There were 18 college bowl games in the 1991-92 season, 8 of them on New Year's Day. But all that football may be saturating the January television viewing market. Such New Year's staples as the Rose Bowl and the Orange Bowl have recently become the victims of the recession, shrinking budgets, and uninspired postseason matchups.

The Big Game

College football teams are ranked subjectively during the season, and it is hard for marketers to predict which bowl games will have the best match-ups. The Fiesta Bowl of 1990 featured No. 18 Louisville against No. 27 Alabama, not the most compelling of television events. Advertising revenues suffer when the teams are not top-rated. When the teams are top-ranked, television networks can ask $225,000 per 30-second spot, as was the case when NBC-TV's coverage of the 1990 Orange Bowl featured No. 1 Colorado against former No. 1 Notre Dame. Even so, the advertising spots were still not sold out three weeks before game time.

Of course, there's always the Super Bowl. While interest in postseason college football games may be declining, public interest in the Super Bowl is still high, according to a 1990 study conducted by Bruskin Goldring Research, a market research firm in Edison, New Jersey.

Although fads come and go, interest in the Super Bowl continues unabated. Just prior to the 1990 Super Bowl, 44 percent of adults expressed more interest in the game than in previous years. Only 33 percent said they were less interested, while 19 percent claimed no change in their interest level. Only 4 percent had no opinion, according to the Bruskin Goldring study.

Among men, the differences were more dramatic—49 percent expressed greater interest in the event, while 30 percent said they had less interest. Pro-football fans, who constituted 43 percent of the total sample, reported a significant increase in interest in the Super Bowl. While 66 percent were more interested just prior to game time, only 20 percent were less interested.

The reasons for an increased interest in the Super Bowl include a greater parity of teams, more competitiveness, and the game itself being more interesting and more exciting. These reasons were mentioned by 18 percent of respondents. An additional 14 percent said their increased interest was based on a better understanding of the game. Twenty-three percent said the Super Bowl was a family affair, and 18 percent said they enjoyed the sport of football more than they previously had. People who were less interested in the Super Bowl had little or no interest in football anyway. They also felt football had become too commercialized.

A TV Extravaganza

A 30-second advertising spot for the 1992 Super Bowl cost nearly $850,000. With that much at stake, sponsors want to be sure they're getting their money's worth.

The Super Bowl has become the country's biggest and most important advertising showcase. Wealthy advertisers devise lavish 60-second spots rather than the usual 15- or 30-second promotions. During the 1990 Super Bowl, for example, Coca-Cola got 22 million viewers to watch a special Diet Coke ad through branded 3-D glasses. For the 1991 Super Bowl, Coke devised an audience-interactive commercial and tie-in contest. The spot, however, was pulled and replaced with a solemn message honoring those involved in the Gulf War. But in 1992, Michael Jordan and Bugs Bunny captured the public's imagination with a 60-second high-tech ad for Nike that combined live and animated action.

While advertising interest has been steadily increasing, Super Bowl ratings have been declining. After the 1982 game, which netted an audience rating of 49.1, meaning that 49.1 percent of all television households were tuned in, the ratings slipped to 41.9 by 1988. It rebounded to 43.5 in 1989. But in 1990, the rating was only 39.0, the third-lowest rating for a Super Bowl game since the big matchup began in the early 1960s. The rating was 40.3 for the 1992 game.

Even with audiences shrinking, advertisers who want to use the Super Bowl as a centerpiece for larger marketing and media plans find the expensive spots worthwhile. ABC, sponsor of the 1991 game, gave advertisers their money's worth by selling the time in a package with pre- and post-game spots, as well as spots in other ABC sports events.

The Super Bowl doesn't only generate television advertising revenues and income from NFL-licensed or player-endorsed products. As one of the most important sporting events in the country, it also promises its host city massive tourism revenue. New Orleans has hosted seven Super Bowls. "We estimate that the economic impact of each game on New Orleans is between $120 and $140 million," says David Jones, president of the New Orleans Chamber of Commerce.

Airlines, hotels, restaurants, taxis, stores, concessionaires, and limousine

THE BLACK CONSUMER

IN 1986, Martin Luther King Day became a national holiday celebrated on the third Monday in January. Because the holiday commemorates the life of one of the most important leaders of the civil rights movement, it is a good time to celebrate the achievements of black Americans and to express appreciation to black customers.

Getting to know your customers is the first step in providing superior customer service. America's 31 million blacks are a large and diverse group. Although many blacks are poor, two-thirds are not. Affluent blacks such as Bill Cosby's television character Heathcliff Huxtable don't represent a majority either, but the upscale black population is growing. In 1990, more than 14 percent of black families had incomes of $50,000 or more, up from less than 11 percent in 1980, after adjusting for inflation. But the share of black families with incomes below $5,000 also grew, from 8 percent to more than 11 percent.

The 7 million black families in this country are generally larger and younger than white families. One in four white family householders is under the age of 35, while the proportion in black families is one in three. Average family size for blacks is 3.49 persons, compared with 3.12 persons for whites. Married couples are the largest and most affluent family type among both blacks and whites. The median income of black married couples was $34,000 in 1990; for white married couples, this figure was $40,000. Between 1989 and 1990, white married couples experienced a 2 percent decline in real income, while the median income of black married couples grew 4 percent.

Blacks are gaining in economic power. Between 1970 and 1990, the number of black-owned businesses more than doubled, the number of black managers and administrators nearly tripled, and the number of black lawyers increased more than sixfold. This translates into greater consumer power, and many businesses recognize this. The automobile industry has actively sought black consumers, according to Edward Lewis, publisher of *Essence*, a magazine for black women. Food companies are also beginning to reach out to blacks, he says. But other advertisers seem to avoid black publications. "The cosmetics industry is flat," says Lewis. "It needs to reach out to new markets."

Some marketers claim they can reach blacks by advertising in general market publications. But according to Eugene Morris, president of a black-owned advertising agency in Chicago, blacks may represent only 10 or 12 percent of a mass-market magazine's readership. "The effectiveness of advertising in a black publication stems from more than just the numbers," he says. "The environment, the relevancy, and the empathy that the reader has with the publication are also important."

Marketers who decide to target blacks may find this new territory rewarding. *Essence* reaches fully 25 percent of its target audience with 4 million readers, primarily black women aged 18 to 49. Everett Staten of *Emerge* says that before his magazine was introduced, "educated blacks were forced to go to the general magazine market."

Blacks spend $250 billion a year, according to the 1990 Consumer Expenditure Survey. "In many cases, targeting blacks can make the difference between breaking even and making a profit," says Staten.

Afrocentric Spending

In the 1990s, minorities of all types have been demanding that business better represent their needs. The list of products and services that can be targeted at minority groups is long, including baby dolls, cosmetics, hair-care products, magazines, history books, cultural events, and even tourist attractions.

The recent dedication of the Civil Rights Memorial in Montgomery, Alabama, is attracting a great number of visitors to that southern city. When blacks visit Memphis, they can see the new National Civil Rights Museum, which is located in the old Lorraine Motel, site of the 1968 assassination of Dr. Martin Luther King, Jr.

Tourist attractions designed to appeal to blacks in search of their own history have been opening up throughout the U.S. In Washington, D.C., one may visit Frederick Douglass's home, or the Willard Hotel, where Dr. King drafted his "I have a dream" speech. The city of Washington also has a Black History National Recreation Trail, under the auspices of the National Park Service and the Parks and History Association, a private group. While not a specific route, the trail highlights sites that illuminate black history in six Washington neighborhoods.

The Black Heritage Trail in Boston also features important spots, including the Abiel Smith School, home of the Museum of Afro-American History, and the memorial to Robert Gould Shaw, the white commander of the black 54th Regiment of the Union Army during the Civil War. Other tourist areas that promote the knowledge of black heritage and history include sites in Chicago, Denver, and Colonial Williamsburg, Virginia.

The designation of Martin Luther King Day as a national holiday was highly significant for the black community. But it is by no means the only day of the year when black Americans celebrate their triumph over adversity. Today, an estimated 5 million blacks celebrate Kwanzaa, an Afrocentric Thanksgiving. The holiday, an American creation of the 1960s, uses African culture, language, and foods to celebrate black America's African heritage. The seven-day celebration takes place from December 26th to January 1st. February marks Black History Month. And throughout the year and across the country, local events celebrate cultural diversity as well as the life and times of black American heros, from Harriet Tubman to Duke Ellington.

services profit from the Super Bowl. Some people travel to a Super Bowl not to see the game, but to take part in the celebrations leading up to the big matchup, says Jones. The economic impact of the Super Bowl is so substantial that cities like Miami, Tampa, Houston, Seattle, Minneapolis, San Diego, San Francisco, and New Orleans send delegations to the NFL to persuade team owners to award them future dates. "These cities are well aware of what the Super Bowl can do for a community. It's more than just the money. The telecast focuses upon the city itself. These cities think it's a great ongoing promotion for tourism," says NFL commissioner Pete Rozelle.

After the Bowl

One week after the 1990 Super Bowl, Bruskin Goldring repeated its survey on public interest. San Francisco had defeated Denver 55 to 10, and people rapidly lost interest in the game. Only 30 percent of people said they were now more interested in the Super Bowl, but fully 42 percent were less interested. In a situation where one team trounces the other so resoundingly, postgame interest declines dramatically, Bruskin Goldring suggests.

However, many enthusiasts show support for their teams long after the season is over. They sport NFL logos on every conceivable piece of clothing. Sweatshirts, T-shirts, sweatpants, and other outfits are splashed with the "official team name and logo." Men are not the only customers for these team outfits. Nearly half of all American women have bought items that bear an NFL logo, according to Simmons Market Research Bureau of New York City. In recognition of the growing prominence of female football fans, a line of women's fashion apparel, NFL Spirit, was licensed by the National Football League in 1991.

Pro football has been attracting more female viewers over the last decade, according to the Simmons Study of Media and Markets. Women now account for 41 percent of those who watch NFL football. Most women are not just fair-weather fans, either. Thirty-seven percent of those who watch games frequently are women, up from 33 percent in 1980, according to Simmons.

WINTER SPORTS
■■■■■■■■■■■

While the Super Bowl often exercises sports fans' voice muscles more than any other part of their bodies, other participatory winter sports get people moving. Downhill skiing, ice-skating, cross-country skiing, and snowmobiling are the four most popular winter sports, according to a 1990 survey conducted by Mediamark Research of New York City.

Winter Sports Enthusiasts

With 4 percent of adults participating, downhill skiing is America's most popular winter sport, according to Mediamark. Those most likely to be downhill-skiing enthusiasts are single men aged 18 to 34 with a college education. Most downhill ski enthusiasts live in New England and the Pacific region of the country.

Ice-skating attracts 3 percent of the adult population. This sport appeals primarily to women aged 18 to 34 who are single and college graduates. The majority live in the Northeast and Midwest, according to Mediamark. Cross-country skiing is the third most popular winter sport, enjoyed by 2 percent of adults. The most avid cross-country skiers are men and women aged 25 to 44. They are most likely to be single college graduates who live in New England and the Midwest.

The fourth most popular winter sport is snowmobiling, which attracts 1.6 percent of the adult population. Snowmobiling appeals to men aged 18 to 34 who have a high school education or better. They live primarily in the Midwest.

I'd Rather Be Skiing

If you flip through the pages of some ski magazines, you might think all skiers are brawny jocks or blonde coeds. But only about one in eight skiers in Colorado is a student, according to a study prepared by the University of Colorado-Boulder's Business Research Division. Almost half are professionals or managers, and almost half have annual incomes greater than $50,000. Thirty-five percent are aged 25 to 34, and 40 percent are aged 35 and older.

"Some marketers are continuing to advertise to the young, active consumer—showing people flying though the air and wearing the wildest clothes. But smart marketers are using people with gray hair and families in their ads, as well as young people," says Jerry Jones, an international resort consultant who lives in Vail.

Jones says that the ski industry now uses sophisticated marketing techniques and has very good businesspeople, but many resort owners did not recognize their problems until it was too late. In the 1960s, the U.S. had 1,400 ski areas. Today, there are fewer than 600, according to Jones. "The baby-boom bulge went right through the ski industry," he says.

Some larger ski areas benefited when nearby competing centers closed, but many potential customers lost access to the sport. Thirty million Americans are now

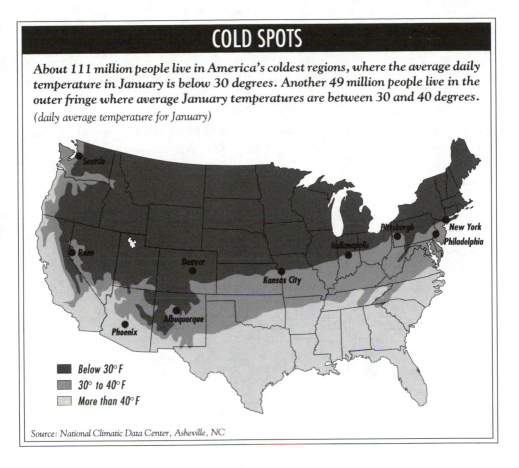

COLD SPOTS

About 111 million people live in America's coldest regions, where the average daily temperature in January is below 30 degrees. Another 49 million people live in the outer fringe where average January temperatures are between 30 and 40 degrees.

(daily average temperature for January)

Seattle

Pittsburgh   New York
Indianapolis   Philadelphia

Reno

Denver

Kansas City

Albuquerque

Phoenix

- ■ Below 30° F
- ▒ 30° to 40° F
- ░ More than 40° F

Source: National Climatic Data Center, Asheville, NC

healthy enough and in the right age range to ski—but only 12 million participate, says Jones.

"We're into mega-resorts," says Jones. "What we've lost is the farm team." By this, he is referring to the smaller local ski areas, where people can learn to ski in a casual, friendly, low-pressure atmosphere. Some resorts that are marketing nationally should be marketing regionally. Skiing must become more accessible to the public through innovative marketing and specialization, he says.

Smaller family-oriented local ski resorts suffer greatly in times of economic difficulty. They are often unable to buy the most sophisticated equipment, such as high-tech ski lifts. People who are used to skiing in mega-resorts come to expect such facilities.

Jones suggests several potentially profitable consumer segments, such as ski resorts with religious themes. One such resort already exists in Colorado. At the end of the day, it serves hot chocolate instead of beer and substitutes church services for parties. Ski resorts that target older adults should consider their clients' dietary needs and perhaps change their image to that of a healthful spa. Mountains at these resorts should be highly groomed, with more intermediate slopes. Ski academies should teach beginners how to ski, what to wear on the slopes, and how to rent or buy equipment. Minorities must also be invited into the sport, says Jones. Few brochures depict blacks or Hispanics sitting around the fireplace at the ski lodge.

Denver Beats Zurich

"Traditional marketing has a lot of problems," says Jones. "But the market is much bigger than we thought—it's a global market." The U.S. is now challenging Europe as a world leader in the ski industry. Europe had a few bad snow years, and the World Alpine Ski Championship was held in Vail in 1989. After that, the number of European visitors to Colorado increased 47 percent.

Jones points out that a flight from London to Zurich costs about the same as a flight from London to Denver. Ski packages in the U.S. are also cheaper than those in the Alps: "You can rent a condominium in Colorado for less than you can rent a hotel room in Switzerland," he says. Jones also points out that ski conditions are superior here and that European visitors get better service than they do on the Continent. "European ski resorts have gotten complacent," he says.

The U.S. can draw skiers from all parts of the world, according to Jones. "There are half as many skiers in Canada as there are in the U.S. There are good ski areas in Canada, but we can offer better packages." And while the number of skiers coming here from Japan is currently small, Jones believes those numbers will become significant.

During the 1980s, the annual number of lift tickets issued in Colorado increased from fewer than 6 million to nearly 10 million. But poor snow conditions caused a 3 percent drop in tickets during the 1989-90 season. Thirteen of Colorado's 27 ski areas reported increased activity that year, while 4 experienced declines of more than 40 percent. "The American ski industry is in a state of flux," Jones says, "but its future potential is limitless."

NEW YEAR'S RESOLUTIONS
■ ■ ■ ■ ■ ■ ■ ■ ■ ■ ■ ■ ■ ■ ■ ■ ■

January is a great time to turn over a new leaf. Bookstores that sell self-help books and audio tapes, organizations that help people quit smoking, and health clubs all see a flurry of activity after the New Year's party favors have been put away. The month is also a good time to take stock of nutritional habits that may have slipped over the holidays. Appropriately, January is National Soup Month, National Oatmeal Month, and National Prune Breakfast Month. For those who mourn the passing of the holiday season, take heart. Every month in the coming year is full of holiday opportunities. People who didn't get enough of noisemakers and parades during the New Year's celebration don't have long to wait for another chance. The Chinese New Year begins on the first full moon between January 21 and February 19.

FEBRUARY WEATHER
■ ■ ■ ■ ■ ■ ■ ■ ■ ■ ■ ■ ■ ■

In February, winter seems like it will never end. Extreme low temperatures include an average of 4 degrees in Bismarck and an average of 9 degrees in Minneapolis. Southern cities like New Orleans and Jacksonville see temperatures in the 40s.

	TEMPERATURE		PRECIPITATION	
	low	*high*	*inches*	*days*
Albuquerque, NM	25.9°F	52.9°F	0.40	4
Atlanta, GA	34.5	55.3	4.43	10
Bismarck, ND	3.7	25.2	0.45	7
Boise, ID	27.9	44.3	1.07	10
Boston, MA	23.7	37.7	3.70	10
Buffalo, NY	17.5	31.4	2.40	17
Burlington, VT	8.8	27.3	1.73	11
Charlotte, NC	32.1	53.6	3.81	10
Chicago, IL	18.1	33.9	1.31	10
Cleveland, OH	19.9	34.8	2.20	14
Dallas, TX	37.8	59.1	1.93	7
Denver, CO	20.2	46.9	0.69	6
Detroit, MI	18.0	33.5	1.69	11
Great Falls, MT	16.8	36.5	0.75	8
Honolulu, HI	65.3	80.4	2.72	9
Houston, TX	43.2	65.7	3.25	8
Indianapolis, IN	21.1	38.5	2.46	10
Jaksonville, FL	43.3	66.8	3.48	8
Juneau, AK	21.9	33.7	3.74	17
Los Angeles, CA	48.6	65.5	2.49	6
Memphis. TN	34.1	53.0	4.33	10
Miami, FL	59.7	75.8	2.05	6
Milwaukee, WI	15.8	30.1	1.33	10
Minneapolis, MN	8.5	26.4	0.85	7
Mobile, AL	43.2	63.9	4.91	10
New Orleans, LA	44.8	64.6	5.23	9
New York, NY	26.6	40.1	3.13	10
Norfolk, VA	32.3	49.9	3.28	10
Oklahoma City, OK	29.4	52.2	1.29	6
Omaha, NE	17.1	37.3	0.91	7
Philadelphia, PA	25.0	41.1	2.81	9
Phoenix, AZ	42.5	69.7	0.59	4
Portland, OR	36.0	50.4	3.93	16
Salt Lake City, UT	24.4	43.7	1.33	9
San Francisco, CA	44.1	59.0	3.23	10
Sault Ste. Marie	5.3	23.1	1.69	15
Seattle, WA	36.8	48.8	4.22	16
St. Louis, MO	24.5	43.1	2.14	8
Washington, DC	29.0	45.9	2.62	9
Wichita, KS	24.1	46.1	0.85	5

Source: U.S. Department of Commerce, Bureau of the Census, Statistical Abstract of the United States 1991. Average daily minimum and maximum temperatures and average monthly precipitation were measured over a standard 30-year period.

FEBRUARY
THE WINTER BLAHS

When all that remains of the holidays is a large balance on your credit-card bills, and almost everyone has the flu or a cold, it must be February. The couch-potato mentality is well entrenched. Americans watch more television in January and February than any other time of year. The right incentive could draw consumers away from their sets, but finding it is the trick.

February is depressing for many Americans. It is the heart of the winter doldrums, and research shows that the blues many people feel in February may be more than just a collection of vague symptoms. For some, they are indicative of a very real malady called Seasonal Affective Disorder—known appropriately by the acronym SAD.

The "blues" aren't the only reason why consumers stay close to home in February. In northern climes, the weather is bad and roads may be hazardous. Influenza and colds force many people to stay in bed. These consumers need medication, food, entertainment, and financial services, but getting out may be a real challenge for them. February could just be "Home Delivery Month."

WINTER ILLS

Millions of Americans suffer from a type of depression called Seasonal Affective Disorder, according to Michael Terman, director of the Light Therapy Unit at the

FEBRUARY'S BEST BUYS

(items most likely to be on sale in February)

- Hosiery
- Housewares
- Major appliances
- Men's clothing
- Toys
- Winter clothing
- Shoes

Source: DOLLAR$ENSE Magazine, *1987*

New York State Psychiatric Institute at Columbia-Presbyterian Medical Center. The further north people live, the more likely they are to have the syndrome. In the southernmost parts of the country, from Florida to southern California, Terman estimates that only about 2 percent of the population experience symptoms characterizing SAD at a clinically severe level. Among those living in the northern latitudes, from New England to Washington state, the share is as high as 10 percent.

Who's Got the Blues?

Victims of Seasonal Affective Disorder may experience social withdrawal, excessive sleepiness, and a weakened sex drive—all characteristics of depression. But SAD victims also tend to overeat and crave carbohydrates. And their symptoms almost always begin to disappear as the days lengthen.

It's not always easy to distinguish SAD from feelings of depression that often occur during the holidays because of long-standing psychological factors. Terman explains that SAD lasts throughout the season, beginning after Thanksgiving and peaking in January and February. The symptoms, he asserts, are pervasive and not tied to social events.

SAD sufferers fall into three groups: those who are truly debilitated by the disease; others, who are bothered but not incapacitated by it; and a third group of people who notice the symptoms but are able to cope with them. For those who wish to escape the blues, psychiatrists prescribe regular doses of bright light at certain times of the day, usually in the early morning. Improvement generally begins in a few days.

Systems for administering controlled doses of light include tabletop units that illuminate a working surface so that people may eat, read, or write in a field of therapeutic light. Also on the market are a visor that contains two small fluorescent lights and a helmet with a fluorescent tube mounted across the front. Portable systems allow people to move about freely so they can take care of children or perform other tasks.

The curative powers of light therapy were not firmly established by researchers until the mid-1980s. Even today, some health-care professionals are not fully aware of the disorder or its cure, and finding help is not always easy.

Some people unable to find the right professional help have taken matters into their own hands. One university professor who suffered from SAD constructed his own light-therapy helmet as an experiment to get him through the winter months. He claimed that wearing the device before his morning lectures gave his spirits a lift and increased his productivity in the classroom. Others might not be so lucky. Using the wrong lighting can easily cause eye damage. But with more people looking for cures to the winter blues, an increase in the availability of light-therapy equipment is inevitable.

Simply turning up the lights in your store or workplace will not cure seasonal depression, and the increased brightness could adversely affect customers and employees who do not suffer from the disorder. So, what can you do to help your customers and employees to cope with the lack-of-sunlight blues? The first step is to recognize that many people simply will not be at their best during the long winter months.

Even people who are not affected by SAD may feel the added pressure of having to cope with so many suffering friends, relatives, and co-workers. Almost everyone is going to need a little coddling and a lot of encouragement to get out of the house. Bright, cheerful promotions and advertisements may provide the necessary motivation for consumers to desert their living room couches and venture out into the world. The right travel incentive could take them even further—to someplace where the sun is shining.

If It's Not One Thing, It's Another

Each flu season is unique, according to the Centers for Disease Control (CDC) in Atlanta. Making projections based on previous years is impossible. But up to 20 percent of the population may be infected with the virus in a typical flu season (October 1 to May 31). The majority of cases occur between January and early March. About 1 percent will require hospitalization, and of those hospitalized, up to 8 percent will die.

While flu tends to be rampant among children, adults are not immune, as figures from the National Center for Health Statistics (NCHS) indicate. In 1989, a bad year for the flu, 62 percent of children under age 5 and 81 percent of those aged 5 to 17 suffered from the disease. About 45 percent of men and 56 percent of women between the ages of 18 and 44 came down with the illness. People aged 45 and older fared a bit better. Just 26 percent of men and 32 percent of women were stricken. By the end of the year, the number of days that Americans spent in bed because of the flu totaled 262 million.

Productivity suffers when employees are down with the flu, and the old adage that plenty of rest is the best cure is borne out by the statistics. In 1989, the flu resulted in 76 work days lost for every 100 employed adults, a higher number than reported for any other malady that year.

Parents make sure that their children see a doctor when they have the flu, but only 31 percent of people between the ages of 25 and 44 saw a doctor themselves in 1989. The share increased to 44 percent of those aged 65 or older, and with good reason. While most flu sufferers are young, those who die from the disease are usually the aged and people with chronic respiratory conditions.

In 1991, the oldest baby boomers turned 45. As they age, their ways of dealing with the flu and other ailments will change. This large segment of the population will visit doctors more often, taking advantage of the availability of flu vaccines to limit their chances of contracting what can be a very serious disease for those in their senior years.

Although it is tempting to associate a cold, snowy, and damp climate with the greatest number of flu cases, the flu can strike anywhere. In 1989, the West had the highest incidence of flu cases (77 percent of the population), while the Northeast had the lowest (33 percent). Fully 58 percent of Midwesterners came down with the flu, but only 39 percent of Southerners did. Even though Westerners suffered the most, only 34 percent of them sought medical attention for the flu. Although the share of Southerners who came down with the flu was relatively low, 44 percent of them went to the doctor.

People sitting in doctors' waiting rooms are a captive audience. *Special Reports*, a multimedia system from Whittle Communications in Knoxville, Tennessee, is now installed in nearly 20,000 waiting rooms for family practitioners, pediatricians, and obstetricians and gynecologists. Participating offices receive three quarterly publications and a 27-inch color television set with a videodisc player. The articles and programs are geared toward family audiences. The system is said to reach 44 million adults, including 26 million mothers.

Self Help

For those who do not see a doctor, and even for many of those who do, symptomatic relief of the flu requires more than soup and sympathy. Over-the-counter medications are purchased annually by almost half of all Americans suffering from colds and flu. Sales of over-the-counter cold and flu remedies amounted to almost $1.75 billion in 1989.

The over-the-counter drug business is growing at a rapid rate, and sales for all segments of the industry are expected to top $12 billion by 1993. There are now some 250 remedies available for the self-treatment of symptoms related to colds and the flu. But pharmaceutical companies time new product introductions to coincide with the winter cold and flu season.

A doctor's recommendation is the most important factor influencing the consumer's decision to purchase over-the-counter drugs, according to the August 1991 issue of *Product Management Today*. When participants in a survey conducted by Ruder Finn, Inc. were asked to evaluate five factors that affect their purchase decisions, 79 percent said a doctor's recommendation was "very important." More than half felt the same about the pharmacist's recommendation, and 29 percent listened to friends and family. Only 8 percent thought what advertisements had to say was "very important."

One of the most rapidly growing segments of the over-the-counter drug market is pediatric medicine. A rise in the birth rate in the late 1980s and early 1990s and development of convenient liquid products have contributed to the success of these products. This segment of the pharmaceutical trade is expected to garner sales of between $75 million and $120 million in 1993, according to the research firm FIND/SVP.

Pediatric over-the-counter cold and flu remedies rely heavily on name recognition. Product-line extensions of adult brands account for almost all of the leading

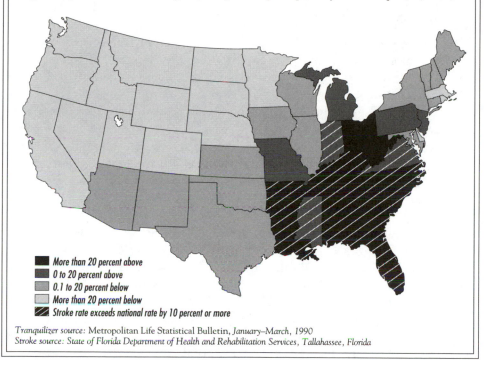

DIFFERENT STROKES

The further south you go, the less likely you are to suffer from Seasonal Affective Disorder. But that doesn't mean southerners are immune to stress, as shown by their stroke mortality rates and use of tranquilizers.

(difference from the national average in per capita new prescriptions of minor tranquilizers, 1989)

- More than 20 percent above
- 0 to 20 percent above
- 0.1 to 20 percent below
- More than 20 percent below
- Stroke rate exceeds national rate by 10 percent or more

Tranquilizer source: Metropolitan Life Statistical Bulletin, *January–March, 1990*
Stroke source: State of Florida Department of Health and Rehabilitation Services, Tallahassee, Florida

child's remedies. Purchases of cold and flu remedies are 13 percent higher in households with children, according to Mediamark statistics. Forty-two percent of householders who purchase more than five cold and flu products during a 30-day period have children between the ages of 6 and 17.

Other groups that rely heavily on over-the-counter flu relief include single parents who cannot afford to miss work and people aged 35 to 44 who generally suffer milder, shorter bouts of the disease. Southerners also purchase a disproportionately large share of over-the-counter products.

Tie-in merchandising—creating a one-stop center for flu relief—is a profitable way to retail cold and flu remedies and to appeal to those feeling under the weather. This includes displaying over-the-counter medications alongside products that offer other creature comforts for the cold sufferer, such as tissues, throat lozenges, magazines and paperback books, canned or packaged soups, teas, and fruit juice.

TELEVISION VIEWING
■ ■ ■ ■ ■ ■ ■ ■ ■ ■ ■ ■ ■

In much of the country, people's moods and the weather are uniformly gray during February. People stay close to home, with a quantity of microwaveable meals, a stack of best-sellers, and the television.

Home Entertainment

"Most people watch television because they don't have anything else to do. When there's nothing else to do, they watch, regardless of what's on," observes George Comstock, a Syracuse University professor of public communications. In February 1990, Americans watched an average of 7 hours and 28 minutes of television a day. In warm sunny July, they had their sets on for only 6 hours and 24 minutes a day, according to the A.C. Nielsen Company.

Americans have a love-hate relationship with television, say George Gallup, Jr. and Frank Newport. They appreciate television's ability to keep them in touch with the world, according to a special Gallup Mirror of America Poll. But many feel guilty about the amount of time they spend in front of their sets.

While there is no evidence that Americans are watching less television than they did 20 years ago, the share saying it is their favorite way to spend an evening is dropping—from almost half in the late 1960s and early 1970s to less than one-quarter in 1990. There has also been a sharp increase in the number of Americans who think they watch too much television—31 percent of adults said they watched too much television in the late 1970s, compared with 42 percent today.

Despite their guilt, 58 percent of Americans say that watching television is a good use of their time. Surprisingly, young adults are the most likely to claim that watching television is a bad use of time. Half of those under age 30 feel this way. Among those aged 55 or older, 70 percent say it's a good use of their time.

Almost half of all Americans say their lives would not be significantly better or worse without television. But over one-third say they would suffer if it was taken away. Thirty-nine percent say they would read more books if they didn't have a television set. Another 16 percent say they would listen to the radio or enjoy music during the time they now spend watching the tube. Spending time with their families, exercising, and other activities were mentioned by less than 5 percent of respondents in the Gallup Poll as alternatives to TV watching.

When asked if they will watch more or less television in the future, 70 percent of Gallup's respondents said they don't plan to change their viewing habits. Only 14 percent said they will be watching less. Even so, only 13 percent of all Americans admit to being hooked on television.

The Sweeps

For television viewers, February is a rich month because it is one of the four "sweeps"

TELEVISION FAMILY AND FRIENDS

During January and February, the household television is turned on almost 7 hours and 30 minutes daily. The average individual spends 4 hours and 30 minutes in front of the tube.

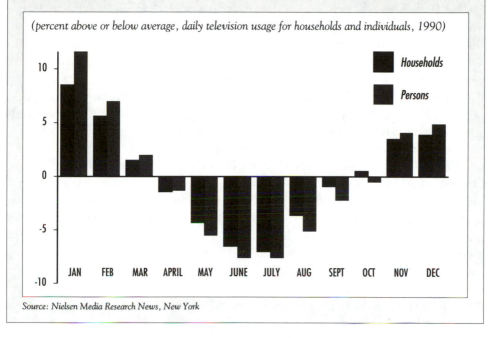

(percent above or below average, daily television usage for households and individuals, 1990)

Source: Nielsen Media Research News, New York

periods on network TV. In February, May, July, and November, Nielsen and Arbitron do a more in-depth rating of television stations on a demographic basis. These four sweeps periods are the only times that ratings look beyond the 25 major markets for which audience statistics are acquired daily. Comprehensive data are collected in all of the more than 200 television markets and serve as the only measure of success for networks on this important local level. The data also become the basis for the prices charged by competing stations within each market. As Comstock puts it in his book, *The Evolution of American Television*, "[The sweeps] are the foundation of the stations' revenues."

The February sweeps begin around January 26 or 27 and run for 28 days. While there is not one special event that can be said to crown this viewing extravaganza, networks help out their local affiliates by showing well-advertised mini-series, first-run movies, and special episodes of popular shows, says Larry Hyams of ABC Television. TV characters are more apt to get married, have children, or resolve major life crises during the sweeps.

With an increased audience in February and a wider variety of top-quality television entertainment to keep the public interested, this is a good month for sponsors to boost their television advertising. Still, Americans have never felt compelled to watch commercials. A 1953 study concluded that increased water consumption during commercials indicated trips to the kitchen and bathroom. Today, advertisers fear that more options have made audiences even less attentive.

For the most part, Americans endure commercials, according to the 1990 Gallup Poll. About 40 percent say they dislike or even hate them. An equal share say they have no strong feelings toward commercials either way. Only 16 percent say they enjoy watching commercials. Still, only 14 percent of Americans say they would be willing to pay for commercial-free broadcasting. But remote controls have given viewers a weapon with which to annihilate ads.

"Remote controls have made it more convenient for the viewer to sample programming," says Comstock. But, he adds, scanning the dial with a remote only slightly reduces the amount of advertising a viewer sees, because commercials are generally aired at the same time.

VCRs "bring people to television who might not otherwise watch," says Comstock. Almost two-thirds of American households with televisions also have video cassette recorders, according to Nielsen. Most recordings are made during prime time and daytime, and over half of these recordings are made when the TV set is turned off. Viewers can then tune in at their convenience to watch the programs they would otherwise have missed. Nielsen points out that 65 percent of the recordings are network programs.

Households that watch the greatest number of hours of television per week are those with three or more people (59 hours and 45 minutes), those with pay cable service (59 hours and 38 minutes), and those with children (58 hours and 43 minutes). On average, women watch more television than men, younger children more than older children, and older adults more than younger adults. Prime-time television, from 8 to 11 pm, attracts the largest audiences.

Women watch more prime time than men or children. The time period they watch the most runs from 8:30 to 9:00 p.m. This half hour is also most popular among all viewers, followed by the 9:00 to 9:30 period. Women also account for the greatest viewer audience during the news hour from 6:00 to 7:00 p.m. By far the favorite night of the week to watch TV is Sunday, followed (in order) by Monday, Tuesday, Thursday, Wednesday, Saturday, and Friday, according to Nielsen.

The television genre that attracts the largest prime-time audience is the situation comedy, followed by feature films and suspense/mystery drama, says Nielsen. While men prefer suspense/mystery dramas, women's first choice for evening viewing is feature films. Sports programming is very popular with male viewers. Of the top 15 regularly scheduled network programs viewed by men in 1989, 5 were sports-related. Teens and children rank situation comedies far above any other program type.

While all the statistics for television viewing look positive, some experts believe that network television is in trouble. "Not because they don't have the audience, but because they don't have the advertisers," says Don E. Schultz, a professor of advertising at Northwestern University. Advertising dollars are "draining into local markets. Even car sales are generated at the local level."

However, the number of families with TV sets is increasing every year. As of 1989, there were 92 million TV households in the U.S., and the average household received 30 stations. Network television still has leverage with the consumer, according to Alec Gerster, vice president of media for Grey Advertising in New York City: "Almost any new product introduction must rely on television to build product awareness. Take, for instance, the movie business. You don't get a $200 million box-office weekend by direct mail."

Kids and TV

Even though America's obsession with television has gotten a lot of bad press, some educators admit it has its place. Ninety-six percent of teachers and 90 percent of school media specialists view the television screen as an important learning tool, according to a 1991 survey released by the New York-based Arts & Entertainment Network. Fifty-six percent of teachers choose PBS as the best source for educational television, followed by the cable channels Arts & Entertainment Network (16 percent) and the Discovery Channel (15 percent).

While 56 percent of teachers agree that educational television is most effective for teaching current events, only 20 percent feel that it is an effective tool for math and science education. And although many teachers would like to use educational television in the classroom, more than 50 percent find it difficult to obtain the video tapes, and 45 percent also have trouble finding a VCR or monitor. Relying on cable TV is also a problem—currently 51 percent of schools are not wired for cable, and only 11 percent plan on having cable access within the next few years.

Since 1989, Whittle Communications has been producing Channel One, a daily news show for the classroom. Participating schools receive two VCRs, classroom televisions, wiring, and a satellite receiver. Channel One's shows are beamed to the classrooms via satellite. While there is no charge to the school, the school must guarantee that a certain number of shows are viewed by students. Two minutes of advertising included in the 12-minute broadcast pay for the system.

Commercials in the classroom have been hotly debated since Whittle's first pilot program, but proponents contend that students are sophisticated consumers and very knowledgeable about advertising. They see advertising on stadium walls, in student newspapers, on wall calendars, and even in their yearbooks. Whittle regrets that its opponents focus on the two minutes of commercials instead of the ten minutes of news. One independent study found that Whittle's viewers are 20 percent more knowledgeable about current events in general than those who are not exposed to this programming.

Channel One has been so successful that Whittle claims the controversy has "all but gone away." In the first five months of the pilot program, Whittle signed up almost 3,000 schools in 34 states. Today, more than 10,000 schools are participating, and the programming is viewed by more than 6 million students. By the fall of 1993, Whittle expects to reach 40 percent of America's teenagers.

HOME ACTIVITIES

Reading is not a lost art. Even though Americans are reading less now than they did in the 1970s, a Gallup poll indicates that the signs are encouraging for a reversal in this trend. About 3 percent of adults admit they'll be reading less in the future, but fully 45 percent say they'll be reading more. Fifty-five percent of young adults aged 18 to 29 plan to read more, compared with 51 percent of those aged 30 to 49 and 30 percent of those aged 50 and older. Young adults are also the most likely to say they'll be watching less television in the future, according to Gallup.

The Book Report

On any given day, 71 percent of adults read a newspaper and 36 percent read a magazine. Thirty-eight percent read a book for school or work, and 33 percent read a book for pleasure. Young adults are just as likely to be reading a book for pleasure as older adults, says Gallup, and they are much more likely to be reading a book for work or school. Men are just as likely to have read a book during the past week as women, but women are more prolific readers. Women say they read 18 books during the year, compared with only 12 for men. The share of all adults actively reading books today is more than double the share that read books throughout the 1950s, according to Gallup.

Among those who read books from cover to cover, the largest share, 55 percent, say the last book they read was a novel. Seven percent read a biography, and 5 percent read a how-to book. Another 10 percent read some other kind of nonfiction book, 5 percent read a textbook, and 2 percent read the Bible. Thirty-nine percent of Americans say they have a favorite author.

Fully 84 percent of Americans have bookcases or bookshelves in their homes, compared with only 58 percent in 1953. The average American home contains 154 books. Only 16 percent have fewer than 20 books. Among college graduates, the average is 249. More than half of Americans say that television is more enjoyable than reading, but about 60 percent say reading is more rewarding and a better way to learn.

Fully 89 percent of today's parents say they read to their children. This is probably the most encouraging sign of all for the publishing industry. When parents read to their small children, they learn to read earlier and they have less difficulty reading when they grow up.

Consumer expenditures on books are expected to rise from $19 billion in 1990 to $28 billion in 1995, according to *Book Industry Trends 1991*, a publication of the

Book Industry Study Group, Inc. in New York City. With an annual growth rate of about 3 percent, publishers' book sales will reach 2.5 billion in 1995. The greatest growth will be in juvenile books, increasing more than 6 percent annually.

Bringing It All Home

Almost any type of product or service can be delivered to the door of home-bound consumers. The pizza delivery business is probably the most well-known, but entrepreneurs have also made a profit delivering videos and popcorn, singing messages and balloons, and oxygen and other medical supplies. Today, 900 numbers pipe astrological consultations and hearing exams into the home.

Now that many homes are equipped with personal computers, these households present an opportunity for businesses to make electronic deliveries of information and services. But just because a business is capable of making a delivery doesn't mean that consumers will want to use its service. During the 1980s, 75 banks offered home banking. But the consumer was just not ready for this service, according to Leonard Berry, director of the Center for Retailing Studies at Texas A&M University, nearly half of the banks that offered this service discontinued it by the end of the decade.

Perhaps it's time to try again. In 1991, Prodigy Services, a computer information service with 1 million customers, began testing a new home-banking service, BillPay USA. Unlike previous services, BillPay does not require customers to bank with any specific company, according to Brian Ek, Prodigy's communications manager: "Many customers don't want to change banks just to get computer banking. Our service allows them to stay with the bank they currently use."

Prodigy's customers are especially suited to banking by computer, according to Ek. "We have a high share of two-career couples, people who want to avoid making extra trips," he says. A large share of Prodigy's customers (35 percent) work for small businesses out of their homes or are small-business owners themselves. "Many of our customers are already using financial services—such as our discount brokerage service—through our network. So we are offering this service to a market that we already have," says Ek.

But just a few months before Prodigy began to offer this new financial service, it had to discontinue its home-delivery grocery service. Prodigy had been trying to provide this service since 1988. Research indicated that it was an important market, but research and reality just didn't match up. "There was only a very small group that wanted this service, and we were never able to build it up. It was very expensive to operate," says Ek.

Computer service companies are not the only ones interested in catching consumers at home. Interactive television promises to deliver many of the same services currently offered by computer services, like home banking, home shopping, and making reservations for airlines, hotels, cars, and entertainment events. With the aid of a special remote control, television viewers will be able to respond to televised polls, participate in educational programs and game shows, and order and pay for pay-per-view programming. The technology exists. A cooperative effort by manufacturers, broadcasters, and advertisers is all that is needed to make this new service a reality for millions of Americans.

The Electronic Cottage

About 25 million Americans work at least part-time at home. These workers have above-average incomes and are more likely than other Americans to be college graduates, according to the 1988 National Work-At-Home Survey by LINK Resources of New York City. They are also more likely than others to have children in their households.

Fifty-five percent of home workers hold professional or managerial jobs, according to a Bureau of Labor Statistics survey of people whose primary work was done at home. About 29 percent are in technical, sales, or administrative support jobs. Fewer than 10 percent are in production, craft, and repair work. Only 3 percent are operators, fabricators, or laborers. The most commonly given reason for working at home is that people feel they can get more work done, reports LINK Resources. Convenience, time with the family, and starting a new business are also very important reasons why people work at home. Only one in five workers works at home because he or she doesn't have a choice.

The trend toward working at home is driving householders to purchase more home office equipment. In 1990, only about 5 percent of home offices had fax machines, according to Technology Futures of Austin, Texas. But Technology Futures expects that a majority will have fax machines by 1995, and practically all will have them by the end of the decade.

As the network of fax machines in home offices and in the workplace grows, many people will be tempted to have them at home for purely personal use. In 1995, Technology Futures anticipates that the price of fax machines will drop to a point where personal transmissions will become economical. It estimates that someone buying a low-end fax ($200) could send 20 letters for as little as 30 cents each, excluding local and long-distance telephone charges.

The availability of home office equipment is making it possible for more people to work at home. But as these items—computers, fax machines, and home copiers—become more commonplace many people will see them as necessities for everyday life.

Home Is Where the Heart Is

Chasing the blues away is more easily accomplished when it's carried out in comfort. But when homebound television viewers look up from their sets, they may see a living room badly in need of furniture.

While the seasonally adjusted retail sales figures for February are generally the lowest of the year, in 1990, furniture, home furnishing, and equipment store sales were second only to May. General merchandise stores also did a booming business,

THE BLUES, NEW ORLEANS STYLE

WHILE OTHER winter-worn Americans cry the blues, the people of New Orleans celebrate them. Mardi Gras, French for Fat Tuesday, celebrates the last day of feasting before the start of the Christian fasting season of Lent. Because the holiday is associated with the astronomically determined Easter season, it can take place as early as February 3rd or as late as March 9th.

The most famous Mardi Gras celebration in the U.S. is held in New Orleans, but other Louisiana cities, as well as places in Alabama, Florida, Mississippi, South Carolina, Tennessee, and Texas, mark the day with parades and other festivities. In both Louisiana and Alabama, Fat Tuesday is an official holiday, and state offices close.

Some say the Mardi Gras parade was started in 1830 by a group of drunken revelers in Mobile, Alabama. They grabbed rakes, cowbells, and other impromptu noise-making equipment from a general store and marched to the mayor's house on New Year's morning. The story goes on to say that this group, known as the Cowbellion de Rakin Society, moved to New Orleans and began the first Mardi Gras parade there in 1856.

Another tradition maintains that a men's literary society first decided to stage a torch-lit procession from its headquarters to the Mardi Gras ball site in the French Quarter of New Orleans. The celebration caught on. After the Civil War, parades began including floats. The floats served both as a mode of transportation for celebrants and as a way to depict the carnival's theme. By the 1880s, float-riders had begun the custom of tossing strings of beads and other baubles to onlookers along the parade route, a tradition that continues today.

The clubs that organize the parade and its fantastic and expensive floats and costumes—known as krewes—once comprised only native-born residents of New Orleans. But in 1968, the Krewe of Bacchus opened its membership to outsiders. The Krewe of Endymion soon followed suit, and these two krewes now compete for celebrities to serve as their festival kings. In 1990, 103 krewes were involved in Mardi Gras celebrations throughout the city. Costumes for krewe kings averaged more than $4,000 each, and the 24,600 float riders each tossed an estimated $420 worth of trinkets to the crowd, according to Dr. James J. McLain of the University of New Orleans, Division of Business and Economic Research.

The frenzied partying, music, and feasting over the last five days of the Mardi Gras celebration in New Orleans culminate with fabulous balls and spectacular parades on Fat Tuesday itself. In 1990, the festivities generated more than $480 million in spending in the greater New Orleans area, according to McLain. The carnival also brought in over $27 million in taxes to local government agencies in Orleans Parish. Revenues were nearly 40 percent higher than in the previous year—despite the approaching recession.

Attendance at the festival has grown steadily, and 1990 was a record-breaking year, with approximately 2.4 million people participating in the celebrations. Most of Mardi Gras's recent growth is attributed to the thousands of hotel rooms added for New Orleans's 1984 World's Fair. "In the mid-1960s, there were 10,000 to 11,000 hotel rooms in the city," says tour operator Andrea Thornton. "Now there are about 19,000 hotel rooms just in the downtown area. The hotels have started to sell themselves."

People from all over North America and from overseas flock to New Orleans for the carnival. In 1990, visitors who stayed in hotels during the five-day height of Mardi Gras season accounted for some $118 million in spending, according to McLain. Each person spent an average of $350 daily.

Mardi Gras spending is by no means restricted only to tourists. Official krewe spending—for dues, parades, balls, dinner dances, and parties—topped $11 million in 1990. Individual spending for dinner-dances and balls, including parking, admission, ball gowns, tuxedos, hairdressing bills, transportation, and champagne and liquor, accounted for $23 million in spending in 1990.

One of the most uninhibited holidays in the U.S., Mardi Gras is known for drunken revelers who consume incredible amounts of alcohol. Unfortunately, violence has also become an element of the festivities. In 1988, three people were killed. In general, however, people just want to have a good time, according to Lieutenant Yvonne Bechet of the New Orleans Police. Arrests have dropped from almost 2,100 during the 12-day celebration in 1986 to only 1,600 in 1988. At the same time, other communities that celebrate Mardi Gras have been promoting their celebrations as more "family-oriented" in order to attract those who may be nervous about going to New Orleans.

as Presidents' Day sales sent many bargain hunters rushing to the stores to take advantage of the savings.

Baby boomers are boosting sales of furniture, home electronics, and appliances as they move into the age group that makes the greatest furniture purchases. Baby boomers are ready to feather their nests, and they plan to do so in a big way. Economic recession led to lower sales in the furniture and home-appliance markets in 1991. But as the economy picks up and new housing starts follow suit, the furniture market is expected to grow.

"Like any group of middle-aged people, baby boomers are becoming increasingly home-oriented. But this generation will define a comfortable home in terms of its access to technology. Home entertainment equipment should grow at twice the rate of overall consumer spending in the 1990s," says Geoffrey Greene, senior economist for DRI/McGraw-Hill in Washington, D.C. "Yet spending on furniture, floor coverings, and other durable accessories will show almost no real growth. Middle-aged baby boomers are likely to express their sophisticated and eclectic tastes by choosing a few pieces of expensive furniture, rather than buying coordinated ensembles."

Understanding the baby-boom furniture market may be challenging for retailers. Some boomers may pursue the "biggest and best" method of home decorating, choosing "ultrapremium" beds that can retail for as much as $3,000, while others sleep on futons and spend their money on electronics equipment. As Valentine's Day approaches, retailers should emphasize the romantic quality of both their bedding and stereo departments.

VALENTINES
■ ■ ■ ■ ■ ■ ■ ■

Valentine's Day is one of the most widely celebrated unofficial holidays of the year. Its bright colors and cheerful themes are in sharp contrast to February's general mood of gloom and despair. Perhaps that's why the holiday is so profitable for many retailers.

Looking For Love
Romance, affection, companionship, and love are the key elements of Valentine's Day. Gestures of love, both traditional and unconventional, abound, from card giving to romantic weekend trips. The market for Valentine's Day runs the gamut from school-aged children to retired couples, and the potential for retailing ideas is as extensive as the market itself.

Most people think that women are more romantic than men, according to a 1990 survey conducted by the Roper Organization. But more than half of men say they have enjoyed a very romantic day or evening within the past month, while only 39 percent of women can make this statement. Fully 20 percent of women say that they have not had a romantic day or evening in a year or more, while only 12 percent of men feel this deprived of romance.

For the most part, men and women agree on what constitutes romance. The majority of both men and women say going somewhere special for the weekend is the most romantic thing two people can do. Over two-thirds of dual-earner married couples are enthusiastic about weekend getaways. Romantic jaunts are also especially appealing to college graduates, upper-income householders, and adults aged 30 to 44.

Red, Red Roses

When lovers can't go on a romantic Caribbean cruise, long-stemmed roses are the next best thing, according to a majority of respondents in the Roper survey. But sending or receiving any type of flower is a big winner.

Floral sales peak during the two days before Valentine's Day as well as on the holiday itself. Marbella Crabb, director of communications for the Society of American Florists, says that while Valentine's Day ranks as the holiday with the third-largest volume of floral sales (after Christmas and Mother's Day), it is the busiest 24-hour period in the floral retailer's year. While floral retailers and wholesalers agree that long-stemmed red roses are still the most popular flowers, they point out that almost anything that is red or pink will sell well.

An American Floral Marketing Council consumer survey notes that women choosing roses for themselves prefer pastel shades of pink or lavender, but when men buy flowers for women, they most frequently select red roses. Of the 75 million roses sold on Valentine's Day in 1991, 80 percent were red.

Men are more intimidated than women by a floral department, according to many floral retailers. They are likely to choose roses or carnations because they are easily recognizable. Prewrapped decorated bouquets are also popular with men, since these products make it easy for the nervous customer to select and purchase a gift quickly. But the experts say that men can easily be convinced to purchase more exotic plants and flowers.

While women are more familiar with different varieties of flowers, they often need help in selecting flowers for men. Trying to find something "masculine" and romantic at the same time may pose a challenge. Suzanne Harris, a floral specialist with Simon David stores in Dallas, suggests cactus or dish gardens, large foliage plants, or arrangements of tropical flowers. Bouquets of daisies or wildflowers are the most popular floral offerings women give to men, according to Marbella Crabb.

Kjell Hollen, director of marketing for the Florida-based Sunpetals, Inc., says that flowers are rapidly moving away from the "for-women-only" image they had in the past, and that more men are receiving flowers as gifts—and enjoying them. Hollen points out that people in their late teens and early 20s especially like flowers as gifts for men. This point is carefully reinforced by floral marketers in print ads aimed at that market.

One profitable approach to floral marketing at Valentine's Day involves cross merchandising—selling floral products alongside stuffed animals, wine, candy, cards, and perfume. Other ideas include retailing flowers along with gourmet foods and gift baskets, or making floral bouquets available in nonfloral departments, such as lingerie, jewelry, paper goods, or accessories.

In 1990, Hallmark Cards began test marketing the sale of fresh flowers in some of its retail stores to target walk-in customers who want flowers and cards for specific occasions. With premade floral arrangements and bouquets ranging in price from $4.50 to $35, Hallmark's cross-merchandising scheme makes it easy for last-minute romantics to find a perfect Valentine's Day gift.

Sales for Valentine's Day averaged $6,200 in supermarket floral departments in 1989, according to a Produce Marketing Association/Food Marketing Institute survey. The 40,000 retail floral outlets in the U.S. also do a booming business on Valentine's Day, as do the wire services and even street vendors.

The Candlelight Dinner

Almost half of the respondents in the Roper survey agree that going out for a candlelight dinner is very romantic. Women are especially likely to feel this way, probably seeing it as a change from the usual cooking routine. They also feel that having a candlelight dinner at home is less romantic, perhaps because they fear they will have to prepare it—or clean up after it. When asked to rate the romantic potential of having breakfast served in bed, women respond more favorably than men.

Valentine's Day is the third most popular holiday for eating out (after Mother's Day and Father's Day), according to the National Restaurant Association in Washington D.C. Adults under age 25 are the most likely to dine out on Valentine's Day (29 percent), followed by those aged 25 to 34 (27 percent) and those aged 35 to 49 (23 percent). Only 17 percent of those aged 50 to 64 and 12 percent of those aged 65 and older said that they celebrate the holiday by dining out.

Tokens of Affection

About 31 percent of women say jewelry is romantic, but only 26 percent of men agree. Affluent adults are the most likely to think jewelry is romantic, but enthusiasm declines among those with lower incomes, and the popularity of jewelry drops after people pass age 60.

Chocolate and other sweets have fallen victim to Americans' obsession with healthy eating. Only 16 percent of respondents questioned by Roper conceded that candy is romantic. Even so, chocolate roses as a Valentine's treat have become increasingly popular—especially among the college crowd—and heart-shaped boxes of candy still appear on retailers' shelves every season. Bonnie Glass of the Hershey Chocolate Company notes that sales of Valentine's Day confections increased in 1990, and buyers of promotional items for the holiday come from all age groups. Candy scores highest among low-income lovers, according to the Roper survey.

An equal share of both men and women (16 percent) feel lingerie is romantic, according to the Roper survey. But young people are more likely than older adults to think sexy undies are romantic. Twenty-three percent of those under age 30 think lingerie is romantic, compared with only 19 percent of those aged 30 to 44, 13 percent of those aged 45 to 59, and 7 percent of those aged 60 and older. Only 8 percent of adults think gifts of clothing (other than lingerie) are romantic.

Messages of Love

Sending or receiving a love letter is considered very romantic by 31 percent of those questioned in the Roper survey. People under age 30 are the most likely to be hoping for a love letter this holiday, but sending Valentine's Day cards is not a practice limited to the younger generation. One billion Valentine's Day cards were exchanged in the United States in 1991, according to Hallmark cards, a figure topped only by cards sent at Christmas (2.3 billion).

The subject matter of Valentine's Day cards and the audiences at which they are aimed have changed over the years. Still popular, of course, are the cards (both romantic and humorous) for spouses, sweethearts, parents, and children. But today's cards also reflect changes in the American family ("Happy Valentine's Day to my father and his wife"), and cards illustrating blacks, Hispanics, and other ethnic and cultural groups are becoming increasingly common.

The messages on Valentine's Day cards reflect changes in our society. While poems to romantic love still predominate, sexually suggestive messages, sarcastic one-liners, and silly puns are also common. Cards for homosexual couples and same-gender friends who are not romantically involved are also becoming more popular. One new segment includes cards from unattached women to other unattached women, commiserating about the scarcity of men with whom to share Valentine's Day.

"The important relationships in the lives of Americans are not necessarily romantic. Since many people are no longer part of extended families, we reach out to friends for support and companionship and nurture these relationships with such gestures as the sending of Valentine's Day cards," says Renee Hershey of Hallmark.

A large segment of the gift- and card-giving population prefers to remain anonymous on Valentine's Day. Cards "from your secret admirer" have always sold well. The desire to mix romance and mystery may be irresistible to people who either find it difficult to express their feelings or prefer the aura of secrecy.

Who are today's romantics? Who is taking advantage of the plethora of cards and flowers available for Valentine's Day giving? Almost everyone. Sixty-six percent of women and 58 percent of men say they tend to be romantic, according to the Roper survey. Sadly, the numbers decrease as people age—74 percent of respondents between 18 and 29 consider themselves romantic, compared with only 44 percent of those aged 60 and older.

Valentine's Day is an occasion to share romantic feelings with that "special somebody." At present, almost three-quarters of Americans have a romantic involvement with another person, according to Roper. A scant 10 percent feel that this special person is not really romantic at all, while 26 percent say their partners are very romantic.

NOT SO BAD, AFTER ALL

Despite the gloomy weather, February has a number of bright spots. It marks Black History Month, Presidents' Day, and American Heart Month. In February, even Groundhog Day becomes a media event. But for the nation's retailers, the month's big day is Valentine's Day.

Winter-weary consumers are looking for love in candy boxes and floral arrangements, but they might just find it in the furniture store, the stereo shop, or anywhere it's available. The search for love could take them a long way from home—to someplace where the weather is warmer.

Although February is not known for its vacation opportunities, several of the month's holidays could inspire homebound consumers to get off their couches and travel. They include Mardi Gras festivities in Louisiana, Presidents' Day weekend ski getaways to Colorado or New England, and romantic Valentine's Day interludes at country inns or Caribbean resorts.

Since inertia tends to slow almost everyone down this time of year, an extra effort is needed to get consumers moving. Because many people think the best thing about February is that it has just 28 days, some understandably dread leap year. But when the right promotion finds the right audience, Sadie Hawkins' Day can turn into another winter opportunity.

P A R T 4

SPRINGING

INTO ACTION

Consumers are anxious
to take advantage of
warm weather activities
from gardening to cycling
and jogging. They'll need
equipment and clothing.
And they don't want to
waste a precious moment.

MARCH WEATHER
■ ■ ■ ■ ■ ■ ■ ■ ■ ■ ■ ■

March temperatures are crazy. Much of the south is experiencing highs in the low 70s, but the highs in many northern cities are not much above freezing.

	TEMPERATURE		PRECIPITATION	
	low	*high*	*inches*	*days*
Albuquerque, NM	31.7°F	60.7°F	0.52	5
Atlanta, GA	41.7	63.2	5.91	11
Bismarck, ND	15.6	36.4	0.70	8
Boise, ID	30.9	51.8	1.03	10
Boston, MA	31.8	45.0	4.13	12
Buffalo, NY	25.6	40.4	2.97	16
Burlington, VT	20.8	37.7	2.20	13
Charlotte, NC	39.1	61.6	4.83	11
Chicago, IL	27.6	44.3	2.59	12
Cleveland, OH	28.4	44.8	2.99	15
Dallas, TX	44.9	67.2	2.42	7
Denver, CO	24.7	51.2	1.21	9
Detroit, MI	26.5	43.4	2.54	13
Great Falls, MT	21.1	41.7	0.93	9
Honolulu, HI	67.3	81.4	3.48	9
Houston, TX	49.8	72.1	2.68	9
Indianapolis, IN	30.7	49.3	3.61	13
Jacksonville, FL	49.3	73.3	3.72	8
Juneau, AK	25.0	37.4	3.34	18
Los Angeles, CA	49.7	65.1	1.76	6
Memphis, TN	41.9	61.4	5.44	11
Miami, FL	64.1	79.3	1.89	6
Milwaukee, WI	24.9	39.2	2.58	12
Minneapolis, MN	20.8	37.5	1.71	10
Mobile, AL	49.8	70.3	6.48	11
New Orleans, LA	51.6	71.2	4.73	9
New York, NY	34.1	48.6	4.22	11
Norfolk, VA	39.4	57.5	3.86	11
Oklahoma City, OK	37.1	61.0	2.07	7
Omaha, NE	26.9	47.7	1.91	9
Philadelphia, PA	33.1	50.5	3.86	11
Phoenix, AZ	46.7	74.5	0.81	3
Portland, OR	37.4	54.5	3.61	17
Salt Lake City, UT	29.9	51.5	1.72	10
San Francisco, CA	44.9	60.6	2.64	10
Sault Ste. Marie, MI	15.4	32.3	2.03	13
Seattle, WA	37.2	51.1	3.59	17
St. Louis, MO	33.0	53.4	3.28	11
Washington, DC	36.6	55.0	3.46	11
Wichita, KS	32.4	55.8	2.01	8

Source: U.S. Department of Commerce, Bureau of the Census, Statistical Abstract of the United States 1991. Average daily minimum and maximum temperatures and average monthly precipitation were measured over a standard 30-year period.

MARCH
WEATHER PERMITTING

If the groundhog saw his shadow in February, then spring is on the way. But if the March breezes are still blowing hard and snow is in the forecast, like the groundhog, consumers will retreat into their dens to watch television for another six weeks. The weather will eventually turn, but consumers are particularly anxious for spring to arrive. The whole family wants new spring outfits for Easter Sunday church services or the Passover seder whether or not the weather cooperates.

March is the month for the Irish and the Irish-at-heart to celebrate St. Patrick's Day and for college kids to enjoy spring break. It is a month of anticipation about what lies ahead. Yet, as spring blossoms unfold, the allergy season begins for many Americans.

THE WEATHER AND CONSUMERS

When sales are slow, many retailers blame the weather. If they look out their windows on a rainy day, they claim bad weather kept the shoppers away. Likewise, if the day is clear and beautiful, they say it was too nice for people to want to spend their time indoors shopping. It's true that the weather can keep customers away, but it's also true that it can send them rushing to the stores for picnic supplies, bathing suits, umbrellas, and fertilizer. When retailers are ready with the right products for the right kind of weather, they won't be left out in the cold.

MARCH'S BEST BUYS
(items most likely to be on sale in March)

- ■ China
- ● Glassware
- ■ Garden supplies
- ● Infants' clothing
- ■ Typewriters
- ● Ski equipment

Source: DOLLAR$ENSE Magazine, 1987

March Winds

In March, the weather ranges from hot and sunny to cold, blustery, and snowy. While New England can see average temperatures of 38 degrees in March with snow or freezing rain, it can be 61 degrees in the Southwest with no precipitation at all. March weather is so fickle that it can bring a little bit of everything to any one particular region—the Midwest, for example, can experience sub-zero temperatures, snow, sleet, rain, and thawing all within the 31 days of March.

Late winter and spring weather can be characterized as violent—the old adage about March coming in like a lion is true. Hail, thunderstorms, lightning, blizzards, and tornadoes—any of these tumultuous weather patterns can occur as winter gives way to spring.

Nationwide, April, May, and June account for the most tornadoes, according to Leo Grenier of the National Severe Storm Forecasting Center (NSSFC) in Kansas City, Missouri. The peak month is May, but storms come earlier the further south you go. In Texas and Alabama, for example, tornadoes are at their peak in March.

In 1990, more than 1,132 storms were reported nationwide, a record year for tornadoes. But the number of tornadoes increases every year. This doesn't mean that the weather is getting worse, but that tornado watchers are becoming more observant, more sophisticated, and more accurate in their reporting.

Forget Dorothy and Toto in Kansas. Texas has the most tornadoes. Between 1961 and 1990, there were 4,100 storms in Texas. Florida was a distant second, with 1,600; Oklahoma came in third, with 1,400. And the number-four state, Kansas, had 1,100 storms, according to NSSFC. Florida may actually be the most tornado-prone state in the country, with almost 10 tornadoes per 10,000 square miles each year between 1961 and 1990. Using this measure, Texas ranks seventh, behind Florida, Oklahoma, Indiana, Iowa, Louisiana, and Mississippi.

While tornadoes are serious business, some retailers make the best of a bad situation. One automobile dealer, Jon Lancaster Chevrolet of Madison, Wisconsin, staged a "scratch-and-dent" sale to help clear the dealership of tornado-damaged vehicles. Labeling the sale cars with bright red "Warning: Tornado-Damaged Vehicle" signs, the dealer was able to recoup some of his losses and gain a lot of free publicity.

Another retailer provided tornado relief for devastated communities and at the same time earned the good will of many people in the area. After a tornado killed 23 people in eastern Kansas in April 1990, all 63 stores in the Dillon Stores supermarket chain got together and collected over $122,000 for relief aid, according to Ken Keefer, director of advertising and public relations for the Hutchinson, Kansas-based company. The chain also initiated a matching grant program to benefit the stricken areas and donated a trailer filled with goods to the Kansas Food Bank.

Russell Anderson, president of Anderson and Associates, an automotive marketing and advertising firm in Fairfax, Virginia, warns that retailers must always walk the fine line of good taste. He cautions retailers to be aware of the negative

ILL WINDS

Between 1961 and 1990, Texas had the greatest number of tornadoes, 4106. But the state with the greatest number of tornadoes per square mile was Florida.

(number of tornadoes per 10,000 square miles per year, 1961–1990)

■ 5 or more
■ 3–4.99
■ 1–2.99
□ Less than 1

Source: National Severe Storm Forecasting Center

publicity a bad-weather sale can generate if there were serious weather-related injuries or fatalities.

Foul-Weather Friends

The weather can affect not only when and how people shop, but also the products they buy. Cold or damp weather makes people long for a cup of hot cocoa or a bowl of soothing soup. A driving rain inspires shoppers to buy umbrellas and suitable outerwear.

One manufacturer has faced the potential of inclement weather head-on. The Campbell Soup Company has a unique agreement with CRN International, formerly the Connecticut Radio Network, for radio spots in 35 storm-prone markets. The manufacturer usually places the first of two radio spots just before a storm is about to hit a particular market. This storm spot alerts listeners to the imminent severe weather and offers a reminder to stock up on essentials, including plenty of Campbell's soup. The second advertisement, usually placed just before or during the storm, tells listeners about the taste of Campbell's soup and its comforting, warming attributes.

Another product that has succeeded because of the weather is the Subaru station wagon. Subaru's introduction to the U.S. market in the 1960s was based on a climatological niche. The car was not advertised as a luxury or economy model— instead, its claim to fame is its dependability in rain and snow. Because of that niche, Subarus became popular first in rural communities and then in cities.

"Initially, we started carving our niche in rural, snowy areas," notes Richard Marshall, spokesman for Subaru of America in Cherry Hill, New Jersey. "We built our network through rural communities." Of the 1.5 million Subarus on the road today, 24 percent are in Subaru's six-state New England region, 16 percent are in the Rocky Mountain region, and 10 percent are in the Northwest, Marshall says. Although Subaru is now looking toward the Sunbelt as its next challenge, the car is still doing best in the Snowbelt areas of the country, where bad weather dictates the need for reliable cars.

Just as snow influences people's car choices, rain is good for umbrella sales. Twelve million Americans buy umbrellas every year, according to a spring 1987 survey conducted by Mediamark Research. The share of people who buy umbrellas rises with household income—peaking among those with annual incomes of $40,000 to $50,000. Nine percent of that higher-income group buy umbrellas in a year, compared with 5 percent of those with incomes of $15,000 or less. Among people with household incomes of $50,000 or more, the share who buy umbrellas in a year falls slightly, to 8 percent.

Although 45 percent of all umbrella buyers live in the South and the West, people in the Northeast and the Midwest are more likely to buy umbrellas. More than 9 percent of Northeasterners buy umbrellas during a year, compared with only 5 percent of Westerners.

Umbrella buyers are most likely to be city dwellers. More than 80 percent of umbrella buyers live in metropolitan areas, and most live in central cities. Fully 82 percent of buyers are white, but blacks are more likely than whites to buy umbrellas. Nearly 10 percent of blacks buy umbrellas during a year, versus less than 8 percent of whites.

Umbrella use is an urban phenomenon, according to Karen Fritz, marketing manager for Totes, a leading marketer of weather-related products. "City people who walk downtown are our biggest customers for umbrellas. Rural people drive from place to place or wear ponchos. The suburban market is better than the rural market, but not as good as the city."

Totes makes all types of rain gear, from boots to apparel, but umbrellas are about 75 percent of its business. The company's aggressive marketing plan has allowed Totes to prosper in a relatively slow-growth industry. "Totes," says Fritz, "is particularly committed to consumer research. We want to solve problems for our customers by making products that work well for them."

Totes' customers are well-educated, middle-income people, and the company takes advantage of market segmentation by offering a variety of umbrella brands designed for people with different income levels. Rain is good for the umbrella business. Sales are stronger in areas where it rains a lot. "Phoenix is not our best market, but New York City is a big umbrella town," observes Fritz. And on a day-to-day basis, sales improve as the weather deteriorates.

SPRING ALLERGIES

While most Americans embrace the first signs of spring with a flurry of gardening and other outdoor activities, millions greet the first signs of the new season with tissues and antihistamines in hand. Some 41 million Americans have asthma and allergies, including more than 22 million who have hay fever, according to the National Institute of Allergy and Infectious Diseases. Hay fever isn't everything it's cracked up to be, says the American Academy of Allergy and Immunology (AAAI) in Milwaukee, Wisconsin. It's not caused by hay and it's not a fever. The correct term is allergic rhinitis, and it results from the inhalation of allergens such as pollens and molds. Ragweed, grasses, and trees are primarily responsible for these wind-borne menaces.

Spring Sneezes

In southern Florida and the Great Plains states, the pollen season can begin as early as January. But for most allergy sufferers, the season begins in February or March and continues through September. Trees pollinate earliest, from February or March to April or May. Grasses follow next in the cycle, beginning pollination in May and continuing until mid-July. Weeds usually don't pollinate until late summer. Outdoor mold spores begin to appear after a spring thaw and reach their peak in either July, August, September, or October in the northern states. Molds can be found year-round in the South.

Allergies tend to run in families. If one parent is allergic, a child has a one in four chance of developing an allergy. If both parents are allergic, two out of three children will also suffer from allergies.

Six million children have hay fever, according to the institute. Ten percent of Americans also have asthma or frequent wheezing at some point in their lives. Virtually all asthma is rooted in allergy, according to a 1989 study in the *New England Journal of Medicine*. Allergies cause asthma in about half of all adults and 90 percent of children who have asthma. Those at greatest risk of death from asthma are persons older than age 50 or younger than age 9.

"Allergies can strike anybody of any age at any time," according to Robin Brown, public information manager at the AAAI. All that anyone can hope for is a slow spring to delay the inevitable spread of irritation-inducing pollen. There is no escape from the itchy eyes, runny nose, and general discomfort that allergies bring, says Brown. Even places like Arizona, thought to be an allergy-free zone, have become pollen-infested as new settlers landscape their environment with many of the same plants they were trying to avoid. Tucson now has one of the fastest-rising pollen counts in the country.

The Cost of Relief

Americans spend more than $4 billion each year trying to keep their allergies and asthma under control. Retail sales of over-the-counter allergy relief top $140 million, according to the National Institutes of Health (NIH). The figure for all allergy medications, including prescription drugs, reaches $600 million. Hay fever sufferers alone spent $224 million on physician services and $297 million on drugs.

One reason that allergy treatment can be so expensive is the fact that there is still no simple test to reveal the exact allergen giving a patient trouble. Diagnosis depends as much on the doctor's skill as it does on the allergy tests administered. If a patient suffers from both allergies and asthma, the diagnosis and medication prescribed to control discomfort can become even more complicated.

Treatments to alleviate the discomfort caused by allergies and asthma range from over-the-counter medications to prescription medications and injections. Side effects of these drugs can include drowsiness, insomnia, and nervousness. Allergies can cause more than mild discomfort. Some 3.5 million work days are lost annually due to hay fever alone, according to the NIH. The loss in wages as a result of sick days from allergies averages $150 million a year.

Children who suffer from asthma and other acute respiratory conditions lose over 129 million school days, or 61 percent of the total school days lost due to illness or injury, according to the National Center for Health Statistics. Asthma is also the most common cause of pediatric admissions to children's hospitals. The parents who must stay home from work to tend to their sick children also lose work time, productivity, and wages.

Allergy sufferers do not have to live in isolation, away from all the outdoor activities enjoyed by so many others. Careful environmental management, both indoors and out, can help them be as allergy-free as possible. Gardeners should consider plants, grasses, and trees that are either virtually pollen-free or that produce pollen that does not readily become windborne. Keeping dust at a minimum in the indoor environment can also be beneficial, but most doctors agree that medication may be the best line of defense for allergy sufferers.

SPRING BREAK
■ ■ ■ ■ ■ ■ ■ ■ ■ ■

In March, the swallows return to Capistrano, and hundreds of thousands of college students descend on America's Sunbelt resorts. But things have changed since the 1960s, when Frankie Avalon and Annette Funicello danced on the beach at Fort Lauderdale.

Where the Boys Are

"Fort Lauderdale is yesterday. So we don't even talk about it," says Joseph Venaglia of College Market Consultants in West New York, New Jersey. Venaglia has over 40 years experience with the college market, and he's seen a lot of changes. "This is totally and completely an electronic generation," he says of the 1990s college kids.

This generation of college students has spent more time alone than any other, and they have become a lot more introspective. "They're not as open to party, party, party. They've been exposed to a great deal of control," says Venaglia. The economic realities of the 1990s have created a fear factor. "Some medical students have $120,000 debt loads—this has never happened before. It is beginning to influence their thinking," he says.

But Spring Breakers have hardly been deserted by the marketing community. "Nintendo sends three semis to set up its exhibits," says Venaglia. In Daytona, Expo America, a trade show for college students, houses exhibits from nearly 100 manufacturers. "Everyone's booth has to be interactive—basketball tosses, prizes, and T-shirts," he says.

Major marketers like the Chrysler Corporation are drawn to the beaches. "Chrysler wants to introduce new vehicles to the youth market," says Richard Tarzian, president of Intercollegiate Communications (ICC) in Leonia, New Jersey. "They have a college financing program—graduates get automatic financing if they have a job." Chrysler, like many of the other marketers on the beach, wants to get its products into the minds of these consumers—for future reference.

Where and When

Spring Break traditionally begins the first Saturday in March and runs to Easter Sunday, lasting from three to six weeks. There are more than 13 million college students nationwide, according to Eric Weil of Strategic Marketing Communications in Ridgewood, New Jersey. However, only about 5 million of them are full-time, year-round undergraduate students at four-year colleges, the people most likely to participate in Spring Break. Fewer than 1 million actually make it to the beach. But a handful of localities get the bulk of these party-goers.

Daytona Beach, not Fort Lauderdale, has become the "in" destination for the 1990s, attracting more than 300,000 students in 1991. But the crowds at Daytona Beach are shrinking, while those at South Padre Island, Texas, and Panama City, Florida, are growing. Either one of these hot sports could challenge the leader for the biggest crowd in any given year. By comparison, Fort Lauderdale gets just a handful of students—about 30,000 in 1991. Spring Breakers are becoming increasingly likely to spread themselves around. Destinations outside the U.S., like the Caribbean, Acapulco, and Cancun, are rapidly gaining in popularity. In fact, representatives from the Mexican Ministry of Tourism attended ICC's annual Spring Break Workshop in 1991.

The market for Spring Break is much larger than the beach crowd, according to

ICC's Tarzian. "Spring Break has always fascinated Americans," he says. "Young people look forward to it when they go to college, and older generations are nostalgic." Television shows that focus on Spring Break draw large audiences. "When '48 Hours' did a report on Spring Break, it had its highest ratings in the show's history," according to Tarzian.

The beach party has moved indoors, thanks to the wonders of electronic technology, ICC, CBS, and MTV. Spring Break America became a feature of CBS late-night television in 1992. On consecutive weekends in March, remotes were broadcast from Daytona Beach, South Padre Island, Cancun, Acapulco, and Palm Springs, and included entertainment, sporting competitions, and beach events, as well as such features as "outrageous moments," "dating techniques," "postcards home," clips from previous Spring Breaks, and fashion shows. Tarzian says the audience for Spring Break ranges from envious 16-year-olds to 50-year-olds who were turned on by Frankie and Annette back in the 1960s.

Good Clean Fun

Daytona Beach, with its 10 miles of ocean frontage and its reputation as a resort and convention area, caters to college students as tourists. By establishing a set of strict guidelines governing public displays of drinking and rowdiness and by having a very visible but nonthreatening police presence, Daytona Beach has managed to strike a happy medium between craziness and civic responsibility.

Thinking of students as tourists, rather than terrorists, is an idea that is catching on in other resort communities. The success of Panama City, Florida, in capturing the Spring Break crowd serves as a lesson to other cities and towns, and not only those in the Sunbelt, says College Market Consultants' Venaglia. He predicts an influx of Spring Breakers at ski resorts in the not-too-distant future.

Spring Break is not just an occasion for bikinis, wet T-shirt contests, and hunk-of-the-year parties. It is also a time for marketers to reach out to an up-and-coming market—the college student. By sponsoring such fun events as basketball and volleyball tournaments, weight-lifting contests, and belly-flop competitions, promoters can gain wide exposure among a crowd whose spending potential will increase as it reaches its prime earning years.

Companies that profit most from Spring Break marketing are those that can build on name recognition and brand loyalty. Chrysler, Nintendo, and Coca-Cola, as well as electronics, video, photography, and computer marketers, all do well with college students.

On the other hand, beer companies have been voluntarily staying away from public displays at Spring Break beach parties. While Philip Morris's Miller Brewing Company used to hand out free samples of beer in Daytona Beach, their 1991 strategy was to line the roads to the beach with billboards that read, "Good beer is properly aged. You should be, too." At the urging of Surgeon General Antonia Novello, the Beer Institute and other individual breweries have followed suit.

"The appeal of being loaded isn't the same," says Strategic Marketing's Eric Weil. "People's awareness of alcohol abuse is extremely high." Students' awareness has been fortified by everyone from the U.S. Surgeon General to local chambers of commerce. No longer do inflatable beer bottles dominate the Spring Break landscape. Beer marketers have not disappeared from the Spring Break scene, but they confine their promotions to bars and retail outlets that cater to the over-21 crowd.

MARCH ACTIVITIES
■ ■ ■ ■ ■ ■ ■ ■ ■ ■ ■ ■

Young people taking a break from the college routine are not the only spring travelers heading to warmer climates. The Southeast hosted more travelers than any other region during spring 1990, according to figures released by the U.S. Travel Data Center. The Southeast was the destination of 75 million visitors during spring 1990, compared with the cold Great Lakes region, which saw only 37 million visitors.

Spring Travel
The majority of people who travel in the spring do so for pleasure, according to the Center—three-quarters of travelers in spring 1990 took pleasure trips. Of these, 48 percent stayed with friends or relatives, while 39 percent stayed in hotels and motels. While 54 percent of spring pleasure travelers cited visits to friends and relatives as the primary purpose of their trips, 17 percent went on vacation for outdoor recreation, and 30 percent went for entertainment.

The most popular means of transportation for spring pleasure trips in 1990 were cars (including rental cars), trucks, or recreational vehicles. Fully 76 percent of spring pleasure seekers drove to their spring destinations. Only 17 percent flew to their vacation spot, according to the Travel Data Center.

Most pleasure trippers (45 percent) spent two or three nights on vacation in the spring of 1990. Twenty-eight percent stayed away from home for four to nine nights, and 12 percent took off for only one night. Eight percent of spring pleasure travelers stayed away from home for ten nights or more, and 7 percent were day-trippers, spending no nights away from home.

The Wearing of the Green
In 1980, 40 million Americans claimed to be of Irish descent—12 times the population of Ireland.* The number of people in Massachusetts with Irish ancestry outnumbered people of any other background. In 42 other states, people of Irish descent ranked second or third in the population. Ancestry data from the 1990 census undoubtedly show that the number of Americans of Irish descent has increased even more.

1990 census data should be available by June 1992.

Each year between 1980 and 1985, the U.S. issued just over 1,000 green cards (alien registration cards) to people from Ireland. In 1986, the number rose to 1,800. In 1987, more than 3,000 residents of Ireland legally immigrated to this country, and almost twice that number came in 1988. This dramatic increase resulted from a change in immigration laws. But even this substantial increase has not accommodated the large number of Irish who would like to move to the U.S.

In 1977, only 26,000 tourists and 4,000 business people came to the United States from Ireland on temporary visas. In 1987, 81,000 tourists and 15,000 business people came here. "It's unlikely that the increase can be attributed to a boom in tourism, considering that Ireland has been in an economic slump during this period," reports *Irish America*, a New York City-based magazine.

In 1987, almost 7,000 Irish residents overstayed their temporary visas. Their overstay rate of 6 percent was more than double the rate of any other country, according to the Immigration and Naturalization Service. This trend is evidence of illegal immigration. Estimates of the number of illegal Irish residents in the U.S. range from 25,000 to 135,000.

High unemployment in Ireland is the major force driving people away. "Fifty percent of our people are under the age of 28. In order to create sufficient employment, we need to work very hard indeed," says Anne Barrington of the Irish Embassy in New York City. Currently, the unemployment rate in Ireland is around 18 percent. But Ireland has a broader definition of unemployment than does the U.S., which keeps its rate higher than the American one, according to Barrington.

Ireland boasts one of the best educational systems in Europe, but many highly educated young people who come to the U.S. illegally find only menial work. A survey of Irish illegals conducted by the *Irish Voice*, a New York City newspaper, found 77 percent of the men in construction and 54 percent of the women in child care or care for the elderly.

Only about 1,300 illegal Irish residents applied for amnesty under the provisions of the Immigration Reform and Control Act of 1986. However, the influx of Irish illegals began when Ireland's economy soured in 1982—so most Irish illegals have not been in the U.S. long enough to meet the requirements for amnesty.

While Ireland struggles with an oversupply of young workers, the U.S. is suffering from a shortage of entry-level workers. The highly skilled, English-speaking Irish immigrants are attractive to American employers, and many American hospitals are actively recruiting nurses from Ireland.

RELIGIOUS HOLIDAYS
■ ■ ■ ■ ■ ■ ■ ■ ■ ■ ■ ■ ■ ■

Spring brings important religious events for Christians and Jews—Easter and Passover. Sixty-three percent of Americans are Protestant, according to a 1989 survey conducted by the National Opinion Research Center (NORC) for Gale Research in

Detroit. Twenty-five percent are Catholic, 2 percent are Jewish, 8 percent have no religious preference, and 2 percent belong to some other religious group.

Religious Events

Easter marks the resurrection or rebirth of Jesus Christ and is celebrated by most Christians between March 22 and April 25. Easter is a time of family celebration and feasting. For some, it is the only Sunday of the year that they attend church services.

While 43 percent of people attend a worship service on a typical Sunday, 68 percent attend on Easter Sunday, according to a 1991 Gallup Poll. Catholics are more likely to attend Easter services than Protestants. While 85 percent of Catholics go to church on Easter, 72 percent of Protestants attend services. And 72 percent of women go to church on Easter, compared with 63 percent of men, according to Gallup. Geographic location is an important factor in determining who will attend Easter services. While only 59 percent of those in the West go to church on Easter, about 70 percent of people in other areas of the country do so.

While church attendance is higher on Easter than on a typical Sunday, many people, especially young people, don't really know what the holiday is about. Only 64 percent of people aged 18 to 29 understand the significance of the day, compared with 85 percent of those aged 30 to 49 and 74 percent of people aged 50 and older, according to Gallup.

God and Family

At a typical Sunday church service, a minister looking over his or her flock may see more women than men, more senior citizens than young adults, and more married people than singles. But the face of the usual congregation is slowly changing, and where seniors were once in the majority, families with children are beginning to make their presence known.

While 45 percent of women attend a religious service on a typical Sunday, only 34 percent of men attend, according to a 1991 survey by the Roper Organization. Because older adults are more likely than younger adults to attend worship services, churches and synagogues may benefit from the aging of the baby-boom generation. On a typical Sunday, only 32 percent of adults under age 30 attend worship services, compared with 36 percent of people aged 30 to 44, 42 percent of people aged 45 to 59, and 53 percent of people aged 60 and older.

Married people are more likely than singles to go to church. Parents of children under age 17 are more likely to go to church if both parents work (49 percent) than if only one works outside the home (37 percent).

Children in a household are a major factor driving baby-boom parents back to church. Baby boomers who were raised on sex, drugs, and rock 'n' roll want to protect their children from the things they toyed with in the 1960s. Sex and drugs have become even more dangerous, with AIDS and crack cocaine epidemics. Rock 'n' roll, with lascivious Madonna videos and x-rated rock and rap lyrics, has also lost any naivete it ever had. Baby-boom parents see the church as a way of returning to traditional family values.

The number of congregations with more than 2,000 worshipers each Sunday climbed from 10 in 1970 to more than 300 in 1991, and is still increasing, according to John Vaughn, publisher of the newsletter *Church Growth Today*. Many of these "megachurches"—usually conservative evangelical denominations like Baptist and Assembly of God—are located in the Sunbelt or in the suburbs of large midwestern cities. Of the 50 largest, 17 are in California, 7 are in Texas, and 6 are in Georgia. Some offer roller rinks, health clubs, and support groups. Others stage Christian pop concerts, lively worship services, and programs to meet every spiritual, emotional, recreational, and entertainment need or interest.

The most actively targeted market for religious organizations is the family-oriented baby boomer. The United Methodist Church's "Reaching for the Baby Boomer" project, introduced in 1990, sponsors workshops like "Sunday Morning with Boomers," and publications like "African American Baby Boomers" to teach its ministers to reach out to baby boomers through Christian education, worship, preaching, and music.

Baby boomers are not the only group that religious institutions can reach. Over 25 percent of the U.S. population will be aged 50 or older by the year 2000. But more than 40 percent of so-called "mainline" Protestants—Episcopalians, Methodists, Presbyterians, and Lutherans—are already aged 50 or older, according to a 1983 survey conducted by the Princeton Religion Research Center.

Many churches are reaching out to their graying congregations by offering retirement planning and guiding older members to new interests. The Episcopal Society for Ministry on Aging runs a referral hotline to help older adults and their families find local programs. The Episcopalian church encourages older and younger members to "adopt" one another and celebrate holidays together.

"Older members can be a resource to younger members," says Lynn Huber, director of the Office of Affirmative Aging for the Episcopal Diocese of Tennessee. Keeping the elderly involved in a church community maintains the credibility of religion, she says. Without evidence of a lifelong commitment to faith, younger generations will view church as a social club and not as an integral part of their lives. "We must find more ways to serve and use the talents of our older members," says Huber. "That is our future."

The New Fundamentalism

They called it "The Second Battle of Atlanta" when over 40,000 delegates descended on the 1986 Southern Baptist Convention. The struggle between moderates and fundamentalists for control over the nation's largest Protestant denomination is rooted in the changing demographics of the South—a struggle that continues today.

About 80 percent of the church's 14 million members live in the South. During

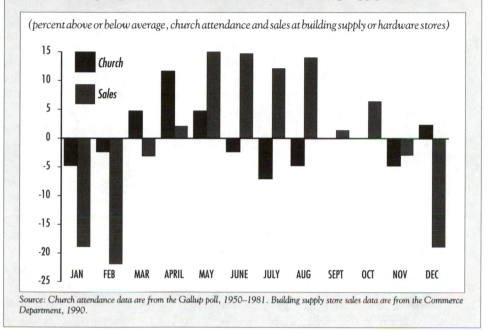

SPRING RITES AND RITUALS

Although church attendance is high in the Christmas season, it's highest during Lent. Other spring rituals mean brisk business at building supply stores.

(percent above or below average, church attendance and sales at building supply or hardware stores)

Source: Church attendance data are from the Gallup poll, 1950–1981. Building supply store sales data are from the Commerce Department, 1990.

the past 25 years, as inmigration and increasing urbanization changed southern culture, a new Southern Baptist leadership emerged with more tolerant ideas about integration, women's roles, and the interpretation of the Bible. But in 1979, the convention elected the first in a series of fundamentalist presidents.

"Fundamentalism has always been a response to more 'modern' ways of believing," says Nancy T. Ammerman of the Center for Religious Research at Emory University in Atlanta. Ammerman's research includes a survey designed to measure individual commitment to fundamentalist ideals. When she polled 1,000 Southern Baptist leaders, only 8 percent disagreed substantially with the fundamentalist beliefs that the Bible is the word of God, that drinking and dancing should be avoided, and that abortion should be unconditionally prohibited.

The survey indicated that adherence to fundamentalism diminished with increasing education and income. Clergy with postgraduate degrees were eight times more likely than those without college degrees to be theologically moderate. Similarly, lay people in professional and managerial households were five times more likely than people in farming or blue-collar households to be moderates.

Ammerman predicts that improving economic conditions in the South will cause fundamentalism to decline, but she also observed an increasing commitment to fundamentalism among the newly urban. Southern Baptists who live in the city but were raised in the country are much more likely to identify themselves as fundamentalists than either rural residents or native urbanites. "People between two worlds—in the new world, but not of it—are more likely to be fundamentalists than any other demographic group," she says.

Passover

The Jewish festival of Passover is celebrated for eight days beginning on the 15th day of the month of Nisan. Following the Western calendar, the holiday begins in late March or April. Passover celebrates the flight of the Jewish people from their enslavement in the land of Egypt. During the festival, many Jews eat matzoh, or unleavened bread, to symbolize the unleavened bread their ancestors ate as they fled Egypt. There are also many other special rituals and traditions that accompany the holiday, including a festive meal, or seder.

Most of America's 6 million Jews are not affiliated with a religious organization, according to Menachem Lubinsky, president of Lubicom, an advertising and public relations firm in New York City. Only about 750,000 Jews observe religious dietary restrictions on a full-time basis. Yet the demand for kosher products is growing rapidly, especially during the Passover season.

Nearly 100 organizations certify kosher foods with a symbol that appears on kosher products. Although sales of these certified products equaled $30 billion in 1990, less than $2 billion were to people who bought the food because it was kosher. However, sales to people who deliberately seek out kosher foods are increasing 15 to 18 percent each year, according to Lubinsky, and some 40 percent of these sales take place during the Passover season.

A growing number of non-Jews are concerned about food purity and are seeking out kosher food. These include Muslims, Seventh-Day Adventists, non-Jewish vegetarians, and others. "Consumers feel more comfortable knowing there's an extra set of eyes inspecting the products," says Rabbi Menachem Genack, rabbinic administrator in the kashruth division of the Union of Orthodox Jewish Congregations of America.

Manufacturers seek and receive kosher certification for between 800 and 1,000 products each year, says Lubinsky. Many of these are health foods, microwaveable products, and low-calorie items. Some are already on the market, and their manufacturers see kosher certification as an added benefit. In 1977, there were about 1,000 certified kosher products on the market. That number reached 20,000 by 1991.

In 1990, Coors became the first American beer to receive kosher certification from the Union of Orthodox Jewish Congregations of America. The brewer supplied itemized lists of all ingredients and suppliers; rabbis then inspected the plants in Colorado and Virginia. An encircled U—the symbol representing certification from this organization—now appears on all Coors products.

Coors beer is available almost anywhere, but some kosher foods are difficult to

MARCH MADNESS

THIS TIME OF YEAR, collegiate basketball finals dominate sports. The battle of the "Final Four" teams is appropriately known to the fans as March Madness.

Basketball was invented in 1891 by Dr. James Naismith, a YMCA physical-education instructor at Springfield College in Massachusetts. Naismith developed the game as a sort of stop-gap measure to fill in the days between the end of football season and the start of baseball season. It is now played by men and women in more than 170 countries around the world. Basketball is one of the few team sports that can be played either inside or outside, so it is a great sport for the unpredictable days of spring.

Americans are addicted to basketball. Between 1987 and 1989, participation rose from 36 million players to 37 million, making it the most popular team sport in the country, according to a 1991 study by the Sporting Goods Manufacturers Association. Also on the rise is the number of people who play the sport frequently (52 days or more a year). Frequent players increased from 7 million to 8 million between 1987 and 1989, a 17 percent increase.

While basketball is a sport enjoyed by men and women alike, the frequent participation levels among males increased 20 percent between 1987 and 1989. The number of frequent female basketball players rose by less than 4 percent. Frequent participation levels for those aged 18 to 44 increased 27 percent over the same two-year period.

Basketball holds a special appeal for America's minorities. In 1987, there were 912,000 nonwhite frequent basketball players. By 1989, that number climbed to over 2.3 million, a 155 percent increase. "There are a number of reasons why basketball is so popular today," says Craig Miller, assistant executive director of USA Basketball. "The work of the Amateur Athletics Association, the YMCA, and the YWCA in the inner cities has influenced a number of youngsters to play. In addition, the attractive marketing campaigns by the National Basketball Association (NBA) have accurately portrayed the sport as fast moving and exciting."

Basketball is as appealing to watch as it is to play. At least, that's the feeling of the millions of Americans who watch NCAA and NBA basketball throughout the season, as well as those who root for the American Olympic team every four years. Between 1976 and 1988, the number of basketball games aired on network television rose 63 percent, according to the A.C. Nielsen Company. The number of hours of basketball television viewing grew almost 72 percent—from 153 hours to 184 hours.

Successful basketball stars have high profiles in the world of television, and when they endorse products, consumers listen—and buy. Michael Jordan, considered one of the greatest basketball players of all time, makes between $15 million and $18 million annually in endorsements alone. But much of his success as a product spokesman lies in the fact that his team, the Chicago Bulls, is positioned in a large television market. This gives him the exposure he needs to make his name a household word. Wheaties and the other products he endorses only enhance his name recognition.

"If you look at three of the biggest basketball endorsers of the past decade, Michael Jordan, Magic Johnson, and Larry Bird, all of them have been from three of the biggest television markets," says Marc Perman of J. Michael Bloom N.Y. "I wonder how much money Larry Bird would have made playing in a market like Utah."

Still, basketball has a universal appeal, and there are professional leagues in Israel, Italy, and Mexico. There are also increasing numbers of foreign-born players on college and professional teams in this country. Some sports enthusiasts boast that there will be a World Cup of basketball similar to the one that already exists for soccer by the 21st century.

As foreigners become more adept at the sport, the American dominance of Olympic basketball becomes more tenuous. Americans dominated the sport until the 1972 Olympic Games, when the U.S.'s 63-game Olympic winning streak was ended by a last-second U.S.S.R. victory. The Russians won 51 to 50, and many American fans are still debating the controversial upset. More controversy and excitement will be in store beginning with the 1992 Olympics, when professionals will be allowed to participate for the first time.

For fans from around the world, there is the Basketball Hall of Fame in Springfield, Massachusetts, where the game was invented. Opened in 1985, the Hall of Fame records all aspects of the game—amateur, high school, college, professional, international, women's, and handicapped. Extensive exhibitions document the creation of the game, its globalization, and its universal appeal. There are bronzed basketball shoes (Bob Lanier's size 22s) and a basketball that traveled around the earth on the Discovery space shuttle. Some 130,000 enthusiasts visited the Hall of Fame in 1990. With the 1991 centennial of the sport, the Hall of Fame launched a commemorative stamp and hosted professional and college Hall of Fame games, giving fans many more reasons to visit the home of one of the most popular American sports.

get in areas thinly populated with Jews. The primary problem is finding meat, according to Rabbi David Kline of Monroe, Louisiana. "Occasionally, you can find a kosher hot dog, but only about three families here stay kosher," he says. "They go to Houston or Memphis to shop. I just gave up meat."

Kline could order from Chicago's Sinai Kosher Foods, which ships its products everywhere from Florida to Hawaii. "We have warehouse clubs. People buy 175 cases of Polish sausage or hot dogs. Five hundred cases may go to one location," says a company spokeswoman.

Kraft General Foods' Maxwell House coffee is perhaps the best-known mass-market brand in the kosher niche. Since 1933, the company has distributed copies of the Passover Haggadah, a prayer book read at the seder table to retell the story of the Israelites' exodus from the land of Egypt. In 1991, the company shipped 2,000 Passover Haggadahs, along with Maxwell House and Sanka instant coffee to Jewish troops stationed in the Persian Gulf.

Some long-distance kosher suppliers advertise in *Chai Today*, a national magazine distributed to members of 50 to 70 synagogues. "I knew that most synagogues had newsletters," says the editor, Rabbi Michael Lozenik, who began the publication in 1989. "So I offered to print their newsletters as custom inserts to a full-color magazine." Producing 70 newsletters and one magazine a month is a lot of work, but Lozenik estimates that his readership now stands at 600,000. He is seeking national advertisers.

Another new publication targeted at affluent Jews was launched in March 1992. MOSAIC claimed to be the first cultural/lifestyle magazine for Jewish consumers interested in the arts. The publication promised it would reach 400,000 readers with a median income of $60,000.

New York State has the largest population of Jews, at nearly 2 million, according to the North American Jewish Data Bank in New York City. California ranks second with more than 800,000 Jews; its urban areas are experiencing the fastest growth in Jewish residents. Communities where the Jewish population is growing rapidly include Napa, Redding, and San Luis Obispo, California; Anchorage, Alaska; Aspen, Colorado; Las Cruces, Los Alamos, and Santa Fe, New Mexico; Vero Beach, Florida; Hartford County, Maryland; and Myrtle Beach, South Carolina.

TIME MARCHES ON

March marks a number of national events, from National Women's History Month and National Nutrition Month to the less serious National Peanut Month and National Frozen Food Month. In Texas, they celebrate the Texas Cowboy Poetry Gathering, while the Wisconsin River National Walleye Tournament is held in Wisconsin. And throughout the country, the first week of the month is Return the Borrowed Books Week.

APRIL WEATHER
■■■■■■■■■■

April is not the rainiest season nationwide. Albuquerque is rainier in the summer, and Seattle is rainier in the winter.

	TEMPERATURE		PRECIPITATION	
	low	high	inches	days
Albuquerque, NM	39.5°F	70.6°F	0.40	3
Atlanta, GA	50.4	73.2	4.43	9
Bismarck, ND	30.8	54.2	1.51	8
Boise, ID	36.4	60.8	1.19	8
Boston, MA	40.8	56.6	3.73	11
Buffalo, NY	36.3	54.4	3.06	14
Burlington, VT	32.7	52.6	2.77	12
Charlotte, NC	48.4	72.1	3.27	9
Chicago, IL	38.8	58.8	3.66	12
Cleveland, OH	38.3	57.9	3.32	14
Dallas, TX	55.0	76.8	3.63	8
Denver, CO	33.7	61.0	1.81	9
Detroit, MI	36.9	57.7	3.15	12
Great Falls, MT	31.3	54.0	1.49	9
Honolulu, HI	68.7	82.7	1.49	9
Houston, TX	58.3	79.0	4.24	7
Indianapolis, IN	41.7	63.1	3.68	12
Jacksonville, FL	55.7	79.7	3.32	6
Juneau, AK	31.3	46.8	2.92	17
Los Angeles, CA	52.2	66.7	0.93	3
Memphis, TN	52.2	72.9	5.77	10
Miami, FL	68.2	82.4	3.07	6
Milwaukee, WI	35.6	53.5	3.37	12
Minneapolis, MN	36.0	56.0	2.05	10
Mobile, AL	57.7	78.3	5.35	7
New Orleans, LA	58.8	78.6	4.50	7
New York, NY	43.8	61.1	3.75	11
Norfolk, VA	48.1	68.2	2.87	10
Oklahoma City, OK	48.6	71.7	2.91	8
Omaha, NE	40.3	64.0	2.94	10
Philadelphia, PA	42.6	63.2	3.47	11
Phoenix, AZ	53.0	83.1	0.27	2
Portland, OR	40.6	60.2	2.31	14
Salt Lake City, UT	37.2	61.1	2.21	9
San Francisco, CA	46.6	63.0	1.53	6
Sault Ste. Marie, MI	29.0	47.1	2.38	11
Seattle, WA	40.5	56.8	2.40	14
St. Louis, MO	45.1	67.1	3.55	11
Washington, DC	46.2	67.1	2.93	10
Wichita, KS	44.5	68.1	2.30	8

Source: U.S. Department of Commerce, Bureau of the Census, Statistical Abstract of the United States 1991. Average daily minimum and maximum temperatures and average monthly precipitation were measured over a standard 30-year period.

APRIL
A CLEAN SWEEP

Many people celebrate the end of the winter by putting their houses in order. But for a growing number of Americans, spring cleaning is more than a time to put the winter woolens in moth balls; it's an occasion to put the whole earth in ecological order. Americans celebrate Earth Day by recycling, using biodegradable products, avoiding such things as Styrofoam and spray cans, and teaching others about ecology.

April is also a time for most Americans to clean up their financial act. As the deadline for filing tax returns approaches, many Americans find themselves hastily gathering all the receipts and financial documents that have been littering surfaces and cluttering drawers over the past year. Some begin wondering if it isn't time to consider their bigger financial picture as well.

THE ENVIRONMENT

When the first Earth Day was organized in 1970, environmentalists were a fringe group, dismissed as crazy, ignored totally, or written off as leftover radicals from the 1960s. But in the 1990s, environmental protection has become a consensus issue among politicians. As people of all demographic groups become concerned about the environment, business and industry are responding with new products, new packaging, and new attitudes toward marketing and manufacturing.

APRIL'S BEST BUYS

(items most likely to be on sale in April)

- ■ Air conditioners
- ● Bathrobes
- ■ Fabrics
- ● Spring shoes
- ■ Vacuum cleaners

Source: DOLLAR$ENSE Magazine, 1987

Every Day Should Be Earth Day

Twenty years ago, only a select group of younger better-educated people were in the forefront of the conservation movement. Today, a majority of every age, education, and income group consider themselves environmentalists, according to a 1989 Gallup Report. Sixty-nine percent of people between the ages of 18 and 29 consider themselves environmentalists, as do 79 percent of those aged 30 to 49 and 77 percent of those aged 50 and older.

Education influences the public's views on environmental issues. While 62 percent of Americans with less than 12 years of education consider themselves environmentalists, 81 percent of those with some college education do, according to Gallup.

The share of environmentalists also tends to increase with household income. Only 70 percent of those with annual incomes below $15,000 say they are environmentalists, compared with 86 percent of those with incomes between $30,000 and $49,999. The share then falls to 79 percent among those with annual incomes of $50,000 or more.

People in all regions of the country are concerned with the environment. But the greatest concentration is the West, where 81 percent of residents call themselves environmentalists. Seventy-nine percent of Northeasterners, 76 percent of Midwesterners, and 70 percent of Southerners also make this claim, according to Gallup.

This new environmentalism directly affects lawmakers, politicians, retailers, and manufacturers. In 1980, 29 percent of Americans believed that environmental regulations were inadequate, while 24 percent felt that the measures in place were too stringent. Today, 55 percent of Americans feel that environmental regulations do not offer adequate safeguards, and only 11 percent feel they have gone too far, according to the Roper Organization.

Environmental concerns have changed the way consumers view the business community. They feel that businesses deserve points for providing jobs and developing new products, but they also see business and industry as doing little to fulfill their obligations to control pollution. Americans tend to blame businesses for the environmental problems they see at local, national, and global levels, says Roper.

More than eight in ten Americans cite industrial pollution as the major cause of environmental problems, and nearly 75 percent of the public say that the products businesses use in manufacturing are harmful to the environment. Six in ten Americans blame businesses for not developing environmentally sound consumer products.

Business and industry have responded to consumer concerns in a number of ways. In some instances, close examination has led to accusations of mislabeling or deception.

Among the best-known environmental flops was Mobil Chemical's degradable Hefty plastic bags. While the company's environmental claim was technically correct, it was misleading, because the bags need sunlight to degrade and do not degrade when buried in a landfill (neither does anything else). A combination of bad publicity and pressure from environmental groups forced Mobil to drop its claim.

The multimillion-dollar diaper market is one of the greatest battlegrounds for environment-based squabbles. Neither proponents of cloth diapers nor advocates of disposables have been able to prove beyond a shadow of a doubt that their products are clearly more environmentally friendly. But both sides have spent large sums of money in advertising, consumer education, and product development.

A measure to ban disposable diapers was brought before the Vermont legislature in 1990. Although it did not pass, it did encourage research in the disposable-diaper industry. Cloth-diaper manufacturers responded by developing more convenient products, such as "pinless" cloth diapers and cloth diapers with reusable plastic outer liners.

Over 60 percent of Americans believe that business misleads the public with environmental claims. And the share is even greater among highly educated consumers, according to Roper. Business must regain the trust of environmentally minded consumers by providing products that live up to their claims.

Package Deal

Sometimes it's packaging, not the product, that is the issue. The sudden disappearance of McDonald's signature Styrofoam "clamshell" hamburger box in 1991 is a good example of a company responding to consumer demand. Although McDonald's claimed that the containers were not a problem and had planned a $100 million recycling campaign, the pressure of ecology-minded customers caused it to withdraw the familiar package and replace it with a type of paper wrapping. The new packaging is not ideal—it is not recyclable and it requires cutting down trees—but it uses 90 percent less space than foam when discarded. In an era when neighborhood dumps are overflowing, McDonald's paper wrappers are still more attractive than the Styrofoam ones.

McDonald's is by no means the only company to take a closer look at its packaging program. Procter & Gamble, Playtex Family Products Corporation, Cosmair's Lancome Division, and other health-and-beauty-aids manufacturers are looking for ways to eliminate the excess packaging of many of their products. Procter & Gamble has eliminated the outside cartons from its Sure and Secret deodorants, while Playtex has done away with the outer boxes it used for many years on Jhirmack hair-care products. Cosmair's Lancome Division is eliminating outer packaging on its cleansers.

The elimination of excess paper and plastic overwrapping has its pluses and minuses for retailers. The products take up less valuable shelf space in supermarkets, but because most products are not uniformly shaped, they cannot stand alone in displays. Products can become damaged more easily. Theft is another worry for health-and-beauty-aids retailers; bulky outer packaging made it more difficult for shoplifters to pocket the products.

However, manufacturers continue to eliminate excess packaging because they know their consumers care about the environment. Half of all Americans object to Styrofoam packaging for fast foods and to nonreturnable glass beverage bottles, according to a 1990 poll by the Roper Organization. Forty percent disapprove of Styrofoam packaging for appliances and to plastic six-pack collars for beverage cans. Those who disapprove of this packaging are most likely to be college graduates or householders with annual incomes of $50,000 or more. About 30 percent of consumers are put off by plastic bottles or by food wrapped in clear plastic. These people are also likely to be well educated and affluent.

To head off its impact on sales, manufacturers have been quick to respond to their customers' complaints. Lever Brothers, for example, now uses some 10 million pounds of recycled plastic annually in packaging liquid laundry products such as Wisk, Surf, and Snuggle. One of its advertising campaigns asks consumers to pitch in by participating in plastic recycling.

Making a Commitment

There is a small group of companies that has always practiced ecologically sound manufacturing. For them, the current interest in the environment has been a boon. Marcal Paper Mills Inc. of Elmwood Park, New Jersey, for example, has been making paper products such as napkins and towels from recycled paper for over 40 years. Aimed primarily at families on a budget, these paper products have until now downplayed their dependence on recycled paper. But their new campaign emphasizes this fact and attempts to appeal to a broader consumer base.

Arm & Hammer has been marketing environmentally sound products for 144 years. Its boxes have been made out of recycled paper for more than a century. Now Arm & Hammer is working to educate consumers about the myriad uses of its ecologically safe products. Concentrating its efforts primarily in supermarkets, Arm & Hammer is winning over many environmentally conscious shoppers.

Sorting through the numerous environmental claims made by different companies confuses many consumers. Environmental advocates are proposing sanctioning "green" or environmentally friendly products with their own seal of approval. One group, the Alliance for Social Responsibility, is introducing a product labeling program designed to help consumers choose safe products.

Recognizing the growing concerns of customers is of major importance for manufacturers, marketers, and retailers. As more people become aware of environmental issues, they will become more selective about the products and services they buy. "Green" consumers may prefer organically grown produce, product packaging made from recycled paper, pedal-powered modes of transportation, and a stock portfolio that concentrates on green-minded corporations. They will also educate their children to be ecologically aware, thus preparing another generation to shop, consume, and invest in with the environment in mind.

A majority of Americans say they are willing to make certain sacrifices to protect the environment, according to Roper. Fully 72 percent say they are ready for mandatory recycling, even though it would cause them some inconvenience, and recycling programs could increase local taxes. Another 72 percent think the federal government should require all states to enact bottle bills that would force consumers to return bottles and cans if they wanted their deposits back. And even though several hundred dollars would be added to the price of a new car, 60 percent of consumers want automobile exhaust systems that further reduce air pollution. Nearly that many think that supermarket customers should supply their own bags.

Less-polluting gasoline is favored by 57 percent of consumers, even though it would add as much as 10 cents to the price of a gallon of gasoline. And 56 percent think refrigerators should stop using chemicals that are harmful to the ozone layer, even though these appliances would use more energy. Banning disposable diapers is favored by a majority (54 percent) of Americans, including those with children in their households, says Roper.

There is a limit to Americans' environmental enthusiasm. Only 46 percent favor changes in refining that would add at least 30 cents to the price of a gallon of gasoline. Just 46 percent believe it would be a good idea to send additional financial aid to South American countries to help save the rainforests. Requiring cars with less than three passengers to stay in certain lanes is condoned by only 40 percent of Americans, according to Roper.

Responding to the environmentally aware consumer will become more important as the 21st century approaches and more people join the environmental movement. But not all consumers are committed to ecology to the same degree, and different aspects of environmentalism are embraced by different groups of consumers. While 16 percent of those in the West avoid products from companies that are not environmentally responsible, only 9 percent of people in the Northeast do, according to Roper. Even though 18 percent of people in the Midwest cut down on pollution by using gasoline with methanol, only 3 percent of Northeasterners do.

Recognizing the environmental concerns of local consumers is a good starting point for establishing a comprehensive environmental policy for a retail business or service industry. Having this policy in place will prove essential as more consumers begin to question the "green-mindedness" of the businesses and industries in their communities.

PLANTING AND LANDSCAPING
■■■■■■■■■■■■■■■■■■■■■■

To some people, the most important spot on earth is their own backyard. The grass is always greener when it's been reseeded, fed, watered, cut, and carefully tended. As the weather gets warmer, more people work outside, planting their gardens or caring for lawns. Of course, April's unpredictable weather, droughts, floods, or unseasonable temperatures can affect regional sales of lawn equipment. But the long-term outlook for this industry is good.

Sprucing Up

The lawn-and-garden-equipment industry—consisting of lawn mowers, Rototillers,™ powered edge trimmers, shredders, snow and leaf blowers, and garden tractors—showed a 1 percent increase in product shipments in 1990. Experts anticipate an annual increase of 2 percent over the next five years, according to the *U.S. Industrial Outlook 1991*, published by the Bureau of Economic Analysis.

Demographic changes account for the growth in the lawn industry. As people have more discretionary income, they are more willing to spend money on things like lawn care. At the same time, more middle- and upper-income Americans favor trading up and getting larger houses with larger lawns to care for.

One of the fastest-growing segments of the lawn-and-garden-equipment industry is reel mowers or nonpower mowers. In 1985, American Lawn Mower Company-Great States Corporation, the largest reel-mower manufacturing company in the United States, had sales of 74,000 units. By 1990, that figure had jumped to 145,000, and it topped 200,000 in 1991.

Reasons for the increase in human-powered mowers include their low price, their quietness, and perhaps most important, their ecological advantages. Reel mowers need no gas or electricity, they emit no exhaust, and they eliminate the need for having cans of gasoline on hand. Sales of reel mowers are highest in southern California, where strict emission standards for automobiles have caused people to consider other ways in which the air can be kept clean. But sales are expected to grow nationwide, as more people become environmentally aware.

Landscaping is an ongoing process. Among all households, 80 percent of households participated in one or more types of indoor and outdoor lawn-and-garden activities in 1990, according to the National Gardening Association (NGA). Landscaping is defined as the installation of new plant material, trees, shrubs, groundcovers, and vines for both original and renovational purposes. Landscaping does not include mowing, fertilizing, watering, weeding, or flower gardening.

Some 29 million households did landscaping in 1990, compared with 20 million households in 1989. Among householders who landscape, three in four are married couples, and nearly half have children at home. Sixty percent of these householders are between the ages of 30 and 49, while the rest of the market is split between younger and older consumers. Suburbanites make up half of the market for landscaping, 40 percent are rural or small-town residents, and 10 percent are city dwellers.

The demand for landscaping rises with income, but fully 40 percent of landscapers have annual household incomes below $30,000. Householders who work in a profession or who are in business make up 51 percent of all landscapers; another one-third are employed as laborers.

Fifteen separate areas of lawn-and-garden activities are charted by the NGA

RAIN AND SHINE

It's a myth that April is the rainiest month across the nation.

(percent above or below average, number of days with precipitation in Peoria and El Paso)

■ Peoria

■ El Paso

JAN   FEB   MAR   APRIL   MAY   JUNE   JULY   AUG   SEPT   OCT   NOV   DEC

Source: The Statistical Abstract of the United States

annually. In 1990, householders spent an average of $284 on their lawns and gardens, according to the NGA. Retail sales for lawn care increased 13 percent, to $6.4 billion.

Flower gardening was also up, and retail sales of annual and perennial plants, seed, and fertilizers increased to $2.3 billion in 1990, from $1.9 billion in 1989. Increases in the number of households participating in vegetable gardening, flower-bulb growing, tree care, landscaping, fruit-tree cultivation, and other aspects of gardening—raising seedlings, container gardening, herb gardening, ornamental gardening, and berry growing—were also noted.

Sprucing up the lawn and garden for spring increases the value of a home. A recent survey conducted by the NGA demonstrated that while 62 percent of all single-family homeowners think that landscaping is a good or an excellent investment, 83 percent of those who have recently purchased a home think so.

Home buyers whose purchase decision is most influenced by landscaping are those who buy single-family houses that are 10 to 20 years old. These homes are most likely to be fully landscaped and not in need of landscape renovation. Buyers of newly built homes are less influenced by landscaping—primarily because 80 percent of new homes have little or no landscaping. On average, homebuyers estimate that landscaping contributed 15 percent to the value of their new home.

Because homebuyers value landscaping, homes that are landscaped have a sales advantage over those that are not. This advantage is especially critical for older homes on the market, but it is not limited to single-family owner-occupied homes. Condominium sales in Florida are linked to landscaping, which improves the market value of multifamily dwellings. Commercial developments such as hotels, office buildings, and shopping malls also profit from landscaping.

Sprouting Up

The number of organic gardeners grew by 4.5 million people between 1988 and 1990, according to a Harris Poll conducted for *Organic Gardening* magazine. Almost 31 percent of Americans grew fruits, vegetables, or herbs in 1990, up from 29 percent in 1988. The share of gardeners who shunned pesticides, herbicides, and synthetic chemical fertilizers leaped from 52 percent to over 60 percent.

Forty-five percent of organic gardeners avoid chemicals because of health and safety concerns. Even 60 percent of gardeners who do use chemicals say they are cutting down on pesticide use because of health concerns. More than 200 new all-natural products—from fish emulsion to sheep manure—are being marketed to the growing number of ecologically aware gardeners.

The most popular organic method is composting, now used by more than one-third of all gardeners. "It's the best way to improve the health and quality of your soil, and it recycles material that would otherwise have to be trucked to a landfill," says Mike McGrath, editor-in-chief of *Organic Gardening*.

Landscaping, lawn care, and gardening are climate-dependent enterprises. In areas of the country where drought conditions have persisted over the last few years, and in areas where dry springs and summers are typical, there is a move toward more environmentally conscious landscaping and gardening. Called xeriscaping (pronounced zir-a-scaping), this technique minimizes water use by emphasizing drought-resistant flora, efficient watering programs, and common sense.

Xeriscaping discourages the cultivation of ubiquitous turf grass, suggesting instead the use of drought-resistant grasses or chip beds. Xeriscaping first gained prominence in Denver, Colorado, where water officials in the late 1970s began to promote it in an attempt to cut down on water consumption. As more people become ecologically sensitive, this landscaping method will undoubtedly gain in popularity.

Forty percent of outdoor water used during the growing season goes towards irrigation. In some drought-stricken parts of the country, this water use is now regulated by local laws. Xeriscaping presents a sensible alternative to conventional landscaping in order to maintain a home's exterior appearance as well as a way of preventing topsoil erosion.

The ecology movement is changing the way people think about gardening, landscaping, and lawn care. But as long as people take pride in the places they live, this industry will continue to bloom.

SPRING CLEANING
■ ■ ■ ■ ■ ■ ■ ■ ■ ■ ■ ■

With the first breath of spring, millions of Americans throw open the windows and let the sun shine in. This move is quickly followed by a concerted effort to clean and polish all those dirty, dusty, and grimy surfaces that have suddenly come to light. Housekeeping products and services have undergone many technological changes, but the demographics of homemakers are changing even faster.

Cleaning Up

Homemakers are defined as those responsible for household shopping, according to Mediamark Research, Inc. of New York City. Over 100 million Americans are homemakers—there are more homemakers than households because some households have more than one person responsible for household shopping. One in five homemakers is a man.

Men are the fastest-growing segment of homemakers. In 1985, they accounted for 14 percent of all homemakers, but by 1989, they were 21 percent, according to Mediamark. Male homemakers differ dramatically from their female counterparts. They are younger than female homemakers, on average, and more likely to be single. Almost 46 percent are under the age of 35, compared with 34 percent of female homemakers. While 63 percent of female homemakers are married, only 23 percent of male homemakers are.

Other differences between male and female homemakers are equally telling. While 45 percent of female homemakers are employed full-time outside the home, 66 percent of male homemakers are. Among male homemakers, only 16 percent have children under age 18 at home. Forty-four percent of female homemakers have children.

Marketers of household cleaning products have been struggling to keep up with the changing needs of homemakers as more women enter the work force. Women homemakers who work outside the home buy fewer household cleaning products, on average, than those who do not work outside the home. The buying habits of these working women homemakers are similar to those of their male counterparts.

Most advertisements for cleaning products avoid the issue of women's employment. They show active women who could be either full-time homemakers or women in the work force. But few ads focus on men. "A lot of men care about household cleaning," says Judith Langer, president of Langer Associates in New York City. "But men don't have the guilt about cleaning that many women do. They're more impressed by a product's strength and effectiveness," she says.

The purchasing patterns of male homemakers show that the marketers of household cleaning products are not reaching these consumers. Female homemakers are twice as likely as male homemakers to be heavy users of household cleaners, glass cleaners, floor wax, toilet-bowl cleaners, and plastic garbage bags, according to

Mediamark. Female homemakers are also more likely than their male counterparts to buy housekeeping appliances, including washers, dryers, and vacuum cleaners.

Because men buy household cleaning products less frequently than women, one might expect them to be heavy users of household cleaning services, but this is not the case. Although the spending gap is small, women still outspend men on these services. Twelve percent of women homemakers use some type of cleaning service during the year, compared with 10 percent of male homemakers. Eight percent of women homemakers hire carpet cleaners, as opposed to 4 percent of male homemakers. Men do outspend women on one type of household cleaning service—maids and housekeepers. Six percent of male homemakers and 5 percent of female homemakers employ a housekeeper.

Only a few marketers have focused their advertising on male homemakers. One television commercial showed single men concerned about spotty glassware. Another ad showed a man using a vacuum cleaner that does everything except fetch the morning paper. But in order to get male homemakers to buy specific products, it may be necessary to adopt a more aggressive approach. Men may not weigh the pros and cons of any one specific cleaning product and may opt instead for a product with brand-name recognition. Because many men were not trained by their parents in housekeeping techniques, they may fail to understand how and when to use cleaning products. Advertisers who target male homemakers should remember that these customers need to be educated about product use and that they want products that are easy to use and efficient.

While household growth will be slow in the 1990s, delayed marriage, divorce, and the blurring of men's and women's roles will continue to spur rapid growth in the share of homemakers who do not fit the stereotypical image of the stay-at-home mom. Male homemakers and working female homemakers are the two segments that will make the difference in the 1990s. Advertisers who neglect their needs will fail to clean up in years to come.

Fixing Up

Spring cleaning can lead to more ambitious home projects. Many people take this time to spruce up and repair their homes, doing interior and exterior painting, carpentry, and even electrical and plumbing tasks. Not everybody is a do-it-yourselfer. Men are much more likely than women to undertake home improvements.

Differences lie not only in gender, but also in household income. Surprisingly, high-income people are more likely to be fixer-uppers than those with lower incomes. While 60 percent of those with household incomes between $30,000 and $50,000 undertake minor electrical repairs, only 36 percent of those with household incomes under $15,000 do, according to a 1991 Roper survey.

Half of adults with incomes between $30,000 and $50,000 paint the exterior of their homes, as do 48 percent of those with household incomes of $50,000 or more. But only 28 percent of people with household incomes of $15,000 or less paint the

FISHING—FOR CUSTOMERS

WITH ALL THE home improvements that spring inspires, the household handyman may occasionally seek escape. April 1 marks the opening of trout-fishing season in New York State. Overnight, sleepy little back roads in central New York turn into massive parking lots for nature-starved downstaters.

One of the most popular fishing areas is the quiet Catskills town of Livingston Manor. Here, fishermen can visit the Catskill Fly Fishing Center and Museum, a 35-acre site on the Willowemoc River that displays row after row of meticulously hand-tied flies, rods, reels, and other fishing memorabilia. The center offers courses in entomology, water testing, acid rain, stream improvements, and fly-fishing techniques, as well as educational programs for anglers between the ages of 8 and 18. The crowds around Livingston are less seasonal than in some places because this part of the state contains "no-kill" fishing areas—areas where fishing is permitted year-round, but anglers may not keep their catch. It's the sport that draws many people to the mountains, not their taste for trout almondine.

"They come up just to go through the ritual," says Robert Bach of the Little Store, a sports supply store in Roscoe, New York. Bach believes that fly fishing has become the "in thing to do." "It's more of a sport than worm fishing," he says. Along with the growing number of New York fishermen, Bach has noticed a lot more out-of-staters, Canadians, British, and Japanese visitors.

The number of active fishermen in the U.S. has more than doubled since 1960. That year, there were about 25 million active fishermen aged 12 and older, according to a national survey of outdoor sports compiled by the U.S. Department of the Interior, Fish and Wildlife Service (FWS) and the Department of Commerce. The number increased to 33 million in 1970, and by 1985, there were over 51 million fishermen aged 12 and older.*

About 86 percent of all fishermen ply their lines in fresh water, according to the 1985 FWS survey. Freshwater fishing accounted for some 734 million

*A new report with 1991 data is due in spring 1993.

fishing trips that year. Saltwater fishing accounts for 30 percent of all fishermen. About 14 million Americans aged 16 and older went fishing in salt water in 1985, accounting for 136 million fishing trips.

Total fishing expenditures in 1985 amounted to more than $28 billion. Of this, 48 percent was spent on equipment, while 47 percent went for trip-related expenses. The final 5 percent was spent on magazines subscriptions, membership dues and contributions, land leasing and ownership, and licenses, stamps, tags, and permits.

The trip-related costs of fishing expeditions provide a seasonal boom for local economies. In 1985, $5.7 billion, or 20 percent of total fishing expenditures, went for food and lodging. Another $3.7 billion (13 percent of the total) went for transportation, while $3.9 billion, or 14 percent, was spent on guide fees, equipment rental, and other trip costs.

Fishing is a sport that appeals to both men and women. In 1985, 37 percent of men and 16 percent of women aged 16 and older went fishing. Of these active anglers, the largest share (49 percent) were aged 25 to 44. Fishing enthusiasm cuts across income lines, although the rates are highest for those living in households with above-average annual incomes. Just 17 percent of those in the lowest household income groups fish. The share of anglers in other income groups ranges from 24 to 31 percent.

The profile of a typical fisherman is hard to capture, because each type of fishing has a different character and feeling, as well as a different type of sports enthusiast. Saltwater fishermen are an entirely different breed from fly-fishermen. And "bait-and-reel-fishers"—fresh-water fishermen who use lures or bait instead of flies—are yet another group.

While all three types of fishing are almost equally popular among people aged 25 to 34, saltwater fishing is much more popular among mature adults, according to a 1990 survey from American Sports Data (ASD) of Hartsdale, New York. Slightly more than 16 percent of adults aged 55 to 64 saltwater fish at least 25 days annually, while only 5 percent are active fly-fishermen. Only 3 percent of people aged 65 or older fly fish, while 12 percent fish in saltwater.

Saltwater fishermen also tend to be more affluent than their freshwater counterparts. Twenty-two percent of saltwater fishermen have annual household incomes of $50,000 or more, compared with 11 percent of fly-fishermen and 13 percent of rod-and-reel fishermen, according to the 1990 ASD figures. Saltwater fishing could experience a giant boost as the baby-boom generation moves into its most affluent years, the time of life when saltwater fishing is most popular.

The future of saltwater fishing depends on more than demographics. The rising cost of fuel and equipment is making this sport more expensive than ever. Government regulations are also making it increasingly difficult for sportsmen and women to bring home the trophies they desire. But saltwater fishermen, like their freshwater counterparts, may be increasingly likely to participate simply for the sport itself, and content themselves with photographs of their catch to relive the memories.

Fishing is a relaxing way to pass the first warm April afternoon, and the first fishing expedition leads to many more trips throughout the spring and summer, fishing, relaxing with friends at the end of the day, and talking about the one that got away.

outside of their homes themselves—perhaps because they are less likely to own their homes. The same pattern holds true of interior painting.

Few of those surveyed undertook any major household repairs—big plumbing jobs or major electrical wiring projects. Well-educated men in upper-income brackets are generally the most likely to do all types of home repair. Perhaps these men see home repair tasks as a way to relax, or maybe they have better skills and equipment to help them get the job done.

Remodeling is becoming more popular as people decide to renovate their present homes rather than move to more costly ones. The businesses that used to cater to professional builders and contractors are now trying to meet the needs of weekend do-it-yourselfers. "You couldn't survive if you concentrated on the builder," notes Robert Sheehan, owner of Regis J. Sheehan Associates, a McLean, Virginia-based management market research consulting firm. "The big building-supply chains have gone to the consumers."

The ten most popular remodeling jobs, ranked by dollar volume, are kitchens, bathrooms, window replacement, carpeting, air-conditioning installation, re-shingling roofs, basement finishing, heating-system replacements, siding replacements, and sunroom additions, according to *Remodeling* magazine. Exterior and interior painting, wallpapering, landscaping, carpeting, bathrooms, air conditioning, window coverings, window replacements, re-shingling roofs, and kitchen remodeling are the most popular jobs ranked by the number of units remodeled.

Residential remodeling expenditures are not solely dependent on household growth. They are influenced by per capita income, the age of housing stock, home values, home equity, and the impact of weather on structures. Despite slow population growth in the Northeast, that area of the country accounts for the largest share of residential remodeling expenditures—29 percent. The housing stock in the Northeast is the oldest in the nation—half of homes were built before 1950. The second-largest share of the remodeling dollar, 20 percent, is spent in the West, where the housing stock is the youngest. Half of western homes were built after 1967. Recent movers often paint and do larger remodeling jobs in order to make their new houses more like homes.

FINANCES AND TAXES
■■■■■■■■■■■■■■■

For many Americans, April is a month fraught with financial anxiety. They begin the month worried and irritated about getting their tax forms completed. After the deadline, they remain worried and irritated because the true state of their finances has been revealed. Household finances are becoming more complex. Rising costs are forcing people to plan for their children's college educations before the children are even in kindergarten. Longer lives mean Americans must plan to spend more years in retirement. Changing lifestyles, dual-earner households, blended and broken families, and home-based businesses further challenge the family bookkeeper. Frequent changes in tax laws add to the confusion.

Adding Up

The number of Americans who dread filling out their tax forms is growing. In 1991, almost one in six people (16 percent) filed their taxes on April 15, according to a survey by Bruskin Goldring Research, a market research firm in Edison, New Jersey. Less than half of Americans (43 percent) filed their taxes more than one month before the deadline. Although the share of earlybirds has remained constant, only 9 percent filed at the last minute in 1983.

Between 1986 and 1989, the number of individual filers who hired someone to prepare their tax returns leaped from 48 million to nearly 53 million—about 48 percent of all filers. And today, consumers are turning to professionals for an even broader range of financial services.

In its projections for the year 2005, the Bureau of Labor Statistics (BLS) lists accountants and auditors among the occupations with the greatest expected job growth. There were 985,000 accountants and auditors in 1990. By 2005, the BLS expects over 1.3 million—a 34 percent increase. The number of financial managers, those who perform a broad range of financial services, is projected to increase from 701,000 to 894,000—a 28 percent gain, compared with 20 percent growth for all jobs in the U.S.

Though the financial planning profession has enjoyed growth in the 1970s and 1980s, a survey of planners certified by the International Board of Standards and Practices for Certified Financial Planners revealed a slump after the 1987 stock market crash. This survey, conducted by the College for Financial Planning in Denver, Colorado, showed that the median value of the average client's stock portfolio dropped 15 percent in the eight months after the 1987 crash. While this decline is considerably less than the 23 percent tumble for the overall market, 80 percent of planners' incomes are typically derived from commissions. A drop in client income quickly hits home.

But bad press may be more damaging to the industry than a bear market. Over the past few years, the media have been rife with stories about planners skipping town with their clients' life savings. Investment advisors are required to register with the Securities and Exchange Commission. However, advisors do not have to take any tests or meet any requirements to register with the commission.

On the other hand, the certification of financial planners, although it is optional, requires testing, and members can lose their certification if they do not live up to a strict code of ethics. Many professionals concerned with their image are calling for required licensing. Certified financial planner (C.F.P.), registered financial planning practitioner, and chartered financial consultant (Ch.F.C.) are all titles that identify qualified financial planners. But most Americans don't know this, and while some public relations efforts have been undertaken, there is no real marketing of the financial planning industry.

Demographic trends portend a bright future for the financial planning industry. Today, almost half of Americans are in the habit of going to a professional for tax advice, and the consumer segments most likely to want a broader range of financial services are growing.

Building Up

As a result of the poor quality of many loan portfolios, 206 commercial banks failed in 1989. The situation among thrifts is much worse. The Office of Thrift Supervision (OTS), the principal federal regulator of the largest segment of the savings institution industry, classifies savings banks based on their overall health, capital levels, and probability of survival. As of 1990, 244 savings institutions were either insolvent and awaiting placement or liquidation, in conservatorship, or expected to fail, according to the U.S. Industrial Outlook 1991. Another 350 exhibited significant weakness because of low capital and poor earnings.

While it is expected that commercial banks will continue to prosper in the years to come, albeit not without a certain amount of vigilance, many observers predict the disappearance of the savings institution industry within several years. Other economists feel that savings institutions specializing in residential finance can continue to be profitable. Savings institutions also make up the largest single investor in the secondary mortgage market, and as long as these mortgage loans are based on safe dependable securities acceptable to investors, thrifts will continue to turn a profit, according to some experts.

The public's loss of faith in banks and the banking system may influence the way in which people save money in the future. Some analysts are predicting a quick rebound in the savings rate as baby boomers hit the age of 45, but "this forecast ignores the slow pace of demographic change. Savers will peak as a share of the population after 2000, but their effect on the savings rate will be partly offset by the increase in the size of a very low-saving age group, those aged 65 and older. The effect of baby boomers reaching their peak saving years will be modest until the end of the 1990s and will not peak until 2010," says Geoffrey Greene, senior economist for DRI/McGraw-Hill, in Washington, D.C.

For many people, saving money means more than simply opening up a bank account, and it is for this reason that financial planning is considered a growth industry for the future. One investment area predicted to remain dependable is mutual funds. The phenomenal growth of mutual-fund investing of the 1980s will not be sustained, but slow and steady growth is anticipated, according to the *U.S. Industrial Outlook 1991*. Aging baby boomers will become valued clients for financial service firms that can assist people in saving and accumulating capital for their retirement.

Mutual funds are changing to meet the requirements of investors, many of whom have specific financial goals in sight. Banks and other financial institutions are also trying to keep their share of the investment dollar. As more Americans begin to consider their financial future, they realize the need to organize now to provide for the future. As more baby boomers reach middle age, the philosophical (and actual) "half-way point," they will realize the need to provide for themselves, their aging parents, and their college-age children. This is the right time for all aspects of the finance industry—from investment specialists and financial planners to the mutual-funds industry and commercial banks—to promote their services and products.

Growing Up

Even though mature consumers may be the most likely customers for financial advisors, young adults may be the most in need of their services. For college students, the credit crunch can start long before graduation. Campus-based financial counselors are finding that students use credit cards to pay for rent, groceries, and gasoline, as well as other essentials. Fifteen percent of 20-to-29-year-olds with college loans owe more than $10,000. Because many parents can't help their children cover all these expenses, college graduates sometimes leave school with a bad credit record.

As if that weren't bad enough, many college students are finding it difficult to get jobs. Two-thirds of the undergraduate class of 1991 left college without full-time employment, according to Challenger Gray & Christmas, a Chicago outplacement firm. Twenty-five percent of people in their 20s report being concerned about losing their jobs in the next year, according to a 1991 *Money* magazine poll. More than half (52 percent) say that they, their spouse, or one of their friends recently lost a job.

Owning a home may be out of the question for many people in this age group. Only 36 percent of householders aged 25 to 29 owned homes in 1991, compared with 44 percent in 1973. Many men and women in their 20s are forced to live with their parents rather than on their own.

Twenty percent of young people do not save or invest any of their income, according to *Money*. Thirty-nine percent of those who said they weren't good at managing their money said that the main reason was that they didn't know enough about finances. Many young people fear losing the American dream. They think they will never be financially able to obtain the quality of life their parents had.

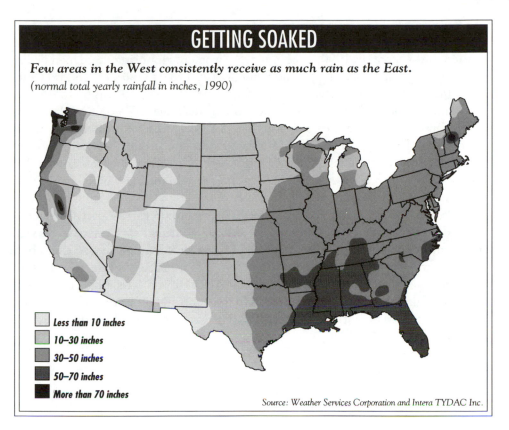

GETTING SOAKED

Few areas in the West consistently receive as much rain as the East.
(normal total yearly rainfall in inches, 1990)

Less than 10 inches
10–30 inches
30–50 inches
50–70 inches
More than 70 inches

Source: *Weather Services Corporation and Intera TYDAC Inc.*

Growing up and taking charge of the future means young adults must think about health insurance, homeowner's or tenant's insurance, life insurance, and a sound investment portfolio for retirement. "Taking control in your 20s helps assure you of emerging financially independent in your 40s and 50s," says Adriane Berg, author of *Your Wealthbuilding Years: Financial Planning for 18-to-38-Year-Olds*, published by Newmarket Press. For many of the twentysomething generation, the sound advice of a financial planner is essential.

APRIL SHOWERS
■■■■■■■■■■■

April showers herald the start of spring, the growing season, and the prelude to summer. It is a time to look ahead, financially, ecologically, and personally, to the near and the distant future. Although Earth Day has become a major event, many of April's other special days are dedicated to the environment, including Arbor Day and John James Audubon's birthday. April is also Keep America Beautiful Month. To take full advantage of longer and warmer days, Americans set their clocks ahead one hour on the last Sunday of the month.

Because April is an important time for reorganization, it is also an appropriate time to celebrate National Secretary's Day. There were almost 5 million secretaries in the United States in 1990; almost all were women. Honoring them has become an April tradition. Cards, flowers, and luncheons let these vital workers know they are valued members of the team.

Thomas Jefferson's birthday is a state holiday in Alabama. People in Maine and Massachusetts celebrate Patriots' Day in April. In New Hampshire, state offices close for Fast Day. In the late 1600s, this day was declared a day of prayer and fasting for the recovery of colonial Governor John Cutt. "Governor Cutt did not survive, but the holiday we know as Fast Day did," says Thomas Manning of New Hampshire's Bureau of Labor Relations.

Although the numbers are shrinking, a few southern states still celebrate Confederate Memorial Day. After the Civil War, the defeated southern states were not permitted to honor their dead on the national day of mourning, so they chose an alternate date to commemorate their own fallen heroes. While not all states picked the same date, April is the most common month for this regional observation.

April Fool's Day kicks off National Humor Month, but April is also National Anxiety Month. The truth about April lies somewhere between these two extremes.

MAY WEATHER
■■■■■■■■■■

When Sault Ste. Marie hits temperatures in the 60s, it's officially spring everywhere in the U.S.

	TEMPERATURE		PRECIPITATION	
	low	*high*	*inches*	*days*
Albuquerque, NM	48.6°F	79.9°F	0.46	4
Atlanta, GA	58.7	79.8	4.02	9
Bismarck, ND	42.0	67.7	2.23	10
Boise, ID	44.0	70.8	1.21	8
Boston, MA	50.0	67.0	3.52	12
Buffalo, NY	46.3	65.9	2.89	12
Burlington, VT	44.0	66.4	2.96	14
Charlotte, NC	57.2	79.1	3.64	10
Chicago, IL	48.1	70.0	3.15	11
Cleveland, OH	47.9	68.5	3.30	13
Dallas, TX	62.9	84.4	4.27	9
Denver, CO	43.6	70.7	2.47	11
Detroit, MI	46.7	69.4	2.77	11
Great Falls, MT	41.1	65.3	2.52	11
Honolulu, HI	70.2	84.8	1.21	7
Houston, TX	64.7	85.1	4.69	8
Indianapolis, IN	51.5	73.4	3.66	12
Jacksonville, FL	63.0	85.2	4.91	8
Juneau, AK	38.1	54.7	3.41	17
Los Angeles, CA	55.7	69.1	0.14	1
Memphis, TN	60.9	81.0	5.06	9
Miami, FL	71.9	85.1	6.53	10
Milwaukee, WI	44.7	64.8	2.66	12
Minneapolis, MN	47.6	69.4	3.20	11
Mobile, AL	64.8	84.9	5.46	8
New Orleans, LA	65.3	84.5	5.07	8
New York, NY	53.3	71.5	3.76	11
Norfolk, VA	57.2	75.7	3.75	10
Oklahoma City, OK	57.7	79.0	5.50	10
Omaha, NE	51.8	74.7	4.33	12
Philadelphia, PA	52.5	73.0	3.18	11
Phoenix, AZ	61.5	92.4	0.14	1
Portland, OR	46.4	66.9	2.08	12
Salt Lake City, UT	45.2	72.4	1.47	8
San Francisco, CA	49.3	66.3	0.32	3
Sault Ste. Marie, MI	38.3	61.0	2.90	11
Seattle, WA	46.0	64.0	1.58	10
St. Louis, MO	54.7	76.4	3.54	11
Washington, DC	56.1	75.9	3.48	11
Wichita, KS	54.6	77.1	3.91	11

Source: U.S. Department of Commerce, Bureau of the Census, Statistical Abstract of the United States 1991. Average daily minimum and maximum temperatures and average monthly precipitation were measured over a standard 30-year period.

MAY
RESURRECTION

Spring propels Americans into action. Everybody wants to be active and outdoors. It's time to look for bathing suits, jogging shoes, T-shirts, and tennis outfits. But those last few pounds have to go before people feel good enough about themselves to face a dressing-room mirror. Getting in shape is a major preoccupation in May.

Whether people are exercising for fun or for fitness is an important question for health-club owners and the manufacturers of sports equipment and clothing. And as Americans age, health and fitness become more important to businesses concerned about their employees and the cost of illness and disability.

Families celebrate Mother's Day by bringing Mom breakfast in bed, showering her with flowers and cards, taking her to dinner at a fancy restaurant, and giving her clothing and jewelry. As families become more extended and more complex, some kids find themselves with more than one mom.

SPORTS ACTIVITIES

There are two seasonal peaks in the fitness business, according to Judy Sheppard Missett, founder and CEO of Jazzercise in Carlsbad, California. "There's an upswing in January, after the holiday season, and another in May, when people begin to realize they're going to be seen in a bathing suit," she says.

MAY'S BEST BUYS

(items most likely to be on sale in May)

- Boys' clothing
- Housewares
- Handbags
- Men's clothing
- White goods

Source: DOLLAR$ENSE Magazine, *1987*

Health Kick

Although all sports, from horseshoe tossing to croquet, provide some level of exercise, there are seven activities that are primarily fitness-oriented: aerobic exercising, calisthenics, cycling, exercise walking, exercising with equipment, running/jogging, and swimming. In order to gain a fitness benefit, people must take part at least twice a week.

One in five adults participates in one of the seven activities twice a week or more, according to a 1987 survey conducted by the National Sporting Goods Association (NSGA). Women are slightly more likely to exercise frequently than men—22 percent of women exercise more than twice a week, compared with 18 percent of men. Women prefer to do aerobic exercise, exercise walk, and cycle. On the other hand, men exercise with equipment and jog more than women.

Education plays a key role in whether or not people exercise frequently. While 27 percent of women with a college diploma are frequent participants in one of the seven exercise activities, only 16 percent of women with less than a high school education are frequent participants, according to the NSGA data. Only 12 percent of men with less than a high school education participate frequently, while 24 percent of college graduates do.

Age is an important factor in determining both how much people exercise and what type of exercise program they participate in. Only 33 percent of adults aged 25 to 34 do not exercise even occasionally. This number increases to just over 40 percent for people aged 35 to 54. Fully 59 percent of people aged 55 and older do not take part in any of the seven fitness exercises even occasionally, according to the NSGA statistics. People who rarely exercise are likely to drop out completely in their older years. But because baby boomers are more committed to exercise than their parents were, this generation may continue their good fitness habits into old age.

This generation has health information that was not available before. They also have a different attitude about their own responsibility for their health. Baby boomers "feel they can do something about their health themselves," says Elaine Turner, a registered dietician at Clemson University's Department of Food Science. Exercising regularly is one way boomers have taken matters into their own hands.

The baby boom is approaching its middle years. After age 45, the average adult's health problems increase significantly. Out of 1,000 adults under age 45, 36 suffer from heart disease. Among 1,000 people aged 45 to 64, fully 119 are sufferers. The rates for high blood pressure, arthritis, and diabetes also increase dramatically after age 45, but baby boomers who are reaching this threshold are well aware of the dangers that await them and how exercise can help them cope with these problems. Even so, their choice of activities may change as they age.

Among those who exercise regularly, 48 percent of participants aged 55 and older exercise walk, while only about 19 percent of 25-to-34-year-olds do. On the other hand, 53 percent of participants aged 25 to 34 run or jog, compared with 8 percent of those aged 55 or older. Swimming is less polarized by age. About 26 percent of participants aged 25 to 34 swim frequently. For those aged 35 and older, the share grows to about 37 percent.

Exercising to maintain strength and endurance can be accomplished without stressing aging joints and muscles. Some makers of exercise equipment are targeting their low-impact solutions for older Americans. NordicTrack is marketing its products on the assumption that aging baby boomers will continue to exercise. Among the products it offers are a machine that simulates the actions of cross-country skiing, a rowing machine that increases cardiovascular fitness, and a "Fitness Chair," designed so arthritis sufferers can increase strength and maintain a good range of movement in their joints.

Some organizations target active older adults. The U.S. National Senior Sports Classic, a competitive event also called the Senior Olympics, involves more than 5,100 competitors at the national level. The games are played in June, but qualifying trials take place throughout most of the year. Athletes aged 55 and older participate in triathlon, basketball, cycling, tennis, track and field, volleyball and archery.

One of the corporate sponsors of the event, General Mills' Whole Grain Total cereal, launched a complete nutrition education program aimed especially at mature adults during the 1991 games. In McDonald's promotional materials for the 1991 games, the company stressed healthy eating, staying active, and job opportunities. In this way, McDonald's extended its "food, folks, and fun" ad campaign to include active older Americans.

For a generation that has grown up on burgers, fries, and pizza, change can be difficult. But fast-food restaurants are jumping on the Surgeon General's healthy eating guidelines and are meeting with approval from their customers.

It's no longer unusual to be able to order a salad at a burger restaurant. Nutritional information, including calories, percentage of calories from fat, and cholesterol amounts for all foods served at the restaurant, are available. When it introduced a 91 percent fat-free hamburger in April 1991, McDonald's positioned itself for a great spring health season.

The Bench Warmers

Nearly half of adults in households with children do not exercise even occasionally, compared with fewer than 30 percent of adults in childless households, says NSGA. Busy parents may find there are just not enough hours in the day to devote to fitness activities. Still, manufacturers of home exercise equipment may find this market promising, especially when the equipment comes at the right price and incorporates safety features. Health clubs that provide child care may also attract many adults who could not participate otherwise.

Time constraints and family responsibilities are not the only reasons people stay away from exercise. Embarrassment may be the main reason why overweight women don't exercise more, according to a 1989 survey published in the *Melpomene Journal*. The survey group was comprised of women with an average weight of 222 pounds.

Fifty-nine percent said they exercised vigorously just once a week or less. Although 33 percent exercised two to three times per week, less than 7 percent exercised more often. The reasons most commonly given for not exercising included fear of not doing well, fear of ridicule, a lack of time, and family obligations.

Older people may also shy away from exercise for similar reasons. They may be too embarrased to work out among young bodybuilders, suggests Tom Dybdahl of *Prevention* magazine. He thinks fitness centers should provide special programs for people aged 50 and older. While the share of people who exercise at all declines with age, older adults are one of the fastest-growing segments of exercise enthusiasts. "Older people who exercise are more concerned about feeling good than looking good," says Dybdahl.

Fitness is important for all people, especially for those who suffer from obesity, high blood pressure, and other medical problems. While the fitness craze is easily accessible to healthy Americans, it has only recently been aimed at people who need it most. In the past few years, a host of diet plans and exercise programs targeted specifically at heart-attack survivors, people with diabetes, and overweight adults have been introduced. Such programs usually include a comprehensive health makeover that aims to change a person's diet, exercise patterns, and psychological outlook.

"It's the age of consumer service," says Jazzercise's Judi Sheppard Missett. "We modify programs for the individual." Jazzercise provides junior classes for children and low-impact classes for older adults and people with special needs. Community-based fitness programs are the foundation of Missett's business, but she has also opened new sports centers complete with juice bars, clothing boutiques, sports equipment, and babysitting service. "We're upscaling," says Missett, "because that's the wave of the future."

When the seasonal customers arrive, Jazzercise is ready for them. "We try to educate them to the benefits of the program," says Missett. "We have a low dropout rate because we use state-of-the-art techniques and emphasize safety—plus, we entertain."

Springing into Action

May is the unofficial "season opening" for all kinds of sports activities, from bicycling and jogging to swimming and sailing. Even though there are some activities like swimming and tennis that can be done indoors year-round, there is a lot more incentive to participate when the weather is warm and beautiful.

Fully 77 percent of Americans consider outdoor recreation a priority, according to a 1991 poll by Peter Hart Research Associates for Recreation Roundtable in Washington, D.C. Fifty-two percent rate outdoor recreation opportunities as "very important," while 25 percent consider them "fairly important." Only 8 percent think outdoor recreation is "not at all important."

Americans love water sports, but women are more likely to swim, while men prefer fishing, according to a Gallup Poll conducted in 1990. While women like swimming, bicycling, bowling, fishing, and aerobics, men ranked fishing, swimming, bicycling, pool/billiards, and camping as their five favorite sports.

Sports and recreation is a $44 billion wholesale industry. Because of the softening economy, growth stagnated in 1989 and 1990, but industry analysts cite increases in certain segments. Wholesale sales of athletic footwear were up 9.6 percent, sports apparel increased 5.3 percent, and sports equipment grew 3.7 percent, according to figures released by the Sporting Goods Manufacturers Association (SGMA).

In 1990, wholesale bicycle sales increased 10 percent, to $1.1 billion, but sales in other recreational transportation categories were down for the second straight year. Pleasure-boat sales declined 19.4 percent to a wholesale figure of $6.4 billion, and recreational vehicle sales also declined 6 percent to $4.7 billion.

The economy is probably the biggest factor contributing to lower sales in such categories as boats and recreational vehicles. Big-ticket items lose their appeal in times of economic stress. Less expensive products such as athletic shoes and sports apparel, however, continue to show steady increases as people maintain their interest in health and fitness.

The Pace Setters

Some 33 million adults own a bicycle that they purchased new. But not all bike owners are created equal, according to a 1990 NFO study by National Family Opinion (NFO) Research. Sixty-nine percent of new bicycle owners are Infrequent Riders who ride only about 25 miles each month. Casual Riders ride about 31 miles each month and account for 21 percent of all new bicycle owners. Moving Up Riders are just 7 percent of new cycle owners, but they put about 83 miles on their bicyles during the month. Enthusiasts, people who average 207 miles of riding monthly, are less than 3 percent of all new bicycle owners. But the NFO study indicates that these small segments can be very important to marketers. Avid sports fans pay more for their equipment and make purchases more frequently than others. They also serve as advisors to others who are thinking about becoming more active in the sport.

The 10 percent of riders who are Enthusiasts and Moving Up Riders account for 83 percent of all new bicycle owners who paid $500 or more for their last bicycle. For one in three Enthusiasts and one in five Moving Up Riders, their last purchase was an additional bike for personal use. Only one in ten less frequent riders bought an additional bike. While Casual and Infrequent Riders are content with one general-purpose bicycle, Enthusiasts and Moving Up Riders have specialized bicycles for different types of activities—road use, racing, or use on rugged terrain.

Making a good impression on bicycling Enthusiasts is the key to survival in the bicycle business. These active riders are crucial because they often influence the purchasing patterns of others. Among new bicycle owners in general, only 14 percent say someone asked for their advice about buying a bicycle in the last year. But

BIKE RIDERS AND BIKE BUYERS

The peak season for bicycle riding is from April to October, but the season for buying is shorter and more intense.

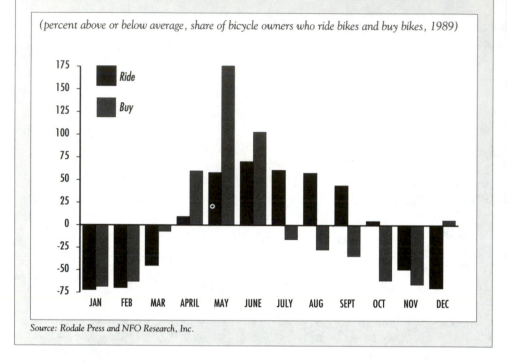

(percent above or below average, share of bicycle owners who ride bikes and buy bikes, 1989)

Source: Rodale Press and NFO Research, Inc.

57 percent of Enthusiasts say someone asked for their advice. Seventy-two percent of these Enthusiasts advised a friend or neighbor, and 40 percent gave advice to a business associate. Almost three-fourths of the Enthusiasts who gave advice said they sometimes recommended a specific brand.

Bicycle riders are customers not only for the cycle itself, but also for all the accessories that go along with it, from helmets and bike shorts to rain gear and cycling shoes. Presenting the customer with a full range of accessories and services is an important consideration for retailers. Forty-five percent of riders bought their last bike in a bicycle shop, but even more intend to make their next purchase in a shop that specializes in bicycles.

More than 80 percent of new bicycle owners bought them sometime between May and August. May and June are the peak months for buying new bikes, accounting for fully one-third of all bicycle sales to adults, according to the NFO survey.

Once active sports enthusiasts decide to buy, however, it may too late for marketers to make a sale. The shoppers may have already made up their minds based on the advertising they were exposed to over the winter months and the discussions they had with people they consider experts. According to NFO, almost 70 percent of adult riders who had a price in mind spent less than three months thinking about their purchase before they hit the store. About 40 percent took less than a month.

Once they got to the store, it didn't take long for the shoppers to become bicycle owners. About 85 percent of shoppers made their purchase in less than a month, and 30 percent took less than one day. When bike shoppers had a brand in mind before they entered a store, they bought that brand 80 percent of the time.

Adults participate in sports for the same reasons that children do. They think sports are fun, and they like to be part of the crowd. But unlike children, adults are aware of the important role sports play in staying fit. Seventy-seven percent of bicyclists ride to stay fit, according to NFO. Fitness is important not only to avid riders but also to those who are casual participants. While 89 percent of adults who cycle frequently say fitness is an important reason to ride, 75 percent of those who ride infrequently agree.

Never underestimate the importance of sports as social activities. Even though some sports, like bicycling, appear to be solitary, there is frequently a people factor that governs participation and purchases. Fully 48 percent of new bicycle owners say that bicycling is important to them as a family activity, and 46 percent say they would ride more if they had someone to ride with. More than one-third of owners say friendly service is important to them when they go to purchase a bike.

SPORTS CLOTHING
■ ■ ■ ■ ■ ■ ■ ■ ■ ■ ■ ■

Athletic clothing is not just for athletes any more. It started with sweatsuits. At first, they were baggy gray outfits worn by runners, joggers, and boxers in training. Today, sweatsuits are seen everywhere from grocery stores to nightclubs. Color-coordinated and decorated with everything from textile paint to sequins, sweatsuits are now high fashion. Sweatsuit fabric is used for other garments, like children's and women's clothes. Bicycle pants, running shorts, spandex tights, and leg warmers have all successfully made the transition from the gym to city streets.

The Sporty Look

Less than 13 percent of total sports-apparel purchases ($3.5 billion) went for clothing bought exclusively for active sports use. The rest went for clothes to wear on the golf course, the aerobics studio, or the shopping mall. In 1991, retail dollar sales of sports apparel reached $28 billion, up 4 percent from 1990, according to the Sporting Goods Manufacturers Association (SGMA).

The most popular outlets for sports-apparel purchases are discount stores, accounting for about 26 percent of 1990 sales. Department stores accounted for another 21 percent. Chain stores like Foot Locker and Athletic Attic captured a 14 percent share, and locally owned sporting-goods stores accounted for only 11 percent of sales.

"Consumers haven't cut back on purchases of sports apparel, even though the economy is in a major slump," announces the SGMA. Men's sports clothing showed the greatest gains in 1991, almost 6 percent. Clothing used specifically for sports activities was especially popular.

What Ever Happened to Sneakers?

Just as jogging suits have become acceptable fashion statements, so too has athletic footwear. But sales of athletic footwear are slowing; their 1990 increase of less than 10 percent was the smallest gain since 1984, according to SGMA figures. In 1991, sales fell 1.5 percent. Even so, the U.S. market hit $12 billion when retailers sold 388 million pairs of athletic shoes in 1991.

Price was a major concern for consumers buying athletic shoes in late 1990. During the last four months of the year, 61 percent of all athletic shoes were bought on sale, compared with 58 percent during the same time period in 1989. Discount stores accounted for the largest share of sales; fully 29 percent of athletic shoes were bought at stores like Kmart. Shoe stores (excluding specialized athletic-shoe stores) and department stores each accounted for 11 percent of sales. Slightly more than 9 percent of athletic shoes were purchased at sporting-goods stores, while just 6 percent were bought at specialized athletic-shoe stores.

Only 9 percent of athletic footwear is designated "for sports usage only." That leaves about 358 million pairs of shoes to be worn for all those nonspecific sports activities—running for the bus, dashing after kids, shopping, walking to work, dancing, and even strolling along on a beautiful May day.

Bathing Suit Time

If swimming is the number-one sport among American women, buying a new swimsuit must be the number-one anxiety. The fear of being seen in a too-revealing bathing suit is common among women over the age of puberty. Until recently, fashion designers encouraged these skimpy and revealing swimsuits. Bathing-suit sales in general depend on the youth market, since young people are the most active sports enthusiasts. But older sports participants also want to have a say in bathing-suit designs, and they are looking for coverage, not courage, when it comes to wearing the latest fashions.

Both high-fashion names and the more anonymous catalog designers have been presenting swimsuits that flatter a wide range of figure types. "Suits that conceal more than they reveal" were touted as 1989's answer to the skimpy looks of the early 1980s. Direct merchandisers, such as the Dodgeville, Wisconsin-based Lands' End, revamped their swimwear lines in 1990 to address the needs of a wider variety of customers, from young active swimmers to more mature women.

The women most able to afford expensive swimwear are the ones least likely to want to be seen in a suit that was designed with an 18-year-old in mind. Women aged 18 to 24 weigh 132 pounds, on average, according to the National Center for Health

CINCO DE MAYO

F OR MEXICANS, May is a very special time of year. Because mothers are venerated for the central role they play in family life, Mother's Day is a very important holiday. In Mexico, May 1st is Labor Day and May 15th is the Feast of San Isidro Labrador, the patron saint of farmers. But one Mexican holiday in particular has crossed the Rio Grande to become one of the most popular spring festivals in the American Southwest.

Cinco de Mayo (the Fifth of May) celebrates the Mexican victory over the French at the Battle of Puebla in 1862. Mexican Americans celebrate with mariachi music, folk dancing, and bazaars of arts and crafts and traditional foods. Fiestas are held in many cities with large Mexican-American populations—most notably in Arizona, California, Colorado, Texas, and New Mexico.

Fiestas, fairs, and other celebrations are perfect vehicles for marketing to Hispanics, according to Chester Swenson, president of Marketing and Financial Management Enterprises in Los Angeles, California. Some 30 food and beverage companies sponsor more than 100 celebrations and fund-raising activities in Mexican communities in Texas and California, he says. Among the sponsors are Mount Gay Rum, Simpatico Beer, and Albertson Food Stores.

The 1990 census counted more than 22 million Hispanic Americans, a 53 percent increase over the 1980 count. By 2010, Hispanics are expected to surpass blacks as the nation's largest minority group. In order to reach this important market effectively, marketers must realize that Hispanics are a very diverse group, says Swenson. The Hispanic market consists of about 20 distinct submarkets, each with its own cultural, racial, and linguistic differences.

People of Mexican origin make up the largest share of Hispanics Americans—60 percent. Although Mexican Americans live throughout the U.S., they are most highly concentrated in the southwestern states from Texas to California. People of Puerto Rican origin make up the next largest Hispanic group, 12 percent. Puerto Ricans dominate the Hispanic-American population in the New York metropolitan area. While they are the majority of Hispanics in south Florida, Cubans are only 5 percent of all Hispanic Americans. Fully 23 percent of Hispanic Americans are "other" Hispanics, who come from Spain as well as South and Central America.

While the U.S. population grew 10 percent during the 1980s, the Mexican-American population increased 54 percent. Puerto Ricans grew 35 percent and Cubans grew 30 percent. The mixed group called "other Hispanics" grew the fastest—67 percent.

With a median age of 39, Cubans are the oldest Hispanics, according to the Census Bureau's 1990 Current Population Survey (CPS). Mexicans are the youngest, with a median age of 24. Fully 20 percent of Cubans aged 25 and older, have attended four or more years of college. The share slips to 15 percent for "other" Hispanics, 10 percent for Puerto Ricans, and 5 percent for Mexicans.

Median household income for all Hispanic Americans was $22,000 in 1989, according to the CPS. At $28,000, Cubans had the highest median. The median for "other" Hispanics was also above average, at about $24,000. The median for Mexican Americans was below average, at $21,000. Puerto Ricans had the lowest median income, $19,000.

Speaking of Hispanics

While nearly all Hispanics speak Spanish, half of Mexican Americans say they cannot easily understand Cubans, Puerto Ricans, or Central Americans, according to Swenson. Even though most Hispanics prefer to speak Spanish at home, 80 percent of Mexican-born permanent residents speak at least some English, and 90 percent of first-generation U.S.-born Mexican Americans speak English well, says Swenson.

Upwardly mobile Hispanics use English in their business and professional lives. While English-language media appeal to this segment of the market, many Hispanics who have just immigrated to the U.S. rely on Spanish-language media as their primary source of information.

A majority of Hispanics think or speak in Spanish in common day-to-day situations—having fun at a party, singing in the shower, gossiping with friends, praying, thinking in moments of privacy, and watching television alone—according to a 1990 Hispanic Monitor survey by Market Development, Inc. of San Diego, California. "Cross-culturally, advertising is more effective when it taps internal drives via the language in which those drives are most spontaneously expressed. This research on situational language usage demonstrates that, for the majority of Hispanics, that language is Spanish," says Dr. Roger S. Sennott, general manager of Market Development.

The number of Spanish-language television stations, newspapers, magazines, and radio stations has increased steadily since the early 1980s. Since 1983, the number of television stations carrying Hispanic programs has increased from 46 to 102. Spanish-language newspapers have risen from 94 to

158, and magazines have increased from 121 to 211. Spanish radio stations have almost doubled from 371 to 661, according to figures released in 1990 by the North Palm Beach, Florida-based Sporting Goods Manufacturers Association.

Nearly seven in ten Hispanics own a VCR, and one-third have cable television, according to Market Segment Research (MSR) of Coral Gabels, Florida. MSR's Fall 1990 Hispanic Product Usage Study focused on 5 key markets: Los Angeles, New York City, Miami, San Antonio, and Chicago. Even among Hispanics who speak Spanish almost exclusively, two-thirds own VCRs.

Credit-card usage varies among the different markets. Half of Hispanics interviewed in Miami use major credit cards, compared with only 18 percent in Chicago. In general, however, credit-card usage is predominant among more acculturated Hispanics. Over half of bilingual Hispanics use credit cards, versus less than 25 percent of Hispanics who rely on Spanish.

Grocery-store purchases reflect the cultural differences between Hispanics and other populations. Frozen entrées are purchased by only 14 percent of Hispanics. The MSR study suggests that newly arrived Hispanic immigrants may not be familiar with frozen entrées and the convenience they offer. Unfamiliarity with products is one aspect of retailing that merchants must deal with.

In order to target the Mexican-American market on Cinco de Mayo, McDonald's introduced chicken fajitas at the end of April 1991. But even as the Hispanic population grows, the market for Hispanic products is expanding to the rest of the population. About 33.5 million women served Mexican food at home in 1990, up nearly 20 percent from 1985, according to *The Lempert Report/ Mediamark Research, Inc.*

Statistics. But women aged 35 to 44 weigh an average of 148 pounds. This weight gain is just one sign that middle-aged women have more than fashion on their minds. Almost three-quarters of baby-boom women are mothers. Two in five have attended college; 75 percent are working. These women want more fashion choices and fewer dictates from the fashion industry. Considering the appeal of swimming as a sport for women of all ages, bathing suits are a good place to make a stand.

MOTHER'S DAY

Since 1914, Mother's Day has been celebrated annually on the second Sunday in May. Mother's Day is big business today. Eighty-five percent of American women are mothers by their 45th birthday. The average woman has had at least two children by then, and that adds up to a lot of cards, flowers, and candy.

A Time for Mother

Just over 1 million women give birth to their first child each year, a number that will decline as baby-boom women age out of their peak childbearing years. But the increasing numbers of adoptions, stepmothers, single parents, working women, and alternate caretakers are changing the Mother's Day market.

Only one married couple in six included a stepchild or an adopted child in 1980. By mid-decade, the number grew to one in five, according to the Census Bureau. During the 1980s, the number of unmarried women heading households with children under the age of 18 grew almost twice as fast as all families. Fewer than 40 percent of mothers with infants worked outside the home in 1980; more than half are at work today.

Birth mothers are now only part of a larger Mother's Day market, which includes other relatives and caregivers. Blended families have created a need to celebrate new emotional bonds. Working mothers want to acknowledge the role other women play in rearing their children. Understanding how changes in the American family affect buying behavior is critical to marketing Mother's Day.

Nearly 60 percent of adults in the U.S. send Mother's Day greetings, according to a 1986 report from the Roper Organization. But changes in the American family have made different messages essential. Each year, Hallmark Cards of Kansas City, Missouri, releases 1,200 different versions of Mother's Day cards, but only 25 percent of the designs are aimed at just plain "mom." The others have no specific titles or are addressed to aunts, stepmothers, grandmothers, great-grandmothers, sisters, friends, and other motherlike figures. There is even a group of Mother's Day cards for widowed, divorced, or single dads who have stepped into a mother's role.

"The concept of Mother has become generic rather than specific," says Renee Hershey, spokesperson at Hallmark Cards. "What is being celebrated is nurturing and caregiving." Hershey points out that there are cards to cover every conceivable situation, including socially awkward relationships that don't fit the traditional maternal image. Included are greetings addressed to "My Father's New Wife" and cards to send to a mother who was never close. There are even Mother's Day cards for the mother-to-be.

Many Mother's Day wishes are also delivered by phone. After Christmas, Mother's Day is the biggest day for placing long-distance phone calls, according to Robin Sayre, public relations manager for AT&T. In 1990, 84.1 million calls crossed the AT&T network on Mother's Day, compared with 60 million calls on an average Sunday. And in 1991, calling on Mother's Day hit an all-time high, with nearly 90 million long-distance phone calls going through the AT&T system.

Gifts from the Heart

Five out of six adults send a card, give a gift, or take someone out for a meal on Mother's Day, according to a 1986 Roper Report. Those younger than age 30 are most likely to do one of these things. Only 5 percent of those under age 30 completely ignore the holiday. That share doubles for people aged 30 to 44 and quadruples for people aged 45 to 59. Observing Mother's Day is least likely among older adults, many of whom do not have a living mother. Still, the majority of adults aged 60 or older give a card, gift, or dinner to someone on Mother's Day.

Almost 90 percent of householders with above-average incomes spend money for a Mother's Day card, gift, or meal, according to the Roper Organization. Participation is average—83 percent—for those with moderate incomes. But only 72 percent of householders with low incomes buy cards, gifts, or dinners. Married people are more likely than average to spend on Mother's Day—especially dual-earner couples. Ninety-three percent of households with children under age 18 buy cards, gifts, or dinners.

The type of Mother's Day gift depends on the giver's household income. About 34 percent of households with incomes of $35,000 or more buy flowers, compared with only 18 percent of households with incomes below $15,000, says the Roper Organization. But high-income people are only slightly more likely than those with low incomes to give candy (8 percent versus 6 percent). Regardless of income, about one in five adults takes someone out for lunch or dinner on Mother's Day.

After birthdays, Mother's Day is the most popular occasion for eating out, according to a 1990 survey released by the National Restaurant Association (NRA) in Washington, D.C. Thirty-nine percent of respondents ate out on Mother's Day. The holiday is family-oriented. Mothers with large families are most likely to get a respite from kitchen duty, with adults in households of five or more people reporting the highest incidence of restaurant visits on Mother's Day (46 percent). Forty-one percent of people in three-or-four-person households go out to eat, as do 37 percent of those in two-person households. Even 33 percent of people who live alone go out to eat on Mother's Day; many are probably elderly widows whose adult children take them out.

Retail and supermarket florists are also busy on Mother's Day. For supermarket floral departments, it is the busiest day of the year, generating an average of $8,120, according to a 1989 survey of supermarket floral retailing by the Newark, Delaware-based Produce Marketing Association and the Food Marketing Institute of Washington, D.C. Average weekly sales for the year were just $1,920.

Flowers pop up everywhere on Mother's Day, from street-corner vendors to variety stores, making it almost impossible for anyone to forget Mother's Day. Flowers are now for sale through computer-based shopping networks. PC Flowers, in operation since 1990, allows its customers to access the FTD (Floral Transworld Delivery) network and order arrangements that can be sent anywhere in the world. There is even a national flowers-by-phone service, 1-800-FLOWERS, that sends reminders to its customers.

Mothers may be many things to many people. In an era when the American family is in a state of flux, with divorces and remarriages becoming more common-place, it is important to maintain a sense of family. The unifying force, especially in families with children, is the mother figure. As a rallying point for the family, Mother's Day can only grow in importance in the years to come.

The Quest for Kids

While Mother's Day is celebrated in the majority of households throughout the country, there are families for whom the day can be a painful reminder of childlessness. Infertility has been at the forefront of media reports over the last few years. But has it reached epidemic proportions in the United States? Some media sources have said that as many as one in six American couples is infertile. But this figure is greatly exaggerated, according to the National Center for Health Statistics (NCHS).

The truth is that the number of couples with fertility impairments has not grown. What's changed is that the number of couples who seek medical solutions for this problem is rising.

Physicians define infertility as the inability of a couple to conceive after a year or more of intercourse without contraception. In 1988, 2.3 million married women between the ages of 15 and 44 reported that they fit this description. That's about 1 in every 13 married couples in which the wife is of childbearing age. This proportion is slightly lower than in 1982 (1 in 12) and is significantly lower than the 1965 estimate (1 in 9).

Since 1965, the infertility experience has changed dramatically. In-vitro fertilization, artificial insemination, surrogate motherhood, and other new technological solutions have brought the public's attention to the problem. The number of women who sought treatment and advice on infertility within the last year climbed 24 percent between 1982 and 1988, to more than 1.3 million.

Because so many women postponed childbirth in the 1980s, the number of childless women aged 35 to 44 who report having difficulty getting pregnant grew from 305,000 in 1976 to 408,000 in 1982 and 418,000 in 1988. But the share of women in this age group who experienced difficulty conceiving has dropped, from over half in 1976 to less than 40 percent today. Fertility rates are rising rapidly among women in their mid-to-late 30s, according to Martin O'Connell, a fertility specialist at the Census Bureau.

This is little comfort for those who cannot conceive. With all the media coverage of infertility issues, most people shy away from what used to be a standard conversational question: "And how many children do you have?" People are afraid to ask if a couple's childlessness is the result of choice or reproductive problems. Women, more than men, feel that this is too personal a question, according to a 1991 Associated Press poll.

People generally believe that remaining childlessness is a couple's choice—67 percent of women and 70 percent of men assume this to be true. But 57 percent of women and 63 percent of men believe that most married couples would be happier if they had children. The only group that is less likely to agree are people between

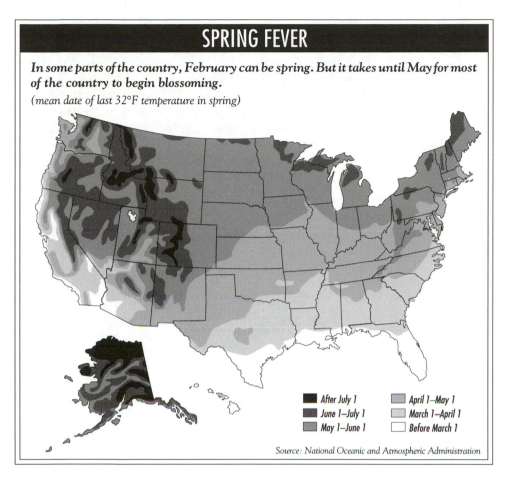

SPRING FEVER

In some parts of the country, February can be spring. But it takes until May for most of the country to begin blossoming.

(*mean date of last 32°F temperature in spring*)

■ After July 1   ▨ April 1–May 1
▨ June 1–July 1   ▨ March 1–April 1
▨ May 1–June 1   □ Before March 1

Source: National Oceanic and Atmospheric Administration

the ages of 35 and 44—the very group that is most likely to be in the midst of parenting themselves. Only 54 percent of this group think parenting can make people happy. Twenty-five percent say "it depends," and 11 percent believe children don't make a marriage happier.

MAY DAYS
■ ■ ■ ■ ■ ■ ■

May is American Bike Month and National Physical Fitness and Sports Month. It's also Older Americans' Month and National Photo Month. The State of Missouri honors Harry S. Truman this month. With expectations of more than 500,000 sales, Hallmark introduced cards for National Nurses' Day in 1992.

    The premier horse-racing event in America, the Kentucky Derby, is run on the first Saturday in May. The Run for the Roses has become a major media and money-generating event. The number of corporate sponsors of the event increased to 324 in 1991 from 75 in 1978, according to the Kentucky Derby Festival, Inc., which has an annual operating budget of $2.5 million.

The Kentucky Derby generates about $100 million in revenues for the City of Louisville, and the organizers use Derby Week to promote the city and state to corporate investors from around the world. About 137,000 people attended the Derby in 1991. For the millions who couldn't get there that year, there was still the option of fixing up a few mint juleps, putting on a straw hat, and settling down in front of the TV. About 13 million people watched the race on television in 1991.

May also has its serious side. On May 30, 1868, Americans first observed Memorial Day by decorating the graves of Northern soldiers killed in the Civil War. After World War I, veterans began selling artificial poppies as a reminder of the poppies that grew on French battlefields. Today, Memorial Day is officially observed on the last Monday in May with parades to local cemeteries, where the war dead are honored with wreaths and 21-gun salutes.

PART 5

SUMMER

AT LAST

Summer's here, and consumers are into having a good time. But marketers should not forget that a lot of joyous events associated with summer—graduations, job changes, weddings, and travel—can also burden consumers with stress when they most want to enjoy themselves.

JUNE WEATHER
■ ■ ■ ■ ■ ■ ■ ■ ■ ■

By June, most American cities are experiencing temperatures in the 70s and 80s, and many are experiencing much higher temperatures.

	TEMPERATURE		PRECIPITATION	
	low	*high*	*inches*	*days*
Albuquerque, NM	58.4°F	90.6°F	0.51	4
Atlanta, GA	65.9	85.6	3.41	10
Bismarck, ND	51.8	76.8	3.01	12
Boise, ID	51.8	79.8	0.95	6
Boston, MA	59.3	76.6	2.92	11
Buffalo, NY	56.4	75.6	2.72	11
Burlington, VT	54.0	75.9	3.64	13
Charlotte, NC	64.7	85.2	3.57	10
Chicago, IL	57.7	79.4	4.08	10
Cleveland, OH	57.2	78.0	3.49	11
Dallas, TX	70.8	93.2	2.59	6
Denver, CO	52.4	81.6	1.58	9
Detroit, MI	56.3	79.0	3.43	10
Great Falls, MT	49.4	74.3	2.75	12
Honolulu, HI	71.9	86.2	0.49	6
Houston, TX	70.2	90.9	4.06	9
Indianapolis, IN	60.9	82.3	3.99	10
Jacksonville, FL	69.1	88.9	5.37	12
Juneau, AK	44.2	61.1	2.98	16
Los Angeles, CA	59.1	72.0	0.04	1
Memphis, TN	68.9	88.4	3.58	8
Miami, FL	74.6	87.3	9.15	15
Milwaukee, WI	54.7	75.0	3.59	11
Minneapolis, MN	57.7	78.5	4.07	12
Mobile, AL	70.8	90.2	5.07	11
New Orleans, LA	70.9	89.5	4.63	11
New York, NY	62.7	80.1	3.23	10
Norfolk, VA	65.3	83.2	3.45	9
Oklahoma City, OK	66.3	87.6	3.87	9
Omaha, NE	61.7	84.2	4.08	10
Philadelphia, PA	61.5	81.7	3.92	10
Phoenix, AZ	70.6	102.3	0.17	1
Portland, OR	52.2	72.7	1.47	9
Salt Lake City, UT	53.3	83.3	0.97	5
San Francisco, CA	52.0	69.6	0.11	1
Sault Ste. Marie, MI	46.7	70.1	3.26	11
Seattle, WA	51.1	69.2	1.38	9
St. Louis, MO	64.3	85.2	3.73	9
Washington, DC	65.0	84.0	3.35	9
Wichita, KS	64.7	87.4	4.06	9

Source: U.S. Department of Commerce, Bureau of the Census, Statistical Abstract of the United States 1991. Average daily minimum and maximum temperatures and average monthly precipitation were measured over a standard 30-year period.

JUNE
RITES OF PASSAGE

The school year is finally over. High school graduates plan one last summer without the responsibilities of college, a civilian job, or a military commitment. College seniors relax after their exams, preparing for careers, marriage, or both. Parents are packing their children's camp clothes and thinking about a vacation for themselves. Many people are moving to new homes, new cities, and new lives. It's summer, and while those long days of relaxation and fun are just around the corner, the next four weeks promise to be exciting, busy, and stressful.

June's rites of passage—graduation, marriage, and moving—can generate a great deal of income for many retail segments. But even though the weather is beautiful this month, the emotional climate is stormy. Joyous events, such as proms, new jobs, and weddings, are fraught with anxieties. For young people, these may be the first independent decisions they have had to make. Planning this summer's events in consultation with partners and family generates tension. And everyone believes their special occasion deserves special attention from the businesses that serve them.

Despite summer hassles, some people can't help but feel nostalgic around this time of year. Almost everyone has fond memories of a graduation ceremony, a

JUNE'S BEST BUYS

(items most likely to be on sale in June)

- Beds
- Building materials
- Floor coverings
- Frozen foods
- Furniture
- Lingerie
- Luggage
- Storm windows and doors
- Summer sportswear
- Toys
- Typewriters
- TV sets
- Wallpaper
- Women's shoes

Source: DOLLAR$ENSE Magazine, 1987

summer love, or a new home, and advertisers can spark these memories with the warm images of June.

HIGH SCHOOL GRADUATION
■ ■ ■ ■ ■ ■ ■ ■ ■ ■ ■ ■ ■ ■ ■ ■ ■ ■ ■

Teenagers on the brink of adulthood face major life decisions concerning higher education, employment, marriage, family, and life goals. These young people may know what they want, but their dreams are not necessarily the ones championed by their parents.

Growing Expectations

Young people today don't see work as a life goal, but as a way to obtain material possessions, say Eileen M. Crimmins, Richard A. Easterlin, and Yasuhiko Saito of the University of Southern California, Los Angeles. Only one in three members of the high school class of 1986 envisaged work as a central part of their lives, according to a survey on the attitudes of high school seniors. Fully one in four students surveyed said that they would not work if they had enough money to live in comfort. One in five teenagers were looking for jobs that provide more than two weeks of paid vacation yearly.

Teenagers have very clear ideas about what they want. Some of these things are aids to family and child-rearing, like two cars, a big yard, and labor-saving devices, but others are strictly luxury goods. Clothes in the latest style, a new car every two or three years, a high-quality stereo system, a vacation home, and a motor-powered recreational vehicle have become increasingly desirable.

Today's young men and women are more interested than ever in marrying and having a family—but not necessarily in the near future. The share of male high school seniors who expected to marry increased from less than 70 percent in 1976 to almost 75 percent in 1986. In both years, about 80 percent of high school women expressed a desire to be married. But both men and women plan to delay marriage. The share planning to wait more than five years after graduation rose 11 percentage points between 1976 and 1986—from 26 percent to 37 percent.

The vast majority of high school seniors wish to have children, but most young women also plan to work outside the home, according to the University of Southern California researchers. In 1986, only 3 percent of high school women expected to be full-time homemakers at age 30, compared with 12 percent in 1976. Only 20 percent of the women in 1986 felt that staying home with preschoolers was important. Among high school men, only 36 percent favored full-time motherhood as a career for their prospective spouses.

Most of the young women in the class of 1986 planned to divide their time between work and home. Even so, fewer than 10 percent felt that both spouses should be employed on a full-time basis when there were preschoolers in the home.

These prospective parents believed it was essential to give their children greater opportunities than they had, but they did not feel that meant spending more time with their children. Instead, they planned to satisfy their children's needs by providing more material goods and services.

The goals today's teenagers believe are extremely important include having a great deal of money, having time for recreational activities, and having a good marriage and family life. But it might take them a while to achieve these ambitions. In 1990, fully 77 percent of people aged 18 to 24 had never married, and two-thirds of those who remained single still lived with their parents.

Working Toward the Future

Because of low birth rates in the 1970s and early 1980s, the number of teenagers in the work force has been declining since 1981. But the number of teenaged workers is expected to rebound after 1993, according to Howard Fullerton, a demographic statistician for the Bureau of Labor Statistics (BLS). By 2000, the total number of young workers, 8.8 million, will still be fewer than in 1981. As a percentage of all workers, teenagers will fall from 8 percent to 6 percent.

In June 1990, 62 percent of 16-to-19-year-olds were either working or looking for work, compared with 53 percent in May. By July, typically the peak month for teenaged employment, the share leaped to 67 percent. These numbers reflect the early effects of the 1990s' recession; in better times, the numbers would be even higher.

Desires for material goods start early. Many teens work summer jobs throughout their high school years in order to save money for stereos, sports equipment, cars, and clothes. Graduation marks an increase in their level of expectation.

Dressed for Success

Graduation is a time for celebration, and the senior prom is the apex of many young people's social lives. Proms are also big business. For many young men, the prom marks their first experience with formal wear. But tapping this market can be a major headache for formal-wear companies.

Traditional media advertising has little effect on teenaged boys, according to Brenda Webster, director of advertising for Westchester, Pennsylvania-based Small's Formal Wear: "Teens don't do much reading, especially newspapers, so the only print ads we usually run are in high school newspapers. Parents may see a newspaper ad, but parents today very rarely influence a high school boy's choice of prom attire. His prom date has much more to say about it."

Since the prom season, primarily May and June, accounts for some 25 percent of a formal-wear-rental company's business, it is essential to target this important segment. Prom magazines, such as *Your Prom* (published by *Modern Bride*), are aimed primarily at high school girls, but a number of tuxedo-rental companies take out full-page ads in these publications. "We find in almost all of our stores that the girls decide what the boys will wear a very large percentage of the time. The girls choose their dress first and then tell the guys what colors to wear," says Dan McDearmid, director of marketing for Mitchell's Formal Wear in Atlanta, Georgia. After seeing the ads in their prom magazines, the young women help their dates find the right stores.

Other ideas for marketing formal wear to young men are even more direct. Some companies recruit students to wear tuxedos during a regular school day and hand out promotional material at the same time. Seeing classmates, especially high-profile classmates, in formal dress is a guaranteed attention-getter. Promotional give-aways, including discounts on rentals, free T-shirts, and offers for graduation announcements, are also useful ways to attract young customers. Formal-wear companies may stage fashion shows in local malls or on school campuses.

Teens' fashion selections throughout the rest of the year are decidedly limited—jeans, jeans, and more jeans. Students at both Parsons School of Design and the Fashion Institute of Technology predict that blue jeans and sneakers will be popular into the 21st century, reports the Columbia News Service. The students agree that while there will always be experimentation in fashion, the trend toward comfort will continue for a long time.

Because of the difficulties in dressing teenagers up, fashion-wear marketers should take a tip from the formal-wear industry. Using high school students—especially young men—as models on campus will probably reach a wider audience than print ads. On-campus and mall fashion shows are important conduits to these young consumers. And knowing how to dress will become increasingly important as young adults start seeking employment.

Risky Business

Teenagers may be interested in attaining material goods and in going to college, but those are not the only things on their minds, especially in the spring and summer months. During summer vacation, adolescents have the greatest probability of having their first sexual experience, according to Joseph Lee Rogers, a psychologist at the University of Oklahoma.

Nearly half of adolescents reported that they lost their virginity during the late spring and summer (May through August) in one survey that Rogers analyzed. Almost 30 percent of respondents became sexually active right after school let out, in June or July. Similar studies of different groups over a 12-year period confirm these findings. This pattern applies to both men and women, and it is strongest among people aged 18 and younger. After people move into their 20s, the pattern weakens but does not disappear.

Despite the growing threat of disease, teenagers are increasingly likely to be sexually active, according to studies by the Alan Guttmacher Institute of New York City. Between 1982 and 1988, the share of sexually active teenagers (aged 15 to 19) increased from 47 percent to 53 percent. Growing participation among white upper-income teenagers has been responsible for much of this increase, and differences based on race, ethnicity, and economic groups are narrowing.

During the 1980s, the pregnancy rate for teenagers remained fairly stable, largely because of increased use of contraception. The proportion of 15-to-19-year-olds using contraception during their first sexual encounter grew to 65 percent in 1988 from 48 percent in 1982. Among all teenagers having intercourse for the first time, the use of condoms doubled. Among Hispanic teenagers, the share using condoms tripled. Still, one-third of all teenagers use no protection the first time they have sex.

Most high school students have a fairly good understanding of AIDS and how it can be transmitted, according to researchers at the Centers for Disease Control (CDC) in Atlanta. A study published in the November/December 1990 issue of *Family Planning Perspectives* showed that almost all teenagers know that AIDS can be contracted through sexual contact or by sharing hypodermic needles. However, a substantial proportion have other ideas about AIDS that could actually place them at risk. Some falsely believe that there may be a cure. Others incorrectly assume that they can tell if people have AIDS just by looking at them.

Learning to Say No

Although a greater number of teenagers are exploring their sexual feelings, drug use among high school seniors has been dropping almost continuously since the early 1980s. In 1990, 48 percent of high school seniors had used an illicit drug at least once in their lives, according to figures released by the U.S. Department of Health and Human Services (HHS). This contrasts sharply with a 66 percent share in the early 1980s.

Cocaine use among high school seniors decreased by nearly 20 percent between 1989 and 1990 alone. The percentage of seniors reporting that they used cocaine within the past year dropped from 6.5 percent in 1989 to 5.3 percent in 1990. Crack use among these students dropped by half—from 1.4 percent to 0.7 percent.

All measures of marijuana use also decreased greatly, but it remains the most widely used illicit drug among high school seniors. The number of students who had used marijuana within the past year decreased to 27 percent in 1990 from 30 percent in 1989. At the same time, the share of current users decreased to 14 percent from 17 percent.

Not only have the rates for drug use decreased—some categories of alcohol use also declined significantly, says HHS. Both daily and binge drinking have declined substantially from their peaks in the early 1980s. But alcohol use among high school students has not declined at the same rate as illicit drugs. Current use of alcohol decreased to 57 percent of high school seniors in 1990 from 72 percent in 1980. About 4 percent of these students use alcohol on a daily basis, and 32 percent of seniors had five or more drinks in a row within the past two weeks.

The HHS survey showed that there was no decrease at all in daily cigarette smoking between 1989 and 1990. The proportion of seniors who smoke at least one cigarette per day has remained around 19 percent since 1984, and the percentage who smoke a half-pack each day has stayed constant at about 11 percent.

While a greater percentage of students now feel that using cocaine and crack can put them at "great risk," alcohol and cigarette use are still very popular among America's young people. The problem is probably more extensive than the HHS survey indicates, because it includes only students who are currently enrolled in school, and drug and alcohol use are higher among dropouts.

COLLEGE AND WORK

Summer partying may be the most immediate concern for young people, but the future looms ominously. Some 2.3 million Americans graduated from high school in June 1990. Of the 1 million graduates who did not go to college, 85 percent successfully crossed over to the adult labor market. The unemployment rate for this group, however, was 15 percent. The jobless rates for recent high school graduates have remained at high levels over the decade, even though the teenage population not in school decreased by 38 percent during the same period, according to the BLS. For the 450,000 students who dropped out of high school, a lack of work experience and education makes it especially difficult to find a job. The unemployment rate for this group was 28 percent.

What's Next?

Sixty percent of the class of 1990 enrolled in college in October of that year, matching the record-setting figure for the class of 1989, according to the BLS. Many of these students are also working. Taking a job to help with college expenses has become more common than it was a decade ago. In 1979, 46 percent of college students also held a job; by 1989, that figure had increased to 53 percent. College students who work put in an average of about 20 hours per week.

June is also the month for college seniors to make a transition from student to full-time employee. In 1990, more than 1 million students graduated from college with a bachelor's degree. About 322,000 got their master's, and another 38,000 received PhDs. Approximately 71,000 students received professional degrees. As today's college graduates enter the work force, they come face to face with the economic realities of the 1990s, and their expectations of job availability and salary have changed along with the country's economic situation.

In 1990, 9 percent of college students expected to obtain first jobs paying more than $35,000, according to a survey conducted by the Philadelphia-based Right Associates. During the recession of 1991, this share dropped to 3 percent. In 1990, none of the students surveyed planned to accept a job that paid less than $15,000. In 1991, 3 percent indicated that this was the most they hoped for.

The opportunity for "advancement" and "challenges" were the two most important factors influencing job choices among students surveyed by Right Associates in both 1990 and 1991. But "salary" moved up to third place from fourth place, while "use of a wide range of skills" dropped from third to fourth. An increased emphasis on salary may reflect uncertainties about the future job market, says Frank P. Louchheim, chairman of Right Associates.

The Job Search

Almost half of the college students surveyed by Right Associates in 1991 began their job search six months before graduation. Many college students are looking for careers rather than jobs, accounting for the longer-than-average time they take looking for the right employer. In order to find a career to match their interests, talents, and academic training, 45 percent made use of personal contacts, 44 percent took advantage of college career centers, 26 percent consulted newspapers, and 15 percent looked for jobs listed in professional journals.

More than 81 percent of those surveyed planned on pursuing advanced degrees, up from 77 percent in 1990. An "improved education" moved from eighth place to one of the top three actions the students believed would secure them better positions—along with "working hard" and "developing a network."

"In 1990, demographic projections indicated a severe shortage in the college-educated labor pool," says Louchheim. But in 1991, potential employers were cutting back or canceling their college recruiting schedules. As a result, students adjusted their expectations. Because many made the decision to add to their education, we may have a much more talented labor pool in the future, according to Louchheim.

As graduates leave college, their financial situation pushes them to secure good jobs. Because of the high cost of education, many parents are unable to cover their children's expenses, and many students must help pay their bills by getting part-time work or taking out loans. The share of recent college graduates with debt is close to 60 percent, and this proportion is growing, according to Diane Saunders, assistant vice president of the New England Education Loan Marketing Corporation (NEELMC).

Students in New England left college with an average loan debt of about $8,200 in 1990, according to the New England Student Loan Survey II (NESLS II), undertaken by NEELMC and the Massachusetts Higher Education Assistance Corporation in 1991. The average loan payment for these college graduates was about $120 per month.

The vast majority of recent college graduates have assumed responsibility for paying their own student loans. Only about 6 percent of those in the NESLS II survey indicated that their parents were paying more than half of their student loans.

Most college graduates also head into the work world burdened with debts on top of their college loans. Some 80 percent of New England's graduates have noneducation debt in addition to their student loans. About 26 percent have monthly car, credit-card, and other loan payments of between $251 and $500, and 10 percent have non-education payments in excess of $1,000 per month.

Better Pay, Better Opportunities

Nearly 10 million workers switched occupations between 1986 and 1987, according to the BLS's *Monthly Labor Review*. Many of these workers were students replacing their part-time jobs with permanent work, but two-thirds were over age 25. Only 13 percent of workers switched careers involuntarily, because they were laid off or otherwise lost their job. The vast majority were looking for better pay, advancement opportunity, and better working conditions.

Career changes are at their peak for workers under age 20. Almost 30 percent of young workers change jobs in a typical year, according to the latest BLS study. Among workers aged 20 to 24, the share is closer to 20 percent, and for those aged 25 to 34, it is just above 11 percent. About 7 percent of men and 9 percent of women aged 35 to 44 change careers in a typical year. Among workers aged 45 and older, less than 5 percent change careers.

The most educated workers are the least likely to career-hop, but rates differ dramatically for various types of occupations. An occupation that requires highly specialized training reduces the worker's ability to change jobs. A substantial share of workers spend their entire lives in one career. Half of people aged 65 to 69 have spent more than 20 years in their current occupation, and almost 20 percent have at least 40 years of experience in their current line of work.

Despite some media hype to the contrary, career changing is no more common today than it was 20 years ago. Between 1965 and 1987, the share of workers who changed jobs fluctuated between 9 and 12 percent, peaking in the late 1970s and early 1980s. However, the demand for career counseling services and personnel agencies has grown significantly since 1965, because the total number of people in the labor force leaped from 76 million to more than 120 million, largely due to women entering the labor force in record numbers.

When making career changes that involve moves, even older adults may be tied to the school calendar. They may have school-aged children in their households. Or they may be going to school themselves. By 2000, over half of college students will be over the age of 25 and nearly one-third will be over 35.

School teachers may be the most likely to make career changes in June. At the end of the 1987-88 school year, 130,000 public school teachers and 40,000 private school teachers left the profession, according to the *OERI Bulletin* of the U.S. Department of Education. When researchers asked those who stayed in the profession what was the best way to keep teachers on the job, two-thirds said "higher salaries" and "better fringe benefits." But only 7 percent of the former public school teachers and 16 percent of the former private school teachers felt this way. Inadequate support from the administration was the major complaint of 26 percent of the people who left public schools and 22 percent of those who left private schools.

Even though older workers are less likely than younger workers to change occupations, workers over age 40 are the ones most likely to look for professional help when changing occupations, according to Paula Mergenhagen Dewitt, a sociologist and researcher in Nashville, Tennessee. Older adults have the skills that headhunters are looking for, and they are more likely than younger people to be able to afford executive search services. During the 1990s, the population aged 40 to 64 should increase nearly 30 percent. This could mean a lot of work for career consultants.

MARRIAGE
■ ■ ■ ■ ■ ■ ■

Weddings are big business. More than 60 percent of Americans have been to a wedding within the last two years, according to the Roper Organization of New York City. Fully 38 percent of adults have attended or participated in a wedding in the last year. But because the demographics of newlyweds are changing, marketers must change their approach to this major market.

Wedding Bells

Young people wait longer before they marry, and remarriages make up a greater share of all weddings. Newlyweds are older and more experienced than their counterparts were a decade ago. That makes them smarter, more sophisticated consumers.

In 1970, half of first-time brides were under age 21, according to the National Center for Health Statistics (NCHS). Twenty years later, their median age was nearly 24 years. First-time grooms also aged over that period, from age 23 to 26. But the number of second-time brides and grooms drives the age of marriage up even higher. The median age for remarriages is 33 for divorced women and 37 for divorced men. One in three marriages is a remarriage for one or both of the partners.

Postponing marriage has contributed to a sharp decline in marriage rates. In 1946, there were 200 marriages for every 1,000 single women aged 15 to 44. During the 1950s and 1960s, this rate hovered around 150. It dropped below 100 in 1982, and to 92 in 1987. Since baby boomers got married in force in the early 1980s, the actual number of weddings did not begin to slump until 1985. This decline will probably continue through the 1990s. But "the change won't be radical," says Barbara Foley Wilson of the NCHS. "The number of couples who marry each year could drop from 2.4 million to 2.3 million."

June is still the most popular month for weddings. A total of 274,000 couples tied the knot in June 1990. More than 9,000 couples took their vows on an average day in June, compared with only 6,700 for the year as a whole. June weddings are so common that in order to reserve popular settings for the ceremony or reception, some couples must book two years in advance.

MARRIAGES AND DIVORCES

Both marriages and divorces peak in June.

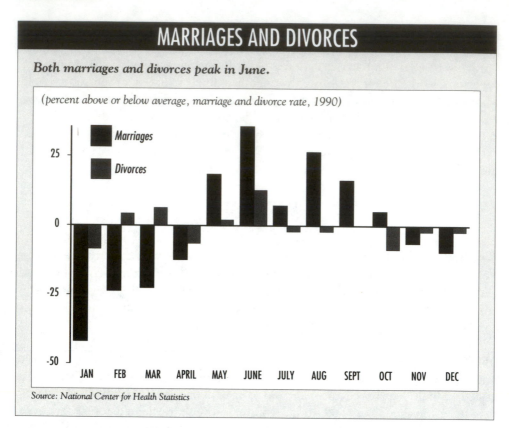

(percent above or below average, marriage and divorce rate, 1990)

■ Marriages

■ Divorces

JAN FEB MAR APRIL MAY JUNE JULY AUG SEPT OCT NOV DEC

Source: National Center for Health Statistics

Spending for the wedding, reception, honeymoon, and incidentals increases annually. In 1989, the total expenditures for couples marrying for the first time were $32 billion, according to estimates by *BRIDE*'s magazine. Of this amount, 10 percent went to engagement and wedding rings; 14 percent paid for honeymoon travel and apparel; 51 percent was spent on wedding apparel, invitations, flowers, the reception, photos, and gifts for the wedding party; and 24 percent was used for the purchase of home furnishings and household equipment. The costs to guests, including travel, lodging, and meals, must also be considered.

A survey of readers of *BRIDE*'s magazine paints an interesting picture of how much Americans are willing to spend on a formal wedding. Spending begins months before the actual event, with payments for such items as the wedding dress, reception, and honeymoon. For the average *BRIDE*'s reader in 1989, the wedding, from the invitations to the reception, cost $16,144—not including the honeymoon.

Some 94 percent of *BRIDE*'s readers considered their weddings to be formal affairs. Wedding receptions were very popular—all respondents to the survey planned to have some type of reception after the ceremony. They planned on entertaining an average of 202 guests and spending nearly $6,000 on the festivities.

Equally important to many couples is a rehearsal dinner. Some 92 percent of

BRIDE's readers have this pre-wedding event. Three-quarters are hosted by the groom's parents, and they cost an average of $500.

Most couples get married on a Saturday (84 percent) and in the afternoon (62 percent), says *BRIDE*'s magazine. Two-thirds spend the first night of their married life in the city or town where they had their reception, and 15 percent stay at an airport hotel. The majority leave for their honeymoon on Sunday. Altogether, 11 percent of weddings and 17 percent of honeymoons take place in June.

Romantic Destinations

All of the newlyweds in the *BRIDE*'s magazine survey took honeymoons. They spent an average of $3,200 for transportation, lodging, food and entertainment, and personal and gift purchases. The actual location of the honeymoon can vary widely, but romance is the key element in choosing a destination.

A 1990 Roper Organization survey quizzed men and women on their ideas of a romantic vacation. Out of 16 different choices, both groups agreed that a Caribbean cruise and a trip to Hawaii were by far the most romantic destinations, and studies show that these are among the most popular honeymoon destinations.

"While the travel and tourist industry has been getting hit hard over the last two years, the honeymoon market is truly very lucrative," says Drew Kerr, a spokesman for *Modern Bride* magazine. Surveys of *Modern Bride* readers taken in 1986–87 and 1990–91 one month before their wedding date indicate that newlyweds aren't going to let a little recession get in the way of their honeymoon plans. Ninety-eight percent of respondents in the early 1990s planned on taking a honeymoon. And these honeymooners were more likely than those in the 1980s to travel by air to far-off destinations.

But are bridal magazine readers representative of the bridal market? Thom Curtin, travel advertising director for *Modern Bride*, says yes: "If you're going to get engaged, plan a wedding, invite guests, purchase a bridal gown, have a ceremony, and take a honeymoon, you're going to read a bridal magazine." He says that bridal magazines are "a darn good reflection of the bridal market's psychographics," but their demographics also hold up pretty well. The average first-time bride's age is about 24.6, according to the National Center for Health Statistics, and the average age of a *Modern Bride* reader is about 24.9.

The changes in the readers' honeymoon plans are also strongly visible in the honeymoon market. While almost half (48 percent) of today's honeymooners say that their destination is within the continental United States, the share of domestic travelers is declining, while the share venturing farther away is growing. Two-thirds of the honeymooners planned on spending at least part of their trip outside the lower 48 states. In 1987, 54 percent of honeymooners took a domestic trip, and 58 percent went farther.

For long-distance honeymooners, Hawaii is the most popular single destination, accounting for 14 percent of all travelers. Mexico is second with a 10 percent share, and the U.S. Virgin Islands is third with a 9 percent share. The Caribbean as a whole accounts for fully one in three honeymoon couples, up from one in four in 1987. Curtin points out that a 1 percent share of the honeymoon market amounts to about $35 million in spending.

Overall, Florida is the most popular destination. But unlike other domestic destinations, Florida's share has grown, from less than 15 percent in 1987 to about 16 percent in 1991. Some of Florida's success might be attributed to its cruise industry. While just 10 percent of honeymooners took a cruise in 1987, 16 percent did in 1991.

Three-quarters of honeymooners traveled by air, 38 percent drove a rental car, and 11 percent drove their own car. In 1987, 69 percent flew, 42 percent rented a car, and fully 38 percent drove their own car. The average length of a honeymoon in 1991 was eight days, unchanged from 1987. About 69 percent of honeymooners made at least some of their travel plans through a travel agent. Half traveled on a honeymoon package.

"Newlyweds today are older, more sophisticated, and willing to travel the long haul for romance and culture," says Curtin. He believes that it's only a matter of time before couples discover Africa, the Fiji Islands, and New Zealand. Beautiful natural scenery is the number-one attraction for a honeymoon destination, he explains.

The Thought That Counts

Gift-giving is another important component of the wedding industry. Brides-to-be estimate that the typical guest will spend about $47 for a wedding gift, according to a 1989 survey conducted by Cahners Publishing and *Modern Bride* magazine. This survey questioned brides-to-be that attended bridal retail store shows. In order to make the selection of an appropriate item easier, 96 percent of these brides register their desires at a store (almost always a department store), and 75 percent register at two or more stores. The grooms-to-be frequently get involved at this point—72 percent of brides register with their fiancés.

The most popular items in a bridal registry include (in decreasing order of popularity) fine crystal stemware, bath linens, fine china dinnerware, bed linens, small kitchen appliances, cookware, sterling silver flatware, table linens, and stainless steel flatware. But brides especially hope to receive china (46 percent), crystal (26 percent), money (12 percent), a microwave oven (12 percent), casual dinnerware (8 percent), cookware (7 percent), and sterling silver flatware (7 percent), according to the Cahners' survey.

What do first-time brides do when they don't receive something they really want? If they think the item is essential, they will simply buy it themselves. In the Cahners' survey, 24 percent of brides wanted a VCR, but only 5 percent expected to get one as a wedding gift, and 41 percent said they would buy one themselves if they had to. An additional 24 percent wished to receive furniture, and while only

DAD'S DAY

T HE THIRD SUNDAY in June was first recognized as Father's Day in 1910. It was an idea publicly supported by President Calvin Coolidge in 1924. But it was not accorded a presidential proclamation until 1966. And only in 1972 was Public Law 92-278 signed, granting Father's Day official status as an annual event. Even so, Father's Day promises to become more important as men take more active roles in their children's lives.

There are 26 million fathers living with their children in America today. Since 1950, the number of households headed by single fathers has increased more than fivefold. The role of fathers has evolved from the "Honey, I'm home. I'll kiss the kids goodnight" image of the 1950s to a strong nurturing style that even some mothers envy. With the ever-increasing number of full-time working women in married-couple households, the role of father is becoming increasingly important.

In households with children aged 13 and younger, 40 percent of mothers said their husbands read to the children regularly, according to a 1989 poll by the Roper Organization. Another 39 percent of mothers claimed their mates regularly put the children to bed, and at least one mother in three said her husband regularly bought toys, cared for sick children, and fixed them dinner.

Overall, mothers gave fathers more credit than fathers gave themselves for performing 15 of the 17 child-care activities covered in the survey, including dressing the children, bathing them, changing their diapers or wet beds, buying them clothes, and getting up at night to feed them.

But for many fathers, jobs still take precedence over child-rearing. Only 16 percent of fathers said they regularly worked at home so that they could be with their children. Only 9 percent said they avoided out-of-town trips to be with the family, and just 5 percent said they regularly left work early to care for their children.

Putting the job first may be a decision made out of necessity rather than choice. A 1989 Gallup Poll found that 78 percent of men and women said that at-home fathers are just as good parents as their female counterparts. Sixty percent of the men questioned in the same poll felt that fathers get greater satisfaction from caring for their families than they do from a job well done at work. For many dads, having to work outside of the home is simply an economic reality over which they have little control.

Remembering Dad on his special day can be a retailing challenge. There are, of course, conventional gifts such as sports accessories, tools, and the ubiquitous necktie. But many children and their mothers are looking for something more unusual. High-tech gadgets, hand-held video games, and all-in-one remote controls for the home entertainment center are gaining in popularity. So are brightly colored power tools, barbecue accessories, and clothing items such as boxer shorts and watches.

Although Mother's Day is the number-one day for flower sales during the year, giving Dad flowers still seems just a bit odd to many gift-givers. But people are starting to buy flowers for men, according to Pam Linder of Linder, Baughman & Associates, a Harbor City, California-based advertising agency specializing in the floral industry. "Men are not always the lion of the jungle. They need nurturing of their artistic side," she says. An advertising campaign from Florists Transworld Delivery (FTD) uses Merlin Olsen, a 240-pound former defensive lineman for the Los Angeles Rams as a spokesperson. Olsen's presence with bouquets and arrangements proves that "real men can get flowers."

Floral gifts for Father's Day are often cross marketed with other products— custom-made gift baskets, decorative duck decoys, and the like. Many gift-givers prefer to give Dad foliage or a flowering plant for his den or office. Retailers can make these gifts more appealing by packaging them in "masculine" containers—rustic baskets, ceramic cache pots, or novelty drinking mugs.

Even if the gift selections are a challenge, finding the right Father's Day card is becoming easier. Hallmark Cards, for example, now has some 850 designs in its Father's Day line, and that number is expected to grow. Dad's special day is not big on sentimental poems. Although Mother's Day cards avoid humor, 40 percent of Hallmark's Father's Day cards are humorous, according to Hallmark spokesperson Renee Hershey.

Even though Dad's getting all the laughs, Americans still take Father's Day seriously. It is the fifth most important occasion for the greeting card industry, and Hallmark reported sales of 150 million cards in 1991. It is also the third-biggest day of the year for long-distance phone calls and the second most popular holiday for dining out.

4 percent expected to get furniture as a wedding gift, 66 percent said they would buy it anyway.

Luxury items meet with a different reaction. A full 50 percent of brides wanted to receive fine china as a wedding gift, and 53 percent expected that this would be the case. But only 28 percent of brides would buy fine china themselves if they did not receive it as a gift. The same holds true for sterling silver flatware—39 percent want to receive it as a gift, and 25 percent expect to, but only 18 percent would buy it themselves.

Registering for wedding gifts is the only way newlyweds can be sure that they will have the things they need to make home entertaining special. With so much money earmarked for essential goods—from a downpayment on a new home to appliances, carpeting, and furniture—newlyweds look forward to receiving luxury items. "I took my registering very seriously. I looked and thought about my choices six months before registering. I feel I will like my choices for many years to come," said one bride who participated in the Cahners' survey.

Some brides-to-be in the Cahners' survey complained about the service they received when registering. Some 42 percent of brides felt the service was only "acceptable/OK" or "not as helpful as I would have liked." "The registry director never seemed to want to take the time to help me select my patterns by telling me about the different brands, etc. They always want you to be ready to tell them what you want," reported one bride. Remembering that brides are excited, nervous, and anxious to be treated as someone special is vital. With this important market, retailers will profit by using a little extra "tender, loving care."

Incidentals for the wedding party include gifts given to attendants, parents, and in-laws. The total retail sales volume for these types of gifts was about $214 million in 1989, according to a survey conducted by the Home Testing Institute (HTI) for *Modern Bride* magazine. The most popular gifts for female attendants include fine and costume jewelry, picture frames, and small silver or crystal items, according to the Cahners' study. Male attendants receive mugs, money clips, pen-and-pencil sets, key chains, jewelry, and billfolds. The overwhelming favorite for a gift to parents is a picture frame, with figurines, vases, and collectors' plates lagging far behind.

The engagement ring, wedding bands, and gifts exchanged on the wedding day between the bride and groom make up yet another important aspect of the wedding market. The total figure for bridal market retail sales of jewelry and watches acquired within the period of six months before to six months after the wedding totaled more than $2.5 billion in 1989, according to the HTI survey. But engagement rings are purchased an average of 11 months before the wedding.

Fine jewelry is by far the most commonly exchanged item between the bride and groom. Crystal, leather, and sterling silver are also popular, and electronic equipment—stereos and VCRs—are gaining a strong following.

First-time newlyweds' annual household incomes average $38,300, and 41 percent of first-timers reported that they own homes or condominiums, according to the HTI survey. Fifty-six percent of first-time brides were college graduates, and 82 percent were employed.

One reason for brides' increasing emphasis on luxury gifts is that the majority of brides today live with their partners before the wedding. Therefore, many of the day-to-day goods that these couples require (from pots and pans to linens) are already part of their premarriage household, and what they really "need" are the fine items. In 1989, sales of fine china dinnerware to brides topped $342 billion, or 75 percent of the total market. Fine crystal stemware and glassware were also high—$187 million, or 46 percent of the market, HTI estimates.

Newlyweds also present an important market for big-ticket items. They are twice as likely as others to get new carpeting, a microwave oven, or a refrigerator. They are three times more likely to get a clothes dryer or bedroom furniture, and almost four times more likely to get a freezer. Small kitchen appliances, cookware, and food processors are also big sellers, and many brides even specify brands.

The bridal market is becoming more profitable as older brides and grooms create a more affluent and sophisticated market for wedding products and services. For all segments of the retail trade, from caterers and equipment rental agencies to travel agents, department stores, fashion houses, and florists, June brides provide a clientele that is all but unrivaled in its consumption of goods and services.

And if June is a good month for weddings, it is also a great month for anniversary celebrations. Seventeen percent of brides plan their weddings around another important family celebration, such as an anniversary, birthday, or reaffirmation, says *BRIDE*'s magazine.

RELOCATION

Lifestyle changes are at their apex in June. Newlyweds, college and high school graduates entering the labor force, and older workers seeking better job opportunities are packing up their belongings and moving. The peak months for moving are June, July, and August, in that order, according to Allied Van Lines. About 40 million Americans move each year.

Life's Highway

Charting American movers isn't easy, according to Larry Long, chief of the demographic analysis staff at the Center for Demographic Studies, Bureau of the Census, in Washington, D.C. Various studies have found that the average American moves every 5, 6, 7, or even 11 years, says Long. But these figures do not clearly differentiate between individuals, families, and homeowners.

Differences in moving patterns depend on the age, economic status, and location of the population. Householders aged 45 to 54 have been in their homes

MOVERS AND SHAKERS

California, Florida, and Texas accounted for more than half of the nation's population growth in the 1980s, and those three Sunbelt states still dominate the nation's moving activity. But in 1990, the inbound and outbound activity in Florida and Texas was about equal. And more movers left California than located there.

(share of moves into and out of states, 1990)

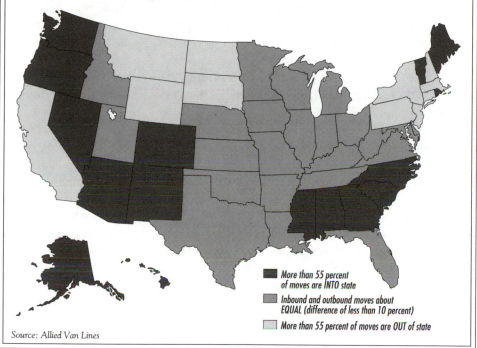

■ More than 55 percent of moves are INTO state

▓ Inbound and outbound moves about EQUAL (difference of less than 10 percent)

☐ More than 55 percent of moves are OUT of state

Source: Allied Van Lines

a median of 8 years, compared with a median of 15 months for 25-to-29-year-olds, and 6 months for those under age 25, according to the 1987 American Housing Survey (AHS).

The number of moves per household varies regionally. The longest average stay in one home is 97 months (just over 8 years) in the nonmetropolitan South. On the other end of the scale, the median is only 30 months, or 2.5 years, in large urban areas of the West.

The relationship between income and moving also varies, according to Long. Some low-income householders never establish a stable residence, while others live for decades in subsidized housing. Average-income householders who can afford to buy a home may stay put for a long time, while those with higher incomes may move more frequently because they can trade up to more expensive homes. Very wealthy people who already live in the best neighborhoods have little incentive to move.

In a typical householder's lifetime, he or she will move almost 12 times. About one-quarter of these moves occur before age 18, and about half occur before age 27. From the early 1950s to the late 1960s, about 20 percent of the population moved each year, according to the Census Bureau's Current Population Survey. In the 1970s, the rate began to decrease. In 1982-83, moves were deterred by the highest-ever mortgage rates and the deep recession. Fewer than 17 percent of householders moved during this period. The rate returned to the 20 percent level in 1985, but has remained below that level ever since.

Whether householders can afford to move or not is significantly influenced by interest rates. In 1988, fully 31 percent of families that currently owned a home could not afford to buy a median -priced home in their region. But if conventional mortgage interest rates had been 2 percentage points higher, the share would have climbed to 33 percent, according to a report from the Census Bureau. The bureau's study also found that 36 percent of all renters could not afford a house at any rate.

Slow population growth will weaken many markets in the 1990s, and homebuilding will grow more slowly than the overall economy between 1991 and 1996, according to the Bureau of Economic Analysis's 1991 U.S. Industrial Outlook.

Over the decade of the 1980s, homeownership rates have been slowly but steadily declining. While the decrease from 64.8 percent in 1982 to 63.9 percent in 1989 may not seem like much, the Census Bureau reports that it is statistically significant. Homeownership rates will continue to decline, as long as housing prices continue to rise and mortgage interest rates remain high. But a reversal of these trends could result in a rebound in the housing market, something that a prolonged economic recession might just cause.

Setting Up Housekeeping

Most people move only about six miles from their previous place of residence, about the same distance they commute to work. This average has not changed much in 40 years. But no matter how short the move, the emotional upheaval can be traumatic. To many American women, the loss they feel when leaving their old home is analogous to dying, according to Audrey McCollum, author of The Trauma of Moving.

To find out how they coped with relocation, McCollum interviewed 42 women over a two-year period. Each of these women had been contacted by the Welcome Wagon, but at the end of the two years, less than one-sixth felt positively connected with their new neighborhood, only one-third were satisfied with their new abode, and just one-half felt at home in their new town. Two-thirds remained without close friends, and one-third were so overwhelmed by anxiety that they sought professional help.

Many newcomers refrained from asking questions about a community for fear of appearing ignorant or nosy, says McCollum. But these people need to know which vendors are the most reliable, who has the fastest services, and where specialized products can be purchased.

It took the typical newcomer to a community six months to locate all the goods and services she needed, according to McCollum. Joining forces with local moving companies, real estate agents, and vehicle-rental agencies to produce and distribute a directory of goods and services to newly established households may be one of the least expensive ways to approach this group.

Some products and services are especially important to newcomers. Many of the women surveyed said that in order to feel at home, their new house must become an expression of themselves. Cleaning, painting, hanging pictures, finding places for memorabilia, and arranging furniture are important steps in re-establishing their identity in their new environment.

More personal manifestations of this identity loss can be seen in a person's need for a new hairdresser or clothes to fit the identity of the community. Some people may seek out new food outlets that stock familiar "comfort foods." The right chili pepper might be as hard to find in Vermont as a fresh bagel is in west Texas. Other newcomers are faced with the challenge of finding new doctors and lawyers.

Many people are shy and uncertain in unfamiliar surroundings. Even though new residents may want to go to a movie or work out at the gym, some may not go if they have to go alone. Ultimately, it is up to the newcomer to join the community, but business can play an important role in making newcomers feel at home. As one of McCollum's interviewees put it, "Feeling at home means going into town and meeting people you know, going to a store and having them call you by name."

Women, for the most part, bear the brunt of the moving experience on behalf of family members and for themselves. Businesses are beginning to recognize this fact. Ryder Truck Rental, for example, is running ads in major women's magazines, emphasizing the features of their vehicles that will appeal to women drivers—power steering, cloth-covered adjustable seats, and automatic transmissions.

Women are the household members most likely to make use of interior decorators, paint and wallpaper retailers, contractors, landscapers, and other services that help "make the house a home." They are the people most likely to seek out supermarkets, clothing stores, dry cleaners, and other facilities in the community. They will also be the household member most likely to find facilities for their children—schools, sports complexes, after-school services, and the products that go along with them.

Children, too, find moving stressful, and tending to their needs is important. Ryder Truck Rental teamed up with KIDVIDZ, a children's video producer, to create a moving guide for children aged 4 to 10. Other businesses that attract a young clientele may also gain the trust of new arrivals by adopting similar methods of reaching out to the children of relocated families.

Moving just adds to a long list of stressful changes that many newlyweds must make, says McCollum. Wives must both establish themselves as members of a new community and recast themselves as equal partners in an evolving relationship—with all the identity problems these situations can bring.

Single women may regard moving in a different light, according to McCollum. Of the seven single women she interviewed, all had seen moving as a catapult into growth and change. This positive attitude toward relocation affected the ways in which these women adapted to their new surroundings.

Americans spent about $6 billion moving in 1988, according to the University of Maryland and the American Movers Conference. More than half used their own truck, van, or car to execute the move, while about 20 percent used rental equipment. Another 20 percent used a moving company. Only 2 percent of those surveyed used their own equipment as well as a moving company.

SUMMER, AT LAST

When the proms, the weddings, and the moves are over, along with the stresses involved in planning these events—sometimes requiring more tactical skill than mounting a small military campaign—it's time to relax and enjoy the first month of summer.

West Virginia celebrates West Virginia Day, Massachusetts celebrates Bunker Hill Day, and Alabama celebrates Jefferson Davis's birthday. There's an Emancipation Day celebration in Texas that is known by the locals as "Juneteenth." June is National Accordion Awareness Month, National Adopt-a-Cat Month, National Drive Safe Month, National Papaya Month, National Pest Control Month, National Ragweed Control Month, National Rose Month, and National Tennis Month. It is also Fresh Fruits and Vegetables Month, Dairy Month, and Zoo and Aquarium Month. But with all the fond memories that June generates, it should be called National Nostalgia Month.

JULY WEATHER
■ ■ ■ ■ ■ ■ ■ ■ ■ ■

You might expect Phoenix to be hot and dry in the middle of July, but don't look for a lot of rain in Seattle, either.

	TEMPERATURE		PRECIPITATION	
	low	*high*	*inches*	*days*
Albuquerque, NM	64.7°F	92.8°F	1.30	9
Atlanta, GA	69.2	87.9	4.73	12
Bismarck, ND	56.4	84.4	2.05	9
Boise, ID	58.5	90.6	0.26	2
Boston, MA	65.1	81.8	2.68	9
Buffalo, NY	61.2	80.2	2.96	10
Burlington, VT	58.6	80.5	3.43	12
Charlotte, NC	68.7	88.3	3.92	11
Chicago, IL	62.7	83.3	3.63	10
Cleveland, OH	61.4	81.7	3.37	10
Dallas, TX	74.7	97.8	2.00	5
Denver, CO	58.7	88.0	1.93	9
Detroit, MI	60.7	83.1	3.10	9
Great Falls, MT	54.4	84.2	1.10	7
Honolulu, HI	73.1	87.1	0.54	7
Houston, TX	72.5	93.6	3.33	9
Indianapolis, IN	64.9	85.2	4.32	9
Jacksonville, FL	71.8	90.7	6.54	15
Juneau, AK	47.4	64.0	4.13	17
Los Angeles, CA	62.6	75.3	0.01	1
Memphis, TN	72.6	91.5	4.03	9
Miami, FL	76.2	88.7	5.98	16
Milwaukee, WI	61.1	79.8	3.54	9
Minneapolis, MN	62.7	83.4	3.51	10
Mobile, AL	73.2	91.2	7.74	16
New Orleans, LA	73.5	90.7	6.73	15
New York, NY	68.2	85.3	3.77	11
Norfolk, VA	69.9	86.9	5.15	11
Oklahoma City, OK	70.6	93.5	3.04	6
Omaha, NE	66.8	88.5	3.62	9
Philadelphia, PA	66.8	86.1	3.88	9
Phoenix, AZ	79.5	105.0	0.74	4
Portland, OR	55.8	79.5	0.46	4
Salt Lake City, UT	61.8	93.2	0.72	5
San Francisco, CA	53.3	71.0	0.03	0
Sault Ste. Marie, MI	51.9	75.1	3.00	10
Seattle, WA	54.3	75.2	0.74	5
St. Louis, MO	68.8	89.0	3.63	9
Washington, DC	69.9	87.9	3.88	10
Wichita, KS	69.8	92.9	3.62	7

Source: U.S. Department of Commerce, Bureau of the Census, Statistical Abstract of the United States 1991. Average daily minimum and maximum temperatures and average monthly precipitation were measured over a standard 30-year period.

JULY
SERIOUS FUN

Leisure time, including summer vacations, is becoming more important as people rethink their attitudes about careers, family, and quality of life.

Half of Americans feel they don't have enough leisure time, according to the Roper Organization in New York City. Before 1985, more Americans thought their work time was more important than their leisure time, 46 percent compared with 33 percent who felt that leisure time was more important. After 1985, the difference began to narrow. By 1989, the larger share (41 percent) thought "leisure time" was more important. Only 36 percent valued their working time over their leisure time.

As time for leisure activities becomes more difficult to find, it becomes more valuable. A 1991 survey by the Hilton Corporation found that two-thirds of adults would take a cut in pay if they could get more time off.

But leisure activities aren't recession-proof. Even though they spell large sales volumes for many retailers, recreational expenditures are among the first to suffer in an economic downturn. For some people, cutting vacation plans may be a necessity. For others, recreational travel may be piggy-backed onto business travel or split into shorter weekend segments. But whatever Americans choose to do, they're looking for ways to make every July day special.

JULY'S BEST BUYS

(items most likely to be on sale in July)

- ■ Air conditioners
- ● Bathing suits
- ■ Handbags
- ● Hats
- ● Infant's needs
- ■ Refrigerators and freezers
- ● Shoes
- ■ Summer sports equipment

Source: DOLLAR$ENSE Magazine, 1987

THE FOURTH OF JULY
■■■■■■■■■■■■■

The Fourth of July is the big party of the summer, celebrated by patriotic outbursts, parades, fireworks, and picnics. But it has not been the same since the tall ships sailed into New York Harbor to celebrate the nation's 200th birthday. Each year brings another centennial, bicentennial, or sesquicentennial. Americans observe the anniversaries of states joining the Union, the incorporation of cities, the establishment of branches of government, the erection of historic monuments, famous battles, the births and deaths of American heroes, and the signing of important documents.

The Spirit of America

When the nation commemorated the 200th anniversary of the signing of the Constitution in 1987, the number of people who visited the Liberty Bell increased nearly 30 percent. Although attendance dropped off the next year, it still exceeded pre-bicentennial levels. In 1990, Constitution Park boosted attendance again with special events and the unveiling of new permanent exhibits in recognition of Benjamin Franklin's death 200 years earlier.

Americans show their patriotism in many ways. During the Gulf War, flags were generously displayed, but so was a relatively new symbol—the yellow ribbon. In the months after the war, sales of yellow ribbons, a welcome-home symbol, slumped. But flagwaving intensified as July 4th approached.

The fighting across the sea was replaced by a battle among American cities to see which city could have the best welcome-home parade. The parade in Washington, D.C., attracted 800,000 people on June 8, 1991. Two days later, the one in New York City attracted nearly 1 million people.

One American in 20 displayed an American flag during a typical week in 1988, according to a poll conducted by the Roper Organization. In the wake of the Gulf War, another Roper survey discovered that fully one in four Americans was flying a flag. Both in 1988 and 1991, older adults were more likely than younger adults to display the flag. Before the Gulf War, Democrats and Republicans were equally likely to fly the flag. After the war, Republicans edged ahead. People who considered themselves political or social activists were twice as likely as others to be flagwavers.

The American Flag Code, drafted in 1942, prohibits the flag from being used in advertising or emblazoned on disposable items. But in the aftermath of the Gulf War and the patriotic outbursts that followed, the American flag was flown atop hamburgers and behind automobile salesmen on television commercials.

Yet "the effectiveness of patriotism-based ad campaigns is not an easy thing to measure," says Eric Marder, an advertising consultant based in New York City. "People on both sides of the issue could be offended," he says. Staunch patriots might feel that such advertising debases the flag; others may feel that an overt display is hypocritical. A lot of money is being thrown away because advertisers don't do enough research before they incorporate Old Glory into their campaigns, says Marder.

One patriotic symbol, the "Made in the U.S.A." label, may provide some real advantages for marketers, according to the Research Advantage, Inc. of Hawthorne, New York. Its studies show that a majority of consumers express more interest in buying goods made in America than in imported goods. Women, older consumers, and residents of the East Coast and the Midwest are the most likely to appreciate American-made products.

Not all products benefit equally from the "Made in the U.S.A." label. Over 80 percent of respondents wanted their fresh foods produced in America, according to the Research Advantage survey. Seventy percent prefer canned and jarred food-stuffs made in the U.S. The majority of respondents expressed a preference for American-made household appliances, clothing, and cosmetics. But only 48 percent preferred American cars, and another 26 percent said it made no difference to them where the car was manufactured.

Over 30 percent of respondents preferred foreign-made personal stereos and VCRs. Cameras were the only product category in which more respondents preferred foreign-made products to domestic, 32 percent versus 31 percent. Only 22 percent of respondents preferred foreign-made wine.

With the globalization of manufacturing, it is frequently difficult for consumers to tell exactly where products are produced. However, the Research Advantage study discovered that it was only important that a product was perceived as American-made. Whether the product was completely manufactured in the U.S., assembled here using foreign parts, or assembled elsewhere using American parts made no difference to the respondents.

Chrysler obviously feels that its "Made in the U.S.A." image is very important. In 1991, the company sponsored a three-hour radio special called "The Americans." The program ran on 300 stations nationwide at various times around the Fourth of July. It featured dramatizations of historical events, patriotic music, and 36 minutes of ad time.

Go Ahead, Eat With Your Hands

Picnic is just another word for fun. Each year, about 40 million householders and their families eat outdoors, according to Mediamark Research of New York City. One in five householders picnics with a cold lunch each year, while one in three barbecues on an outdoor grill.

While eating outdoors has been a favorite pastime for many generations, it is especially popular among young families today. Over half of householders aged 25 to 44 eat outdoors at least once a year. Almost 40 percent picnic or barbecue at least once a month, according to Mediamark.

Families with children under age 18 are 57 percent more likely than others to eat outdoors regularly. Families with children aged 5 and younger are the most likely to eat a meal outside. Forty percent of these families picnic or barbecue at least once a month, compared with one-third of families with teenagers.

Half of households that frequently eat outdoors have two incomes. This may explain why 40 percent of enthusiastic outdoor picnickers and barbecuers had household incomes above $44,000 in 1990 dollars, compared with 30 percent of all households.

Northeasterners are most likely to picnic frequently, and Westerners are most likely to barbecue frequently. Participation in the Midwest is average. People in the South are the least likely to picnic or barbecue. Perhaps they take their warm weather for granted, while those in the Northeast celebrate every sunny day.

Summertime, the peak barbecue and picnic season in much of the country, makes for booming sales in soft drinks, cold cuts, chips, bread, pickles, and mayonnaise. Only 9 percent of all households are heavy purchasers of mustard, compared with 14 percent of frequent picnickers, according to Mediamark. Seventeen percent of all households consume great amounts of meat sauce, in contrast with 25 percent of frequent barbecuers.

Summer is a big time for beer drinkers, too, says Coors' spokesperson Don Shook. A five-year analysis of the brewer's sales indicates that August is the peak month for beer consumption, followed by May, July, and June. Households that picnic at least once a month are 22 percent more likely than average to be heavy beer drinkers, and those who barbecue frequently are 41 percent more likely to be heavy beer drinkers, according to Mediamark data.

To capitalize on the July outdoor eating craze, many food stores extend their lines of ready-to-eat products. Stocking premade salads and appetizers that can withstand at least some exposure to the heat (pickled salads, vinegar-based coleslaws, and fruit desserts) is a good idea during this time of year. Another marketing strategy is to have popular products prepackaged in convenient sizes, ready to take out.

Sales of barbecue meats also increase during the summer months. Hot dogs, hamburgers, and chicken are perennial favorites. Many food stores sell premade items such as ready-to-cook hamburger patties and skewers of marinated chicken or beef and vegetables. Making food preparation convenient for busy homemakers is a good idea any time of year. But it's especially appropriate during the summer months when working parents are trying to squeeze some leisure time in between the meals.

The Picnic Basket

Leisure-seekers don't want to spend a lot of time cleaning up after themselves. Frequent barbecuers and picnickers are heavy consumers of a variety of disposable items. Frequent picnickers are 28 percent more likely than other householders to buy disposable plates, according to Mediamark, and 19 percent more likely to buy disposable cups.

Even with environmental issues making front-page news, paper plates are part of the current American experience, with some 42 million female homemakers buying these products. While there may be a trend back to washable dishes for daily use, disposable plates and cups will probably always be popular for outdoor eating.

During the year, people who eat outdoors are more likely than others to buy coolers, picnic jugs, charcoal or gas grills, and ice-cream makers. Picnickers and barbecuers make up nearly 60 percent of the buyers of porch and lawn furniture, according to Mediamark. They also are 63 percent more likely than households in general to be heavy film buyers, so that they can record their happy gatherings.

Businesses have responded to a large market for products related to outdoor cooking and eating by introducing new products to make such events easier and more fun. Some products, like quick-lighting charcoal, aim to please busy families. Designer picnic baskets, complete with champagne flutes and a compartment to hold the bubbly, are targeted at affluent picnickers. For those who desire convenience and luxury, many catering services will pack a gourmet lunch to order. Other recently introduced outdoor-eating products include lightweight fire extinguishers, portable barbecue grills, safety lighters, and barbecue chips made from grapevines.

Merchandising products such as barbecue grills alongside cooking tools, charcoal, mitts, and aprons attracts more interest and generates higher sales. Barbecues and picnics are an American tradition with cross-generational appeal. That's why images of the family picnic are commonly used in the media. Each week, ABC's "Wonder Years" begins with a backyard barbecue. And advertisers who want to place their products in familiar surroundings often display them on a red-checkered picnic tablecloth. Not much can go wrong with this marketing strategy for barbecue and picnic goods—except perhaps the weather or some overly aggressive ants.

Beating the Bugs

Bugs don't scare away avid nature lovers anxious to take full advantage of the splendid weather in July. People who want to spend time in the great outdoors simply make sure that they are equipped to ward off the insects that could cast a cloud over otherwise pleasant days. Home entertainers are equally aggressive about making sure that their special events aren't bugged.

Frequent barbecuers are 44 percent more likely than the average household to be heavy users of insect repellent, and frequent picnickers are 65 percent more likely than householders in general to buy quantities of bug spray. Insect repellents, both for personal use and for use in the surrounding atmosphere, are big sellers, especially in summer months.

Their use varies greatly by region. Southerners are the greatest purchasers of indoor insecticides, according to a 1990 Mediamark survey. More than 11 percent of Southerners buy two or more containers in a six-month period, compared with 7 percent of people in the West and Northeast and 6 percent of Midwesterners.

Despite the warm climate, however, Southerners are not any more likely than others to use outdoor insecticides. About one-fourth of households in all regions buy at least one container of outdoor insecticide in a six-month period. People in the Northeast are the most likely to use flying insect spray, Midwesterners are the most likely to use outdoor foggers, and Southerners are the most likely to use powders like Sevin.

Southerners are also less likely than the average American to use personal insect repellents, like Avon Skin-So-Soft or Off! (products that users apply to their own bodies). About 30 percent of Americans buy at least one can in a 30-day period during the bug season, according to Mediamark. Midwesterners are most likely to be heavy purchasers, and Westerners are least likely. Homemakers are 40 percent more likely than average to be heavy purchasers of personal repellents when they have children aged 2 to 11 in their households—perhaps because children spend more time outdoors and are sensitive to insect bites.

In the Northeast and other parts of the country where Lyme disease is a concern, sales of insect repellents are up. The deer tick that carries the disease is especially active during May, June, and July. A number of new products aimed specifically at the deer tick have been launched over the past few years. S.C. Johnson & Son's Ticks Off! is distributed in areas where Lyme disease is prevalent. CBR Laboratories' Identitick kit enables consumers to tell if a tick is infected with Lyme disease. Commercial laboratories have also developed home diagnostic urine tests for Lyme disease.

The public has become more knowledgeable about the dangers of insect-borne disease as a result of the Lyme disease epidemic. For example, 38 percent of adults know that roaches can carry and spread allergies, and 31 percent know that these insects can carry and spread hepatitis and salmonella, according to a 1991 survey conducted for Black Flag.

Although a majority of adults (52 percent) would be embarrassed if a roach scrambled across the floor while they were entertaining guests, hardly any (1 percent) would be frightened, says the Black Flag study. Two-thirds of adults would kill the bug with their shoe. Ten percent would pretend they didn't see it. Fourteen percent of women would ask someone else to kill it, compared with just 3 percent of men. Two percent of adults would catch the bug and set it free outside.

While it is true that insect repellents are effective, they also contain many chemicals that may, over time, prove to be harmful to "friendly" insects, groundwater, and the environment. Some products may even cause adverse health effects in humans. In 1991, New York State warned consumers not to use products with high levels of DEET. This ingredient can cause skin rashes and in some rare cases neurological problems. Repellents that contain ethylhexanediol were banned in Canada in 1991. While Health and Welfare Canada was not aware of any adverse effects on humans, the ingredient was linked to birth defects in lab animals. Environmental advocates are urging consumers to use organic and nontoxic repellents, such as boric acid, to control roaches and eucalyptus extract to repel fleas.

In the Black Flag study, however, only 1 percent of respondents chose boric acid to solve their roach problem. The largest share of respondents, 28 percent, said they used sprays to kill roaches. Nineteen percent turned to a professional exterminator, while 16 percent used roach traps and 13 percent used foggers. About 6 percent chose disk products, which poison the roach slowly, allowing it to carry the poison back to the nest. Three percent selected roach powders.

STAYING COOL
■ ■ ■ ■ ■ ■ ■ ■ ■

When people say, "It'll be a cold day in July," don't expect them to change their minds too soon. July sets the standard for being hot. The average daily temperature in July is commonly used as an indicator of an area's most extreme highs.

Beating the Heat

Although warm temperatures make it possible for Americans to enjoy the great outdoors, staying comfortable during hot sunny days is a priority for many. While some coat their bodies with protective lotions that allow them to enjoy the sun's most powerful rays, others hide away in air-conditioned refuges.

Almost 70 percent of America's homes have some form of air conditioning, according to the 1989 American Housing Survey. Almost 60 percent of those with air conditioning have central air, while 27 percent limit themselves to one air-conditioning unit.

Not surprisingly, the South leads in air conditioning, with more than 88 percent of its households taking advantage of its cooling powers. About 72 percent of Midwesterners and 59 percent of Northeasterners have air conditioning, versus 45 percent of western homes.

In the Northeast, where the nation's housing stock is the oldest, only 27 percent of people who have air conditioning use central air. In the Midwest, the share is 56 percent. Sixty-eight percent of air-conditioned homes in the South and the West are equipped with central air.

Climate control has resulted in a dramatic decline in regional distinctiveness. Air-conditioning systems promote urban high-rises and suburban shopping malls. They eliminate the need for front porches, breezeways, and shade trees. By bringing people indoors, they reduce sociability. Even so, much of the South's recent development could not have occurred without air conditioning.

In 1955, only 10 percent of southern households had air conditioning, but by 1970, they were installed in the majority of homes, according to Ray Arsenaut, an historian with the University of South Florida. By the mid-1970s, climate control was in place in 90 percent of the South's offices, 80 percent of its automobiles, most of its classrooms, and many of its tractors, barns, and chicken coops.

There are still 9 million homes in the South that currently use room units. These households are good candidates for central air. Upgrading systems with quieter, smaller, more energy-efficient units will also keep the market strong nationwide.

Worshipping the Sun

It's almost impossible to spend the entire summer in an air-conditioned room—even in the South. And while many people would rather avoid the summer sun completely, others only reluctantly give up their quest for a perfect tan.

Overexposure to the sun's rays can cause skin cancer, premature aging, and wrinkled, damaged skin. But this hasn't stopped many Americans from worshipping the sun. To find out why, *Self* magazine and the American Academy of Dermatology (AAD) sponsored a survey conducted by the Opinion Research Corporation. Because women between the ages of 25 and 35 comprise 30 percent of the $500 million sun-care product market, the 1988 *Self*/AAD survey polled a representative sample of 500 women in that age group.

While 62 percent of the women surveyed said that they spent less time in the sun than they had a decade ago, only 16 percent claimed they rarely spent time in the sun. Almost 75 percent of young mothers said they were more careful about their children's skin than their own.

"Fear of skin cancer" and "lack of leisure time" were the two most frequently cited reasons for getting less sun. Nearly two-thirds of women between and ages of 25 and 35 use sunscreens, according to the survey. Products with a sun-protection factor (SPF) of grade 15 are the most popular. Sixty percent of the women use products with an SPF of grade 8 or higher.

Despite the dangers, 68 percent of the women surveyed felt that they looked more attractive and healthier with a tan. This image affects not only the amount of time they spend in the sun, but also the skin-care products they buy, the clothes they wear, and the places they go on vacation. Thirty percent base their choice of spring and summer clothing on how they will look with a tan, and 27 percent pick winter vacation spots where they can get the best tan.

The *Self* survey shows that young women still want to worship the sun. American businesses have responded by producing more products that help them get a tan in as safe and healthy a manner as possible. Sun-care products are more technically sophisticated than they were in the 1970s. Up to half the products on the market today were developed during the last decade, and everything with an SPF over 15 is new. During the late 1980s, the first sun-care product specifically for children was introduced.

Products that are waterproof, unscented, and non-oily have become especially popular. New products target golfers, tennis players, and other outdoor sports enthusiasts with formulas that are sweat-resistant, nongreasy, and long-lasting. Other products include sunscreens with SPFs as high as 45 in cosmetically elegant formulas aimed at providing broad-spectrum protection against premature aging and wrinkling.

For those who want a healthy-looking tan without the sun's harmful rays, new "sunless tanning" products are becoming popular. Sunless tanning products have been around since the 1960s, but complaints about such results as streaky color and

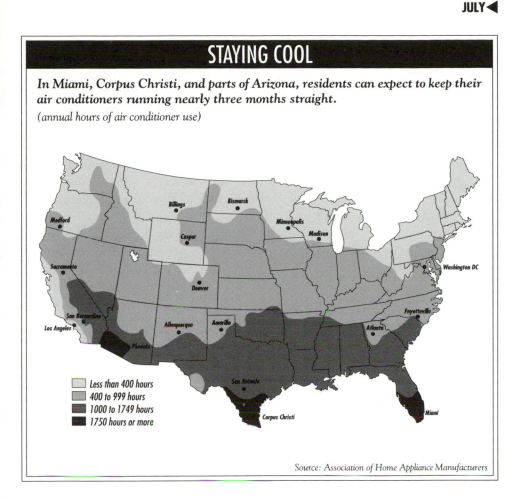

STAYING COOL

In Miami, Corpus Christi, and parts of Arizona, residents can expect to keep their air conditioners running nearly three months straight.

(annual hours of air conditioner use)

Less than 400 hours
400 to 999 hours
1000 to 1749 hours
1750 hours or more

Source: Association of Home Appliance Manufacturers

color on the palms of users' hands have led to a reformulation of the products. New formulas introduced over the last two years provide a more even tan.

"Sunless tanning products may be at their zenith right now," says Doug Petkas of Schering Plough HealthCare Products. But these products do not contain sunscreens. The sensible sun worshipper should use a sunless tanning product to simulate a tanned complexion and then cover up with a sunscreen when going out of doors, according to Petkas.

Sun-protection products range from floppy hats and sunglasses to high-tech gadgets. One particularly creative product is a wristwatch that monitors exposure to ultraviolet B (UVB) rays. Sunwatch, introduced by Saitek Industries Ltd., contains a UVB sensor and microprocessor. Sunworshippers program the watch with their skin shade and the SPF of the lotion they use. When they are exposed to just the right amount of UVB rays, an alarm goes off.

The market for sun-care products is still growing. Nearly all women aged 25 to 35 use sunscreen when they go to the beach, but fewer than half use it when they exercise outdoors. Only one in five uses cosmetics that contain a sunscreen, and just one in ten uses sunscreen products throughout the year. Manufacturers are responding to all these challenges by providing more and varied product lines. But until women get the message, many will continue to limit their use of sun-care products to the hot days of July.

Quenching Big Thirsts

A cold drink may be a necessity on a hot summer's day, but it's also part of the fun. The beverages associated with summer—cold beer, cold sodas, fruit punch, and iced tea—all make great subject matter for lively TV commercials, colorful print advertisements, and snappy radio jingles.

Perhaps no drink is more tied to the season than iced tea. When the Nestlé company tried to apply psychographic analysis to consumers of Nestea, its instant iced tea, the company found it couldn't segment this market, reports *Media Decisions* magazine. At first, researchers were disappointed because the analysis was supposed to help them determine which media would best reach their market. Then they realized that their findings were very significant.

The sales of Nestea were highly concentrated in late spring and summer. During this time of year, almost everyone was a prospective customer. Nestlé decided to use a broad media approach. Its commercial theme, people falling backward into a clear-blue pool of water, gave the impression that the product was both refreshing and fun.

Soft drinks account for the largest share of beverages consumed at fast-food restaurants—64 percent. The volume consumed between 1987 and 1990 declined slightly, but the total volume of beverages consumed at fast-food restaurants was down fully 7 percent.

Soft-drink sales are doing much better in grocery stores. Between 1989 and 1990, they grew by more than 6 percent—to nearly $9.3 billion in supermarket sales. Diet and caffeine-free drinks accounted for most of the growth. John Lucey, a buyer for Waldbaum's Food Mart Division in Holyoke, Massachusetts, told *Progressive Grocer* that the market for soft drinks is aging: "People who drank soda as youngsters are still drinking soda, but they're trying to avoid the sugar and the caffeine for health reasons."

Other beverage sales have also benefited from America's health kick. Between 1989 and 1990, fruit-juice sales in supermarkets were up 7 percent, according to *Progressive Grocer*. Apple juice was the biggest single winner, with an increase of nearly 9 percent. Orange juice, cranberry juice, and grape juice all increased significantly, but were below average in the category. Grapefruit and pineapple juice experienced declining sales, while other miscellaneous fruit juices saw nearly a 20 percent increase over the previous year.

Sales of bottled water in supermarkets increased 10 percent between 1989 and 1990 and now total more than $1 billion. When Perrier was taken off the shelves because health authorities found traces of benzene in some bottles, consumers

LOOKING FOR COOL CUSTOMERS IN JULY

F OR WINTER SPORTS promoters, ski resort owners, and winter clothing and equipment retailers, it must seem as though customers melt away with the spring thaw. But summer is a great time to remind customers that winter sports are worth the wait. How can you reach winter athletes when the temperature is 95 degrees? Target the groups most likely to contain ski enthusiasts and other winter athletes, and be prepared to reap additional benefits. The people who enjoy the same summer activities as skiers are likely to become skiing's newest customers as well.

Almost 10 million adults ski during the year, according to 1988 estimates by the Simmons Market Research Bureau in New York City. Three-quarters of them downhill ski, nearly half cross-country ski, and 20 percent do both.

But what do they do when they aren't on the slopes? When summer comes, skiers can be found on the greens. Golf attracts almost 23 million Americans annually, and the majority of skiers golf. Tennis is another very popular sport, attracting one in four downhill skiers annually.

The differences between the groups have to do with age and attitude. Many people aged 45 and older are physically capable of enjoying demanding sports, but they may view skiing as too demanding—especially if they have never participated. Even so, over 13 million golfers are under the age of 45—peak years for skiers—and one in six golfers already knows the thrill of downhill skiing. Ski advertising targeted at golfers should keep in mind that these athletes are older and more likely to have families than the average skiers.

The difference in age is not so great for tennis players. Still, only one in nine tennis players also downhill skis, possibly because the greatest number of tennis players lives in the South, skiing's weakest territory. These athletes will be particularly concerned about transportation to the winter slopes.

Golfers and tennis players can be easy targets for advertising, because they are tied to the facilities of the tennis court and golf course. Both tennis players and golfers are three times more likely than the population in general to belong to a country club. Advertising in special publications targeted to these audiences and promotions during major tournaments may attract both experienced and potential ski buffs.

One in ten powerboaters and one in six sailors also snow skis. Among the nation's 7 million water skiers, almost one in five takes to the slopes in the winter months. Because the demographics of pleasure boaters and water skiers parallel those of snow skiers, they are particularly worthwhile targets for ski advertising.

Another potentially attractive market is backpackers and hikers. Among the 2.3 million backpackers in America, one in five downhill skis. People who enjoy downhill skiing are twice as likely as other adults to go hiking. Love of the outdoors may draw backpackers to many of the same areas that skiers enjoy. But they are not as tied to facilities as other athletes, and seeking them out could be a real marketing challenge.

Another place to look for skiers, both in and out of ski season, is at the gym. Downhill skiers strive to stay in shape. One in five plays racquetball, one in six weight trains, and one in seven does aerobics.

It is easy to find skiers away from the slopes. Just look for sports enthusiasts everywhere. Among the 22 million fishermen who are drawn to mountain streams and lakes each year, over 1 million ski. Large numbers of skiers bowl, roller-skate, and fitness walk. But these sports are so popular that skiers are only a small portion of all participants. In other sports, like archery, piloting a private plane, and long-distance running, skiers make up a large share of the participants. In many of these activities, however, the total market may not be large enough to justify advertising expenses. The decision to target other sports for ski advertising depends on many factors.

Special opportunities may arise. Tournaments for these other sports may be held in ski territory, or sports publications may focus on winter activities. Because skiers are all-around athletes, other sports activities capture their attention. When ski areas have facilities for horseback riding, fitness training, or racquetball, the season can be extended to attract a broader variety of athletes.

simply turned to other brands. In table-service restaurants, the volume of bottled water consumed swelled 131 percent between 1987 and 1990, according to the National Restaurant Association.

Among the hottest sellers in the cold-drink market are "energy drinks" or "isotonic drinks." These high-energy beverages demonstrated a retail sales growth of 17 percent in 1989, according to *The Lempert Report*, which expects the trend to continue through the 1990s, anticipating a 15 percent annual growth rate and sales topping $1 billion in 1995.

The best-known energy drink, Gatorade, controls 96 percent of the market, although some 50 products have challenged Gatorade for a share of the action. With an estimated 231 million gallons of isotonics consumed in 1989, it would not be surprising if even more manufacturers tried to break into the market.

While energy-drink sales have boomed, the alcoholic cooler market has gone bust. In 1986, 72 new wine coolers—sweet, carbonated, low-alcohol beverages—were introduced, according to *The Lempert Report*. By 1989, the number of introductions dropped to less than a dozen. Possible reasons for the decline include a high calorie count, an overt sweetness that does not appeal to many people's tastes, and the bad press many of these products received as alcoholic beverages that appeal primarily to teenagers.

Wine sales at supermarkets showed a respectable gain of 6 percent between 1989 and 1990. *Progressive Grocer* points out that most of this increase has resulted from a greater public interest in quality wines. Sales of four-liter bottles of table and domestic wines are declining, while sales of higher-priced, higher-quality Chardonnays and Cabernets are rising. The increase in wine sales at table-service restaurants was below the increase for beverages in general between 1987 and 1990, according to the National Restaurant Association.

Supermarket beer sales were uninspiring between 1989 and 1990. *Progressive Grocer* explains that beer's poor performance was primarily due "to the recession, the Persian Gulf War, a doubling of the federal excise tax on beer, and an increasing emphasis on moderation in consumption." However, between 1987 and 1990, consumption of malt beverages was up fully 30 percent at table-service restaurants, according to the National Restaurant Association. Part of the increase may be the result of a 10 percent decline in liquor consumed. Summer drinks are part of summer fun. But even here, there is a shift toward healthier, more responsible consumption.

SPORTS
■ ■ ■ ■ ■

Not all of July's leisure activities are laid back. The many professional athletic events that take place this month inspire all types of amateur and armchair athletes. Wimbledon gets the tennis enthusiasts out on the court, while the Tour de France sets the pace for bicyclists. In the U.S., the baseball season is well underway, and golf tournaments abound. July 4th is known as Cowboy Christmas because there are so many rodeos. Sports enthusiasts might even catch a preseason football game in July.

Playing Hard

Sports participants vary dramatically, and marketing to them requires an in-depth study of each individual sports niche. People who fish don't all use the same type of tackle. The equipment they use depends on whether they fish in fresh or salt water and what size fish they expect to catch. Understanding the niches within a market has been extremely profitable for the sports-shoe industry. Twenty years ago, there was a limited selection of sports footwear. Today, the choices seem almost endless.

But just as surely as different sports need different equipment, each market possesses a distinct personality—unique to its sport. Swimmers who do laps probably have a different view of health and fitness than those who just bob in the surf. Advertising campaigns selling beer or bathing suits are likely to get a completely different response from each sports niche. An analysis of different types of pleasure boaters illustrates this point.

While powerboaters and sailors have a lot in common, there is a big difference in the way they go about their sports. Sailing, especially sailboat racing, is a very involved activity, requiring concentration and attention to detail. Powerboat racing, on the other hand, requires more technology and less physical activity. Cruising presents the opposite picture. Cruising in a sailboat is relaxed, but powerboaters tend to relax only when they have reached their destination. "The different demands of the two sports tend to develop different personality types," according to Lloyd Yanis, manager of Miami's 1988 International Boat and Sailboat Shows.

The two shows (held in September) are located miles apart and joined only by a shuttle bus. The decision to separate the powerboat and sailboat events was "definitely a marketing decision," according to Yanis. He points out that when the two boating events were combined, the needs of the industries were not being properly addressed.

Of 15 million pleasure boaters, only 10 percent both sail and powerboat during the year, according to the Simmons 1986 Study of Media and Markets. Although 4.5 million people sail, twice as many go powerboating every year. Both types of boaters are active, affluent, and youthful. But there are important demographic differences between the two groups.

Half of powerboaters are men, versus nearly 60 percent of sailors. Only 40 percent of the total adult population is aged 18 to 34, compared with 50 percent of powerboaters and 60 percent of sailors. About 60 percent of powerboaters and only half of sailors are married, according to Simmons.

Despite their youth and single status, sailors—like powerboaters—are 50 percent more likely than other adults to be affluent, according to Simmons. In the U.S., fewer than one in five adults is a college graduate, but one in four powerboaters and one in three sailors has a college degree.

Although pleasure boaters are twice as likely as "landlubbers" to go sport fishing, powerboaters are 106 percent more likely to go fly-fishing and 55 percent more likely to go saltwater fishing. Boaters are more likely to view themselves as "brave" than the population in general, according to the Simmons survey. But a larger proportion of powerboaters than sailors identify themselves as brave.

It is important for retailers to keep in mind that boaters, like many other sports enthusiasts, cannot be viewed as a homogeneous group. Differences exist between sailors and powerboaters, just as they do between power walkers and joggers or swimmers and divers. To be successful, zoom in on the audience you want to target and focus on its specific characteristics.

TRAVEL
■ ■ ■ ■ ■

Summer fun is always more enjoyable when you can get away. In June, July, and August 1990, nearly 223 million trips* were taken, according to the U.S. Travel Data Center. Summer accounted for fully one-third of all trips taken that year. Three-quarters of summer trips are taken for pleasure, and July was the peak month for pleasure travel.

Getting Away From It All

Between 1985 and 1990, summer vacation trips increased almost 19 percent. During the 1991 recession, summer vacation trips increased only slightly. Many Americans modified their travel plans because of the economic situation.

Americans were looking for ways to stretch the travel budget in 1991, says Doug Shifflet, president of the McLean, Virginia, travel research firm D.K. Shifflet & Associates. Changes in travel, based at least in part on the economic realities of the 1990s, include shorter trips, smaller travel parties, and increasing diversity of travelers' wants and needs. Instead of one long vacation, over half of leisure travelers planned to take short leisure trips, and 25 percent planned to stay closer to home than they did in the past, according to a 1991 Shifflet survey.

In 1990, Americans spent an average of $1,146 on each vacation trip, according to Roper. Executives and professionals spent the most (average $1,567), followed by college graduates ($1,479), people aged 45 to 59 ($1,465), and people from the Northeast ($1,450).

People on vacation want to be good to themselves. They try to save money by bringing along snacks and eating at fast-food restaurants. But they are actually more likely to eat at midscale and upscale restaurants than they would be at home, according to a 1990 study conducted for the National Restaurant Association. Over half of the meals that vacationers eat at restaurants are in fast-food places, but when they are not away, almost 70 percent of eating out is done at fast-food places.

The share of visits to midscale restaurants when away from home increases from 23 percent to 32 percent, and the share of visits to upscale restaurants increases from 8 percent to 14 percent. Vacationers under age 35 are the least likely to visit midscale and upscale restaurants. People aged 50 to 64 are the most likely to visit upscale restaurants (17 percent). Travelers over age 65 are the least likely to go to fast-food places (39 percent) and the most likely to dine at midscale restaurants (47 percent).

People say that lack of money and family commitments are the two major reasons they don't have the quality leisure time they want. Lack of money restricts leisure plans for about 70 percent of Americans, according to the Roper Organization. About 80 percent of people in low-income households, those with children,

*A "trip" is counted each time one or more adults travels 100 miles or more away from home and returns.

and those under age 30 say that financial difficulties sometimes take the fun out of their spare time.

Family commitments restrict leisure activities for about 60 percent of Americans. In two-income families and families with children, 75 percent say that family commitments sometimes interfere with leisure activities, says Roper. Upper-income households are more likely than lower-income households to say family commitments interfere with leisure plans.

Spending time with family is an important part of leisure activities. Three out of four Americans say "being together as a family" is a primary reason for taking a summer vacation trip, according to a 1991 poll conducted by the U.S. Travel Data Center. At least 70 percent say "getting away from the daily work routine" is an important incentive for taking a trip. Less than 30 percent claim that "pampering themselves and indulging in luxury" is reason enough to take a vacation. "The need to relax with the family and get away from the daily work routine seems to outweigh the possible economic restraints," explains Suzanne Cook, executive director of the center.

Adjusting to Hard Times

The pattern of summer trips changes to fit the economic situation. In a recession, summer vacations are shorter, and people visit friends and relatives more, according to the U.S. Travel Data Center. The center estimates that the duration of overnight summer vacation trips declined from an average of 5.1 nights in summer 1990 to 4.9 nights in 1991. Trips of one to three nights become more popular during times of financial stress. Still, 63 percent of U.S. residents, nearly 90 million Americans, took at least one summer trip of 100 miles or more during the recession of 1991.

Not only is the duration of the typical summer vacation changing, but the aim of the vacation is also changing, according to the Roper Organization. In 1987, 51 percent of those surveyed wanted a vacation in which they could go away and do many things, while 23 percent wanted to go away and relax. Only 17 percent wanted to stay at home and relax. But in 1990, only 44 percent wanted to go away and do many things. Twenty-five percent wanted to go away and relax, and 22 percent wanted to stay home and relax. The aging of the population and the busy lifestyle of two-earner couples is driving the trend toward more relaxing vacations.

People over age 60 and low-income people are more likely than others to spend their vacations at home relaxing. High school dropouts are the most likely to spend their vacations at home. But the majority of all vacationers would prefer to get away.

Younger people, singles, and those with a college education are more adventuresome than others. Some 57 percent of people between the ages of 18 and 29 want vacations that involve travel and a variety of activities, as do 51 percent of singles under age 45 and 53 percent of college graduates.

Almost half of those surveyed would like to spend their vacation exclusively with their spouse or companion. This attitude was especially prevalent among those aged 30 to 44 (55 percent). Traveling with a partner is also preferred by college graduates and by people with above-average incomes. Adults under age 30, however, are by far the most likely to travel with a group of friends.

No matter how a vacation is spent—sightseeing, sunning, or relaxing—the majority of Americans enjoy their time away from home. Some 72 percent of those surveyed expressed satisfaction with their last vacation, and a full 80 percent of those aged 60 and older were very satisfied, according to Roper. The enjoyment factor is important, since 31 percent of Americans choose their vacation spot because they have been there before and liked it.

Dreaming of a Vacation

When choosing a destination, the largest share of vacationers head for the ocean or beach, according to the U.S. Travel Data Center. In 1991, 30 percent of summer vacationers chose the beach as their destination, while 14 percent chose the mountains. An additional 14 percent traveled to small or rural towns, while 13 percent chose to vacation in cities. Lake areas were the destination of 10 percent of those surveyed, while 8 percent chose a state or national park, and 7 percent opted for a theme or amusement park.

If vacation travelers could go wherever they wanted, where would they go? Among dreamers, the most popular destination is Europe, according to a poll conducted for *Travel & Leisure* magazine. While only 1 in 20 respondents had been to Europe in the past year, fully 1 in 3 wanted to go. One in 10 wanted to visit Great Britain in particular, and the other would-be European travelers would have spread themselves across the continent.

Sunny spots were the next most popular destination. Hawaii, the South Pacific, and the Caribbean are all favorite choices of armchair travelers. Asia, Africa, the Middle East, and South America would gain tourists if people followed their dreams, and so would Alaska. Travel in the lower 48 states would suffer. Florida and California would not be among the top choices, and states like New York would see their tourist industry crumble.

But economic realities keep many travelers well within the confines of North America. With discretionary funds at a premium for most vacationers, a trip to an American destination, preferably one that is accessible by car, is the most popular current choice. Airline travel, battered by economic and political woes, declined in 1991. Some 82 percent of vacationers reached their destination by car, while only 14 percent flew. Bus and train travel accounted for only 4 percent of trips, according to the U.S. Travel Data Center.

Airlines are trying to reverse this trend by offering fare reductions, travel packages, and combination deals for both domestic and international travel. Enticements include half-price tickets for children flying with adults, low "introductory" fares to celebrate the establishment of new routes, and much more innovative promotions. On April 23, 1991, British Airways gave away all 50,000 of its seats worldwide. The giveaway launched a six-month campaign that included theater and hotel discounts as well as various prizes. But as the price of foreign travel increases, most Americans still opt for domestic travel.

To capture as many potential tourist dollars as possible, some states have increased their travel office budgets. Overall, the total budget of state travel offices has increased from $114 million in 1980-81 to $356 million in 1990-91. About one-third of that is earmarked for advertising, according to the U.S. Travel Data Center. But the recession has hit hard, and some states have been forced to reduce their tourism advertising budgets drastically. This can spell trouble for states like Alaska, where tourism is the third-largest industry, but its tourism advertising budget was slashed by 40 percent in 1990.

However, there are optimistic projections that domestic travel will continue at a high level. While a weekend in Paris sounds exotic, it is not as practical as a quick jaunt to the Big Apple or Disney World. With less leisure time on their hands, many Americans want to spend their vacations at their destinations, not getting there.

Seeing the U.S.A.

The travel industry has recognized the need to let people know that there are many options available in the U.S. to satisfy every type of traveler, from the family that doesn't want to stray too far from home to the most adventuresome explorers who are looking for off-beat destinations.

The "Discover America" campaign, developed by the National Council of State Travel Directors in conjunction with the USA Marketing Council, publicizes events throughout the country. This campaign makes state and even local events known to a wider audience and provides numerous options for all types of vacationers.

Summertime is the perfect occasion to take advantage of the beauty and grandeur of America's national parks, and it is no surprise that July is National Recreation and Parks Month. Among the most popular national park areas are the National Capital Parks in Maryland and Washington, D.C., visited by 7.5 million people in 1990, according to the National Park Service.

Historically significant parks serve not only as prime recreation areas, but also as meaningful destinations for the patriotic tourist. Independence National Historical Park, in Pennsylvania, had 3.3 million visitors, while the Vietnam Veterans Memorial in Washington, D.C. was visited by 2 million people. Valley Forge National Historical Park in Pennsylvania saw 1.7 million visitors the same year.

For many people, getting away from it all is more relaxing when it's done on one's own turf. Between 1973 and 1990, the number of householders who owned recreational property increased 50 percent, to 7.2 million, according to a study conducted by Ragatz Associates of Eugene, Oregon. Most of this increase was due to simple household growth. In 1973, 7 percent of householders owned vacation homes, condominiums, campsites, or other property for recreational purposes. By 1990, that share had edged up to only 7.6 percent.

BUSINESS AND PLEASURE

July is the biggest month for pleasure travel, but businesspeople do their most intensive traveling in August.

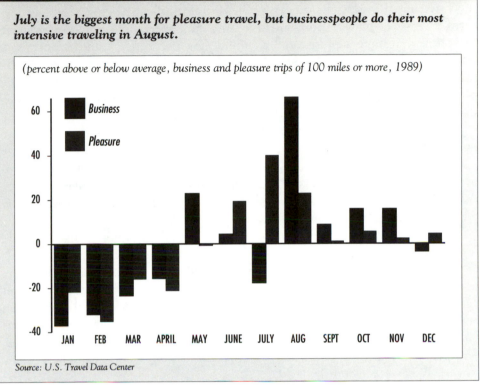

(*percent above or below average, business and pleasure trips of 100 miles or more, 1989*)

■ Business

■ Pleasure

Source: U.S. Travel Data Center

Currently, baby boomers account for 44 percent of all householders but only one-third of recreational property owners. Householders aged 45 to 64 are less than 30 percent of all householders, but fully 48 percent of recreational property owners. Over the next 20 years, recreational property ownership should rise dramatically as baby boomers enter this age group.

Happy Campers

Every summer, individuals face the problem of whether they should do what they really want to do or go somewhere with the family. Mom and dad may think lolling around at the lake is a great way to spend a summer vacation, while the kids envision roller coasters and bumper cars. The emotions generated by this dilemma range from guilt to righteous indignation, but families are finding ways to solve these conflicts.

Although summer camps have been the butt of comedy routines and the topic of horror movies, they are enjoying a new popularity as growing numbers of dual-earner couples seek a respite from their camp-aged children. Fifty-six percent of fathers and 70 percent of mothers would be interested in taking a vacation without their children, according to a 1991 Gallup Poll. The popularity of summer camp will undoubtedly increase as the number of dual-income families with children increases in the years ahead.

Day camps have become more popular as working parents explore summer day-care options. Sleep-away camps are becoming more specialized as marketers strive to appeal to a more sophisticated clientele. Theater, tennis, sailing, horseback riding, and art camps are perennial favorites, but today's camping opportunities also include law camps for high schoolers, ice hockey and figure-skating camps, college-prep camps, fat camps, and ecology camps. Ringling Brothers-Barnum & Bailey Circus even offers a circus camp for youngsters aged 6 to 16.

Camps can stretch the budget of many households. Two months at a private overnight camp can range from $2,700 to more than $4,000. Day camp can set parents back between $900 and $2,300 for an eight-week session. Clothes, equipment, and extras are not included. But summer camping is still popular, and more than 5 million kids attended summer camp in 1991, according to Gary Abell, public relations manager of the American Camping Association.

For parents who just can't bear to be away from their children that long, the travel industry is responding with a variety of alternatives. In 1989, Hyatt Hotels began its new family program: Camp Hyatt Passport. "We realized that the people who stay with us for business were choosing other hotels when they traveled on vacation with their kids," says Hyatt spokesperson Julie Halpern. The program rewards children with a backpack after four stays at Hyatt Hotels. Individual Hyatts offer special activities. Depending on the season, Kamp Kachina at the Scottsdale, Arizona, Hyatt, offers a summer day camp, pizza-making lessons, catered birthday parties, and even ice skating.

With the baby-boom generation in the years when they are most likely to have children at home, even Club Med is offering child care. Michael Kubin, president of Club Med Sales Inc., says family vacations are now the fastest-growing part of his business.

THE TIME OF YOUR LIFE.

For many Americans, July really is the best month of the year. The weather is fabulous, there's plenty to do in the great outdoors, and it seems like everyone has decided to have a good time. July marks National Hot Dog Month, National Baked Bean Month, National Ice Cream Month, National July Belongs to Blueberries Month, and National Picnic Month—the ingredients of a great summer day. Consistent with July's patriotic theme, Utah celebrates Pioneer Day this month.

More Americans travel for pleasure in July than in any other month of the year. But even those who stay at home aim to enjoy themselves. From the backyard barbecue to the softball field, from a few laps in the pool to a couple of drinks on the veranda, people are practicing the fine art of taking it easy.

ABOUT THE AUTHORS
■■■■■■■■■■■■■■■

AS RESEARCH EDITOR OF *American Demographics*, Judith Waldrop is responsible for the statistical content of the magazine. To her credit, the American Statistical Association presented its 1989 Award for Outstanding Statistical Presentation in the Media to the magazine for its "high quality of statistical analysis, for selection of interesting applications of statistical data, and for publicizing statistical data sources."

Ms. Waldrop is an award-winning journalist whose writing has been honored by the American Diabetes Association, the National Religious Public Relations Council, the National Easter Seal Society and American Association of Disability Communicators, and others. Her articles have been cited in many major news publications, and her television and radio interviews include CBS Nightwatch and National Public Radio's Morning Edition.

Ms. Waldrop joined *American Demographics* full-time in 1987, but her first article appeared in the October 1980 issue. Currently, she writes a monthly column on seasonal variations in consumer markets. She received an MPA from Florida Atlantic University in 1983. Prior to American Demographics, she worked as a city planner in Alabama.

MARCIA MOGELONSKY is a free-lance writer in Ithaca, New York.

---

indicates a map or chart

---

* indicates a map or chart